The
Economist

POCKET
WORLD IN
FIGURES

2020 Edition

Published by
Profile Books Ltd
3 Holford Yard
Bevin Way
London WC1X 9HD

Published under exclusive licence from
The Economist by Profile Books, 2019

Material researched by
Andrea Burgess, Lisa Davies, Graham Douglas, Mark Doyle,
Ian Emery, Conrad Heine, Carol Howard, David McKelvey,
Georgina McKelvey, Christopher Wilson, Pip Wroe

The greatest care has been taken in compiling this book. However,
no responsibility can be accepted by the publishers or compilers
for the accuracy of the information presented.

Typeset in Econ Sans Condensed by MacGuru Ltd

Printed and bound in Italy by L.E.G.O. Spa

A CIP catalogue record for this book is available
from the British Library

ISBN 978 1 78816 279 1

Contents

Introduction

This 2020 edition of *The Economist Pocket World in Figures* presents and analyses data about the world in two sections:

The **world rankings** consider and rank the performance of 185 countries against a range of indicators in five sections: geography and demographics, business and economics, politics and society, health and welfare, and culture and entertainment. The countries included are those which had (in 2017) a population of at least 1m or a GDP of at least $3bn; they are listed on pages 250–53. New rankings this year include topics as diverse as sex ratios, urban concentration, populations displaced by conflict, most road deaths and fastest growth of car ownership, modern slavery, unpaid work and gender pay gaps, most costly out-of-pocket-health spending, countries with the fastest broadband speeds and those that drink the most wine. Some of the rankings data are shown as charts and graphs.

The **country profiles** look in detail at 64 major countries, listed on page 109, plus profiles of the euro area and the world.

Test your *Pocket World in Figures* knowledge with our **World Rankings Quiz** on pages 242–7. Answers can be found in the corresponding world rankings section.

Notes

The extent and quality of the statistics available vary from country to country. Every care has been taken to specify the broad definitions on which the data are based and to indicate cases where data quality or technical difficulties are such that interpretation of the figures is likely to be seriously affected. Nevertheless, figures from individual countries may differ from standard international statistical definitions. The term "country" can also refer to territories or economic entities.

Definitions of the statistics shown are given on the relevant page or in the glossary on pages 248–9. Figures may not add exactly to totals, or percentages to 100, because of rounding or, in the case of GDP, statistical adjustment. Sums of money have generally been converted to US dollars at the official exchange rate ruling at the time to which the figures refer.

Some country definitions
Macedonia was officially known as the Former Yugoslav Republic of Macedonia until February 2019 when it changed to North Macedonia. Data for Cyprus normally refer to Greek Cyprus only. Data for China do not include Hong Kong or Macau. For countries such as Morocco they exclude disputed areas. Congo-Kinshasa refers to the Democratic Republic of Congo, formerly known as Zaire. Congo-Brazzaville refers to the other Congo. Swaziland was officially changed to the Kingdom of Eswatini in April 2018. Sources use both names, but Swaziland is used throughout this book for consistency. Euro area data normally refer to the 19 members that had adopted the euro as at December 31 2017: Austria, Belgium, Cyprus, Estonia, Finland, France, Germany, Greece, Ireland, Italy, Latvia, Lithuania, Luxembourg, Malta, Netherlands, Portugal, Slovakia, Slovenia and Spain. Data referring to the European Union include the United Kingdom, which in June 2016 voted in a referendum to leave the EU. Negotiations over the country's departure are due to run until at least October 2019 if no deal is agreed. For more information about the EU, euro area and OECD see the glossary on pages 248–9.

Statistical basis
The all-important factor in a book of this kind is to be able to make reliable comparisons between countries.

Although this is never quite possible for the reasons stated above, the best route, which this book takes, is to compare data for the same year or period and to use actual, not estimated, figures wherever possible. In some cases, only OECD members are considered. Where a country's data are excessively out of date, they are excluded. The research for this edition was carried out in 2019 using the latest available sources that present data on an internationally comparable basis.

Data in the country profiles, unless otherwise indicated, refer to the year ending December 31 2017. Life expectancy, crude birth, death and fertility rates are based on 2020–25 estimated averages; energy data are for 2014 and 2015 and religion data for 2010; marriage and divorce, employment, health and education, consumer goods and services data refer to the latest year for which figures are available.

Other definitions

Data shown in country profiles may not always be consistent with those shown in the world rankings because the definitions or years covered can differ.

Statistics for principal exports and principal imports are normally based on customs statistics. These are generally compiled on different definitions to the visible exports and imports figures shown in the balance of payments section.

Energy-consumption data are not always reliable, particularly for the major oil-producing countries; consumption per person data may therefore be higher than in reality. Energy exports can exceed production and imports can exceed consumption if transit operations distort trade data or oil is imported for refining and re-exported.

Abbreviations and conventions
(see also glossary on pages 248–9)

bn	billion (one thousand million)	km	kilometre
		m	million
EU	European Union	PPP	purchasing power parity
GDP	gross domestic product	TOE	tonnes of oil equivalent
GNI	gross national income	trn	trillion (one thousand billion)
ha	hectare		
kg	kilogram	...	not available

World
rankings

Countries: natural facts

Countries: the largest[a]

'000 sq km

1	Russia	17,098	34	Pakistan	796
2	Canada	9,985	35	Mozambique	786
3	United States	9,832	36	Turkey	785
4	China	9,563	37	Chile	757
5	Brazil	8,516	38	Zambia	753
6	Australia	7,741	39	Myanmar	677
7	India	3,287	40	Afghanistan	653
8	Argentina	2,780	41	Somalia	638
9	Kazakhstan	2,725	42	Central African Rep.	623
10	Algeria	2,382	43	Ukraine	604
11	Congo-Kinshasa	2,345	44	Madagascar	587
12	Saudi Arabia	2,150	45	Botswana	582
13	Mexico	1,964	46	Kenya	580
14	Indonesia	1,914	47	France	549
15	Sudan	1,879	48	Yemen	528
16	Libya	1,760	49	Thailand	513
17	Iran	1,745	50	Spain	506
18	Mongolia	1,564	51	Turkmenistan	488
19	Peru	1,285	52	Cameroon	475
20	Chad	1,284	53	Papua New Guinea	463
21	Niger	1,267	54	Morocco	447
22	Angola	1,247		Sweden	447
23	Mali	1,240		Uzbekistan	447
24	South Africa	1,219	57	Iraq	435
25	Colombia	1,142	58	Paraguay	407
26	Ethiopia	1,104	59	Zimbabwe	391
27	Bolivia	1,099	60	Norway	385
28	Mauritania	1,031	61	Japan	378
29	Egypt	1,001	62	Germany	358
30	Tanzania	947	63	Congo-Brazzaville	342
31	Nigeria	924	64	Finland	338
32	Venezuela	912	65	Vietnam	331
33	Namibia	824	66	Malaysia	330

Largest exclusive economic zones[b]

Marine area divided by land area

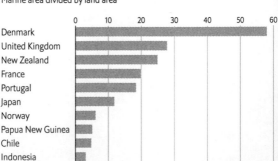

a Includes freshwater.   b Area extending 200 nautical miles (370km) from the coast.

Mountains: the highest[a]

		Location	Height (m)
1	Everest	China-Nepal	8,848
2	K2 (Godwin Austen)	China-Pakistan	8,611
3	Kangchenjunga	India-Nepal	8,586
4	Lhotse	China-Nepal	8,516
5	Makalu	China-Nepal	8,463
6	Cho Oyu	China-Nepal	8,201
7	Dhaulagiri	Nepal	8,167
8	Manaslu	Nepal	8,163
9	Nanga Parbat	Pakistan	8,126
10	Annapurna I	Nepal	8,091

Rivers: the longest

		Location	Length (km)
1	Nile	Africa	6,695
2	Amazon	South America	6,516
3	Yangtze (Chang Jiang)	Asia	6,380
4	Mississippi-Missouri system	North America	5,969
5	Ob'-Irtysh	Asia	5,568
6	Yenisey-Angara-Selanga	Asia	5,550
7	Yellow (Huang He)	Asia	5,464
8	Congo	Africa	4,667

Deserts: the largest non-polar

		Location	Area ('000 sq km)
1	Sahara	Northern Africa	8,600
2	Arabian	South-western Asia	2,300
3	Gobi	Mongolia/China	1,300
4	Patagonian	Argentina	673
5	Syrian	Middle East	520
6	Great Basin	South-western United States	490
7	Great Victoria	Western & Southern Australia	419
8	Great Sandy	Western Australia	395

Lakes: the largest

		Location	Area ('000 sq km)
1	Caspian Sea	Central Asia	371
2	Superior	Canada/United States	82
3	Victoria	East Africa	69
4	Huron	Canada/United States	60
5	Michigan	United States	58
6	Tanganyika	East Africa	33
7	Baikal	Russia	31
	Great Bear	Canada	31
9	Malawi	East Africa	30

a Includes separate peaks which are part of the same massif.
Notes: Estimates of the lengths of rivers vary widely depending on, eg, the path to take through a delta. The definition of a desert is normally a mean annual precipitation value equal to 250ml or less.

Population: size and growth

Largest populations
m, 2017

1	China	1,409.5	37	Poland	38.2
2	India	1,339.2	38	Canada	36.6
3	United States	324.5	39	Morocco	35.7
4	Indonesia	264.0	40	Afghanistan	35.5
5	Brazil	209.3	41	Saudi Arabia	32.9
6	Pakistan	197.0	42	Peru	32.2
7	Nigeria	190.9	43	Venezuela	32.0
8	Bangladesh	164.7	44	Uzbekistan	31.9
9	Russia	144.0	45	Malaysia	31.6
10	Mexico	129.2	46	Angola	29.8
11	Japan	127.5	47	Mozambique	29.7
12	Ethiopia	105.0	48	Nepal	29.3
13	Philippines	104.9	49	Ghana	28.8
14	Egypt	97.6	50	Yemen	28.3
15	Vietnam	95.5	51	Madagascar	25.6
16	Germany	82.1	52	North Korea	25.5
17	Congo-Kinshasa	81.3	53	Australia	24.5
18	Iran	81.2	54	Ivory Coast	24.3
19	Turkey	80.7	55	Cameroon	24.1
20	Thailand	69.0	56	Taiwan	23.6
21	United Kingdom	66.2	57	Niger	21.5
22	France	65.0	58	Sri Lanka	20.9
23	Italy	59.4	59	Romania	19.7
24	Tanzania	57.3	60	Burkina Faso	19.2
25	South Africa	56.7	61	Malawi	18.6
26	Myanmar	53.4	62	Mali	18.5
27	South Korea	51.0	63	Syria	18.3
28	Kenya	49.7	64	Kazakhstan	18.2
29	Colombia	49.1	65	Chile	18.1
30	Spain	46.4	66	Zambia	17.1
31	Argentina	44.3	67	Netherlands	17.0
32	Ukraine	44.2	68	Guatemala	16.9
33	Uganda	42.9	69	Ecuador	16.6
34	Algeria	41.3	70	Zimbabwe	16.5
35	Sudan	40.5	71	Cambodia	16.0
36	Iraq	38.3	72	Senegal	15.9

Largest populations
m, 2040

1	India	1,605.4	11	Congo-Kinshasa	157.1
2	China	1,417.5	12	Philippines	139.5
3	United States	374.1	13	Egypt	137.1
4	Nigeria	333.2	14	Russia	135.8
5	Indonesia	312.1	15	Japan	115.2
6	Pakistan	277.5	16	Vietnam	111.2
7	Brazil	231.6	17	Tanzania	109.1
8	Bangladesh	196.3	18	Turkey	93.0
9	Ethiopia	166.1	19	Iran	91.9
10	Mexico	157.7	20	Uganda	83.6

Note: Populations include migrant workers.

Fastest-growing populations
Total % change, 2010–20

1	Oman	69.3	26	Afghanistan	32.1
2	Qatar	56.9	27	Benin	31.8
3	Equatorial Guinea	47.9	28	Gabon	31.2
4	Niger	46.6	29	Madagascar	30.9
5	Kuwait	43.5		West Bank & Gaza	30.9
6	Jordan	42.1	31	Cameroon	30.0
7	Angola	40.5		Nigeria	30.0
8	Uganda	39.1	33	French Guiana	29.8
9	Lebanon	38.8	34	Congo-Brazzaville	29.6
10	Congo-Kinshasa	38.7	35	Kenya	29.4
11	Chad	37.0	36	Liberia	29.3
12	Bahrain	36.8	37	Togo	28.9
13	Burundi	36.2	38	Ethiopia	28.6
	Tanzania	36.2		Guinea-Bissau	28.6
15	Gambia, The	35.5	40	Ivory Coast	28.3
16	South Sudan	35.2	41	Yemen	28.1
17	Iraq	34.9	42	Rwanda	27.7
	Zambia	34.9	43	Guinea	27.4
19	Mali	34.6	44	Saudi Arabia	26.6
20	Burkina Faso	34.0		Sudan	26.6
21	Malawi	33.7	46	Maldives	25.9
22	Somalia	33.6	47	Zimbabwe	25.5
23	Mozambique	33.4	48	Ghana	25.4
24	Senegal	33.2	49	Sierra Leone	24.6
25	Mauritania	32.5	50	Timor-Leste	24.5

Slowest-growing populations
Total % change, 2010–20

1	Latvia	-10.7	24	Spain	-0.7
2	Syria	-10.0	25	Belarus	-0.6
3	Lithuania	-8.7	26	Guadeloupe	-0.5
4	Andorra	-8.6	27	Albania	0.1
5	Georgia	-7.9	28	Russia	0.4
6	Bulgaria	-6.3	29	Kosovo	0.6
7	Bosnia & Herz.	-6.0	30	Macedonia	0.8
8	Bermuda	-5.2		Montenegro	0.8
9	Romania	-5.1	32	Czech Republic	0.9
10	Croatia	-4.9		Slovakia	0.9
11	Ukraine	-4.8	34	Cuba	1.4
12	Portugal	-4.1	35	Slovenia	1.8
13	Serbia	-3.6	36	Germany	2.0
14	Hungary	-3.1	37	Armenia	2.1
15	Greece	-3.0		Mauritius	2.1
16	Estonia	-2.4	39	Barbados	2.9
	Martinique	-2.4	40	Netherlands	3.0
18	Puerto Rico	-1.8	41	Taiwan	3.1
19	Japan	-1.6	42	Thailand	3.3
	Moldova	-1.6	43	Jamaica	3.4
21	Virgin Islands (US)	-1.2	44	Uruguay	3.6
22	Italy	-1.0	45	Trinidad & Tobago	3.7
	Poland	-1.0	46	South Korea	3.9

Population: matters of breeding and sex

Total births

Average annual number of births, 2015–20, '000

1	India	25,224.0		26	Mozambique	1,156.6
2	China	16,346.0		27	Niger	1,048.4
3	Nigeria	7,381.2		28	Japan	1,027.8
4	Pakistan	5,445.2		29	Myanmar	942.4
5	Indonesia	4,882.4		30	Algeria	900.0
6	United States	4,120.6		31	Ivory Coast	897.0
7	Congo-Kinshasa	3,431.6		32	Ghana	880.6
8	Ethiopia	3,295.4		33	Yemen	877.2
9	Bangladesh	3,057.2		34	Cameroon	865.4
10	Brazil	2,895.8		35	Madagascar	852.2
11	Egypt	2,461.2		36	United Kingdom	805.6
12	Philippines	2,419.4		37	Mali	788.8
13	Mexico	2,291.6		38	France	760.0
14	Tanzania	2,189.4		39	Argentina	750.0
15	Uganda	1,808.8		40	Burkina Faso	745.0
16	Russia	1,780.6		41	Colombia	729.0
17	Vietnam	1,558.6		42	Germany	728.0
18	Kenya	1,547.2		43	Morocco	689.0
19	Sudan	1,330.4		44	Thailand	688.6
20	Turkey	1,281.0		45	Malawi	688.2
21	Iran	1,266.8		46	Zambia	655.8
22	Iraq	1,260.6		47	Uzbekistan	649.8
23	Angola	1,248.0		48	Chad	644.6
24	South Africa	1,166.8		49	Somalia	644.2
25	Afghanistan	1,158.0		50	Saudi Arabia	631.8

Total births among teenage women

Average annual number of births, women aged 15–19, 2015–20, '000

1	India	1,359.8		23	Iraq	156.2
2	Nigeria	1,070.2		24	Malawi	148.8
3	Bangladesh	657.8		25	Sudan	142.2
4	Congo-Kinshasa	535.0		26	Cameroon	136.0
5	Indonesia	529.2			Chad	136.0
6	Brazil	510.0		28	Afghanistan	133.0
7	Ethiopia	381.6		29	Venezuela	118.0
8	Tanzania	358.4		30	Thailand	116.4
9	Mexico	345.6		31	South Africa	109.6
10	Pakistan	344.0		32	Burkina Faso	109.4
11	Philippines	301.2		33	Argentina	108.4
12	Uganda	261.0		34	Ghana	97.4
13	Angola	248.4		35	Nepal	96.6
14	China	238.0		36	Colombia	94.4
15	Mozambique	223.8		37	Guinea	92.6
16	Niger	223.0			Yemen	92.6
17	Kenya	220.8		39	Zimbabwe	92.0
18	Egypt	207.0		40	Vietnam	90.0
19	United States	195.4		41	Turkey	85.4
20	Ivory Coast	177.0		42	Somalia	82.0
21	Mali	170.8		43	Zambia	81.2
22	Madagascar	156.6		44	Myanmar	71.6

Number of males per 100 females, 2020

Highest		Lowest	
	0 100 200 300		0 100
Qatar		Martinique	
UAE		Hong Kong	
Oman		Latvia	
Bahrain		Lithuania	
Saudi Arabia		Guadeloupe	
Kuwait		Ukraine	
Maldives		Russia	
Equatorial Guinea		Belarus	
India		El Salvador	
China		Estonia	
Kosovo		Armenia	
Malaysia		Portugal	
Afghanistan		Hungary	
Brunei		Virgin Islands (US)	
Pakistan		Georgia	
Gabon		Barbados	
Papua New Guinea		Moldova	
French Polynesia		Sri Lanka	
Timor-Leste		Macau	
Nigeria		Puerto Rico	
West Bank & Gaza		Croatia	
Jordan		Poland	
Paraguay		Uruguay	
Fiji		Réunion	
Iraq		Swaziland	

Women[a] who use modern methods of contraception

2017, %

Highest			Lowest		
1	China	82.5	1	Chad	5.9
2	United Kingdom	79.0		South Sudan	5.9
3	Finland	78.4	3	Guinea	7.9
4	Nicaragua	77.1	4	Congo-Kinshasa	10.6
5	Costa Rica	77.0	5	Gambia, The	11.2
6	Brazil	76.9	6	Eritrea	12.2
7	Uruguay	76.5	7	Benin	13.4
8	Thailand	75.9	8	Equatorial Guinea	13.5
9	Colombia	75.3	9	Nigeria	13.7
10	France	73.7	10	Angola	14.3
11	Hong Kong	72.4	11	Mali	14.4
12	Cuba	72.2	12	Sudan	14.5
13	Chile	72.0	13	Ivory Coast	16.1
14	Belgium	71.1	14	Mauritania	16.7

a Married or partnered women aged 15–49; excludes traditional methods of contraception, such as the rhythm method.

Population: age

Median age[a]

Highest, 2017

1	Monaco	52.0
2	Japan	47.1
3	Italy	46.7
4	Germany	46.2
5	Portugal	44.8
6	Martinique	44.5
7	Greece	44.1
	Spain	44.1
9	Bulgaria	44.0
10	Hong Kong	43.8
11	Austria	43.7
12	Slovenia	43.6
13	Channel Islands	43.2
	Croatia	43.2
15	Latvia	43.1
16	Andorra	43.0
	Lithuania	43.0
18	Finland	42.6
	Switzerland	42.6
20	Netherlands	42.5
21	Hungary	42.4
22	Guadeloupe	42.3

Lowest, 2017

1	Niger	15.0
2	Uganda	16.0
3	Mali	16.2
4	Chad	16.3
5	Angola	16.6
	Somalia	16.6
7	Congo-Kinshasa	16.9
8	Burkina Faso	17.2
	Gambia, The	17.2
10	Zambia	17.3
11	Mozambique	17.4
12	Tanzania	17.5
13	Burundi	17.6
	Timor-Leste	17.6
15	Malawi	17.7
16	Afghanistan	17.8
17	Central African Rep.	18.0
	Nigeria	18.0
19	Benin	18.4
20	Cameroon	18.5
	Ivory Coast	18.5
	Senegal	18.5

Most old people

% of population aged 65 or over, 2020

1	Monaco	32.2
2	Japan	28.2
3	Italy	23.9
4	Portugal	22.7
5	Finland	22.3
6	Germany	22.2
7	Bulgaria	21.5
8	Greece	21.1
9	Croatia	20.9
10	Malta	20.8
	Slovenia	20.8
12	France	20.7
13	Martinique	20.6
14	Latvia	20.5
15	Spain	20.4
16	Estonia	20.3
	Sweden	20.3
	Virgin Islands (US)	20.3
19	Czech Republic	20.2
	Denmark	20.2
21	Hungary	20.1
22	Netherlands	20.0
23	Austria	19.9
24	Lithuania	19.6

Most young people

% of population aged 0–19, 2020

1	Niger	60.8
2	Mali	58.1
	Uganda	58.1
4	Chad	57.5
5	Angola	56.9
	Somalia	56.9
7	Congo-Kinshasa	56.4
8	Gambia, The	55.5
9	Burkina Faso	55.4
10	Zambia	55.2
11	Burundi	55.0
	Mozambique	55.0
	Tanzania	55.0
14	Timor-Leste	54.5
15	Malawi	54.2
16	Nigeria	54.1
17	Central African Rep.	53.9
18	Afghanistan	53.3
19	Ivory Coast	52.7
	Senegal	52.7
21	Benin	52.6
	Cameroon	52.6
23	Guinea	52.2
24	Sierra Leone	52.1

a Age at which there is an equal number of people above and below.

City living

Biggest cities[a]

Population, m, 2017

1	Tokyo, Japan	37.4	26	Lahore, Pakistan	11.3
2	Delhi, India	27.6	27	Bangalore, India	11.0
3	Shanghai, China	24.9	28	Paris, France	10.8
4	Mexico City, Mexico	21.5	29	Jakarta, Indonesia	10.4
5	São Paulo, Brazil	21.4	30	Bogotá, Colombia	10.3
6	Mumbai, India	19.8	31	Chennai, India	10.2
7	Cairo, Egypt	19.6		Lima, Peru	10.2
8	Osaka, Japan	19.3	33	Bangkok, Thailand	9.9
9	Beijing, China	19.2		Seoul, South Korea	9.9
10	Dhaka, Bangladesh	18.9	35	Nagoya, Japan	9.5
11	New York, United States	18.8	36	Hyderabad, India	9.2
12	Karachi, Pakistan	15.0	37	London, United Kingdom	8.9
13	Buenos Aires, Argentina	14.9	38	Chicago, United States	8.8
14	Kolkata, India	14.6		Tehran, Iran	8.8
15	Istanbul, Turkey	14.5	40	Chengdu, China	8.7
16	Chongqing, China	14.3	41	Wuhan, China	8.1
17	Manila, Philippines	13.3	42	Nanjing, China	8.0
18	Rio de Janeiro, Brazil	13.2	43	Ho Chi Minh City, Vietnam	7.9
19	Lagos, Nigeria	13.0	44	Ahmedabad, India	7.5
	Tianjin, China	13.0		Luanda, Angola	7.5
21	Kinshasa, Congo-Kinshasa	12.6	46	Hong Kong	7.4
22	Los Angeles, United States	12.4	47	Dongguan, China	7.3
23	Guangzhou, China	12.3		Kuala Lumpur, Malaysia	7.3
	Moscow, Russia	12.3	49	Xi'an, China	7.2
25	Shenzhen, China	11.7	50	Foshan, China	7.1

City growth[b]

Total % change, 2015–20

Fastest

1	Malappuram, India	44.1
2	Can Tho, Vietnam	36.7
3	Suqian, China	36.6
4	Kozhikode, India	34.5
5	Abuja, Nigeria	34.2
6	Suzhou, China	32.5
7	Putian, China	32.2
	Sharjah, United Arab Emirates	32.2
9	Muscat, Oman	31.4
10	Kollam, India	31.1
11	Dar es Salaam, Tanzania	31.0
12	Wuhu, China	30.8
13	Thrissur, India	30.2
14	Batam, Indonesia	28.9
	Yaoundé, Cameroon	28.9
16	Port Harcourt, Nigeria	28.8
17	Antananarivo, Madagascar	28.7

Slowest

1	Khulna, Bangladesh	-6.5
2	Detroit, United States	-2.7
3	Bucharest, Romania	-2.5
4	Daegu, South Korea	-2.0
5	Fushun, China	-1.2
	Pittsburgh, United States	-1.2
	Volgograd, Russia	-1.2
8	Karaj, Iran	-1.1
9	Kharkiv, Ukraine	-0.9
10	Cleveland, United States	-0.8
	Naples, Italy	-0.8
12	Hiroshima, Japan	-0.7
	Osaka, Japan	-0.7
14	San Juan, Puerto Rico	-0.6
15	Samara, Russia	-0.4
16	Athens, Greece	-0.3
	Changwon, South Korea	-0.3

a Urban agglomerations. Data may change from year to year based on reassessments of agglomeration boundaries.
b Urban agglomerations with a population of at least 750,000 in 2015.

City liveability[a]
100 = ideal, 0 = intolerable, 2018

Best

1	Vienna, Austria	99.1
2	Melbourne, Australia	98.4
3	Sydney, Australia	98.1
4	Osaka, Japan	97.7
5	Calgary, Canada	97.5
6	Vancouver, Canada	97.3
7	Tokyo, Japan	97.2
	Toronto, Canada	97.2
9	Copenhagen, Denmark	96.8
10	Adelaide, Australia	96.6
11	Zurich, Switzerland	96.3
12	Auckland, New Zealand	96.0
	Frankfurt. Germany	96.0
14	Geneva, Switzerland	95.9
	Perth, Australia	95.9

Worst

1	Damascus, Syria	30.7
2	Lagos, Nigeria	38.5
3	Tripoli, Libya	39.1
4	Dhaka, Bangladesh	39.2
5	Karachi, Pakistan	40.9
6	Port Moresby, Papua New Guinea	41.0
7	Harare, Zimbabwe	42.6
8	Douala, Cameroon	43.3
9	Algiers, Algeria	43.4
10	Caracas, Venezuela	46.9
11	Dakar, Senegal	48.3
12	Tehran, Iran	49.5
13	Kathmandu, Nepal	51.0
	Lusaka, Zambia	51.0

Tallest buildings[b]
Height, metres, 2018

Burj Khalifa, Dubai
Shanghai Tower, Shanghai
Makkah Royal Clock Tower, Mecca
Ping An Finance Centre, Shenzhen
Lotte World Tower, Seoul
One World Trade Centre, New York
CTF Finance Centre, Guangzhou
CITIC Tower, Beijing
Taipei 101, Taipei
World Financial Centre, Shanghai
Int. Commerce Centre, Hong Kong
Vincom Landmark, Ho Chi Minh City
IFS Tower T1, Changsha
Petronas Twin Towers, Kuala Lumpur
Zifeng Tower, Nanjing
Willis Tower, Chicago
KK100, Shenzhen
Int. Finance Centre, Guangzhou
432 Park Avenue, New York
Marina 101, Dubai
Trump Int. Hotel & Tower, Chicago
Jin Mao Tower, Shanghai
Princess Tower, Dubai
Al Hamra Tower, Kuwait City

a EIU liveability index, based on factors such as stability, health care, culture, education and infrastructure.   b Completed.

Urban growth

Average annual change, %, 2015–20

Fastest			Slowest		
1	Burundi	5.7	1	Latvia	-0.9
	Uganda	5.7	2	Bermuda	-0.4
3	Oman	5.3		Romania	-0.4
4	Tanzania	5.2	4	Andorra	-0.3
5	Burkina Faso	5.0		Lithuania	-0.3
6	Mali	4.9		Poland	-0.3
7	Ethiopia	4.6		Ukraine	-0.3
8	Congo-Kinshasa	4.5	8	Bulgaria	-0.2
	Madagascar	4.5	9	Croatia	-0.1
10	Bahrain	4.4		Guadeloupe	-0.1
	Mozambique	4.4		Japan	-0.1
12	Angola	4.3		Moldova	-0.1
	Equatorial Guinea	4.3		Puerto Rico	-0.1
	Mauritania	4.3		Serbia	-0.1
	Niger	4.3	15	Estonia	0.0
				Martinique	0.0
				Slovakia	0.0

Urban concentration

Cities[a] that hold most of a country's total population, %, 2015

1	Hong Kong	100.0	13	Libreville, Gabon	38.7
	Macau	100.0	14	Beirut, Lebanon	38.1
	Singapore	100.0	15	Santiago, Chile	36.7
4	San Juan, Puerto Rico	67.0		Yerevan, Armenia	36.7
5	Kuwait City, Kuwait	65.2	17	Buenos Aires, Argentina	33.9
6	Montevideo, Uruguay	49.8	18	Riga, Latvia	32.4
7	Tel Aviv, Israel	45.9	19	Manama, Bahrain	32.1
8	Ulaanbaatar, Mongolia	45.8	20	Auckland, New Zealand	31.8
9	Asunción, Paraguay	44.7	21	Tallinn, Estonia	31.6
10	Panama City, Panama	42.2	22	Lima, Peru	31.3
11	Port of Spain, Trinidad & Tobago	40.1	23	Tokyo, Japan	29.1
12	Brazzaville, Congo-Brazzaville	39.2	24	Athens, Greece	28.2
				Monrovia, Liberia	28.2

Biggest rural populations

m, 2017

1	India	889.2	12	Congo-Kinshasa	45.6
2	China	592.6	13	Tanzania	38.4
3	Pakistan	125.2	14	Myanmar	37.2
4	Indonesia	119.7	15	Russia	37.0
5	Bangladesh	105.6	16	Kenya	36.5
6	Nigeria	96.4	17	Thailand	35.1
7	Ethiopia	83.6	18	Uganda	32.9
8	Vietnam	61.9	19	Brazil	28.7
9	United States	58.2	20	Afghanistan	26.6
10	Egypt	55.9		Sudan	26.6
	Philippines	55.9	22	Mexico	26.0

a Cities with a population of at least 300,000.

Migrants, refugees and asylum-seekers

Foreign-born populations
% of total population, 2017

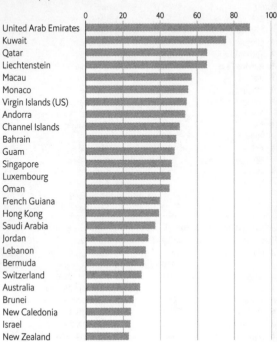

	0	20	40	60	80	100
United Arab Emirates						
Kuwait						
Qatar						
Liechtenstein						
Macau						
Monaco						
Virgin Islands (US)						
Andorra						
Channel Islands						
Bahrain						
Guam						
Singapore						
Luxembourg						
Oman						
French Guiana						
Hong Kong						
Saudi Arabia						
Jordan						
Lebanon						
Bermuda						
Switzerland						
Australia						
Brunei						
New Caledonia						
Israel						
New Zealand						

Refugees[a], country of origin
'000, 2017

1	Syria	6,308.7	8	Central African Rep.	545.5
2	Afghanistan	2,624.3	9	Eritrea	486.2
3	South Sudan	2,439.9	10	Burundi	439.3
4	Myanmar	1,156.7	11	Iraq	362.5
5	Somalia	986.4	12	Vietnam	334.1
6	Sudan	694.6	13	Rwanda	259.0
7	Congo-Kinshasa	620.8	14	Nigeria	239.0

Countries with largest refugee[a] populations
'000, 2017

1	Turkey	3,480.4	8	Sudan	906.6
2	Pakistan	1,393.1	9	Ethiopia	889.4
3	Uganda	1,350.5	10	Jordan	691.0
4	Lebanon	998.9	11	Congo-Kinshasa	537.1
5	Iran	979.4	12	Kenya	431.9
6	Germany	970.4	13	Chad	411.5
7	Bangladesh	932.2	14	Cameroon	337.4

a According to UNHCR. Includes people in "refugee-like situations".

Applications for asylum by country of origin

'000, 2017

1	Afghanistan	149.9	16	Honduras	35.1
2	Iraq	127.9	17	Ukraine	34.4
3	Syria	124.7	18	Bangladesh	33.9
4	Venezuela	112.4	19	Haiti	30.7
5	Congo-Kinshasa	109.3	20	Ethiopia	29.3
6	El Salvador	60.3		Sudan	29.3
7	Nigeria	57.2	22	Mexico	29.2
8	Pakistan	56.7	23	Turkey	27.3
9	Eritrea	56.3	24	Myanmar	24.0
10	Somalia	44.8	25	Russia	23.8
11	Iran	42.2	26	Guinea	23.6
12	Burundi	40.4	27	Serbia[a]	19.9
13	China	38.6	28	India	19.3
14	Albania	36.7	29	Cameroon	18.9
15	Guatemala	36.6	30	Colombia	17.7

Countries where asylum applications were lodged

'000, 2017

1	United States	334.7	15	Spain	31.7
2	Germany	222.7	16	Egypt	30.4
3	France	154.0	17	Japan	28.2
4	Turkey	126.9	18	Malaysia	26.2
5	Italy	126.5	19	South Africa	24.2
6	Uganda	72.0	20	Austria	22.5
7	Greece	70.4	21	Kenya	19.8
8	Sweden	56.9	22	Belgium	18.4
9	Canada	52.7	23	Netherlands	18.2
10	Australia	49.9		Zambia	18.2
11	United Kingdom	48.4	25	Switzerland	18.1
12	Tanzania	36.5	26	Israel	15.4
13	Peru	34.2	27	Mexico	14.6
14	Brazil	33.8	28	Russia	14.1

Stock of a population displaced by conflict

'000, as of end 2017

1	Syria	6,784	15	Central African Rep.	689
2	Colombia	6,509	16	Myanmar	635
3	Congo-Kinshasa	4,480	17	Philippines	445
4	Iraq	2,648	18	Bangladesh	432
5	Sudan	2,072	19	Azerbaijan	393
6	Yemen	2,014	20	Mexico	345
7	South Sudan	1,899	21	Georgia	289
8	Nigeria	1,707	22	Pakistan	249
9	Afghanistan	1,286	23	Guatemala	242
10	Turkey	1,113	24	Cameroon	239
11	Ethiopia	1,078	25	West Bank & Gaza	231
12	Somalia	825	26	Cyprus	217
13	India	806	27	Libya	197
14	Ukraine	800	28	Honduras	190

a Includes Kosovo.

The world economy

Biggest economies
GDP, $bn, 2017

1	United States	19,485	23	Sweden	536
2	China	12,238	24	Poland	526
3	Japan	4,872	25	Belgium	495
4	Germany	3,693	26	Thailand	455
5	India	2,651	27	Iran	454
6	United Kingdom	2,638	28	Austria	417
7	France[a]	2,583	29	Norway	399
8	Brazil	2,054	30	United Arab Emirates	383
9	Italy	1,944	31	Nigeria	376
10	Canada	1,647	32	Israel	353
11	Russia	1,578	33	South Africa	349
12	South Korea	1,531	34	Hong Kong	341
13	Australia	1,323	35	Ireland	331
14	Spain	1,314	36	Denmark	330
15	Mexico	1,151	37	Singapore	324
16	Indonesia	1,015	38	Malaysia	315
17	Turkey	852	39	Colombia	314
18	Netherlands	831		Philippines	314
19	Saudi Arabia	687	41	Pakistan	305
20	Switzerland	679	42	Chile	277
21	Argentina	637	43	Finland	252
22	Taiwan	575	44	Bangladesh	250

Biggest economies by purchasing power
GDP PPP, $bn, 2017

1	China	23,190	24	Nigeria	1,121
2	United States	19,485	25	Pakistan	1,061
3	India	9,597	26	Malaysia	933
4	Japan	5,427	27	Netherlands	924
5	Germany	4,199	28	Argentina	918
6	Russia	4,027	29	Philippines	877
7	Brazil	3,255	30	South Africa	766
8	Indonesia	3,250	31	Colombia	709
9	United Kingdom	2,930	32	United Arab Emirates	696
10	France	2,854	33	Bangladesh	691
11	Mexico	2,464	34	Iraq	655
12	Italy	2,324	35	Vietnam	649
13	Turkey	2,186	36	Algeria	630
14	South Korea	2,035	37	Singapore	536
15	Spain	1,778	38	Belgium	531
16	Saudi Arabia	1,777	39	Switzerland	523
17	Canada	1,764	40	Sweden	518
18	Iran	1,640	41	Romania	485
19	Australia	1,254	42	Kazakhstan	478
20	Thailand	1,240	43	Hong Kong	456
21	Egypt	1,204	44	Chile	453
22	Taiwan	1,193	45	Austria	441
23	Poland	1,129	46	Peru	430

Note: For a list of 185 countries with their GDPs, see pages 250–53. "Advanced economies" refers to 39 countries as defined by the IMF.
a Includes overseas territories.　b 2017　c IMF coverage.

Regional GDP

$bn, 2018		*% annual growth 2013–18*	
World	84,740	World	3.6
Advanced economies	51,070	Advanced economies	2.1
G7	38,854	G7	1.9
Euro area (19)	13,669	Euro area (19)	1.9
Other Asia	19,146	Other Asia	6.7
Latin America & Caribbean	5,247	Latin America & Caribbean	0.7
Other Europe & CIS	4,157	Other Europe & CIS	2.6
Middle East, N. Africa, Afghanistan & Pakistan	3,478	Middle East, N. Africa, Afghanistan & Pakistan	2.9
Sub-Saharan Africa	1,643	Sub-Saharan Africa	3.1

Regional purchasing power

GDP, % of total, 2018		*$ per person, 2018*	
World	100.0	Worldb	17,100
Advanced economies	40.8	Advanced economies	51,573
G7	30.1	G7	53,148
Euro area (19)	11.4	Euro area (19)	45,538
Other Asia	33.3	Other Asia	12,487
Latin America & Caribbean	7.5	Latin America & Caribbean	16,220
Other Europe & CIS	8.0	Other Europe & CIS	23,324
Middle East, N. Africa, Afghanistan & Pakistan	7.4	Middle East, N. Africa, Afghanistan & Pakistan	14,193
Sub-Saharan Africa	3.0	Sub-Saharan Africa	4,112

Regional population

% of total (7.5bn), 2018		*No. of countriesᶜ, 2018*	
World	100.0	World	194
Advanced economies	14.3	Advanced economies	39
G7	10.3	G7	7
Euro area (19)	4.5	Euro area (19)	19
Other Asia	48.3	Other Asia	30
Latin America & Caribbean	8.4	Latin America & Caribbean	33
Other Europe & CIS	6.2	Other Europe & CIS	24
Middle East, N. Africa, Afghanistan & Pakistan	9.4	Middle East, N. Africa, Afghanistan & Pakistan	23
Sub-Saharan Africa	13.4	Sub-Saharan Africa	45

Regional international trade

Exports of goods & services *% of total, 2018*		*Current-account balances* *$bn, 2018*	
World	100.0	World	348
Advanced economies	63.0	Advanced economies	372
G7	33.2	G7	-121
Euro area (19)	26.3	Euro area (19)	404
Other Asia	18.1	Other Asia	-25
Latin America & Caribbean	5.1	Latin America & Caribbean	-100
Other Europe & CIS	6.6	Other Europe & CIS	65
Middle East, N. Africa, Afghanistan & Pakistan	5.6	Middle East, N. Africa, Afghanistan & Pakistan	79
Sub-Saharan Africa	1.7	Sub-Saharan Africa	-43

Living standards

Highest GDP per person

$, 2017

1	Monaco[a]	168,011	31	Guam	35,676
2	Liechtenstein[a]	164,993	32	Virgin Islands (US)	34,899
3	Luxembourg	105,713	33	Bahamas	32,661
4	Bermuda[b]	85,748	34	Italy	32,132
5	Switzerland	80,643	35	Puerto Rico	31,581
6	Macau	77,415	36	South Korea	29,750
7	Norway	75,514	37	Spain	28,378
8	Iceland	72,390	38	Brunei	28,278
9	Ireland	68,723	39	Malta	27,707
10	Qatar	62,826	40	Kuwait	26,863
11	Singapore	59,990	41	Cyprus	25,955
12	United States	59,895	42	Bahrain	24,399
13	Denmark	57,380	43	Taiwan	24,390
14	Australia	55,958	44	Slovenia	23,502
15	Sweden	52,924	45	Portugal	21,334
16	Netherlands	48,555	46	Saudi Arabia	21,153
17	Austria	47,384	47	Czech Republic	20,410
18	Hong Kong	46,091	48	Estonia	20,241
19	Finland	45,938	49	Greece	18,898
20	Canada	45,224	50	Slovakia	17,627
21	Germany	44,771	51	Barbados	17,463
22	Belgium	43,672	52	Oman	17,128
23	New Zealand	41,350	53	Uruguay	16,942
24	Israel	40,560	54	Lithuania	16,864
25	France	40,046	55	Trinidad & Tobago	16,107
26	United Kingdom	39,975	56	Latvia	15,653
27	Andorra	39,147	57	Panama	15,198
28	Japan	38,344	58	Chile	15,128
29	United Arab Emirates	37,733	59	Argentina	14,588
30	New Caledonia	35,815	60	Hungary	14,264

Lowest GDP per person

$, 2017

1	South Sudan	234	17	Liberia	755
2	Burundi	312	18	Rwanda	774
3	Malawi	325	19	Haiti	784
4	Central African Rep.	389	20	Guinea-Bissau	794
5	Mozambique	426	21	Tajikistan	801
6	Niger	434	22	Guinea	802
7	Madagascar	448	23	Chad	812
8	Congo-Kinshasa	449	24	Ethiopia	817
9	Somalia	478	25	Benin	833
10	Sierra Leone	506	26	Nepal	849
11	Afghanistan	570	27	Mali	854
12	Togo	615	28	Yemen	895
13	Burkina Faso	643	29	Eritrea	980
14	North Korea	685	30	Tanzania	1,064
15	Uganda	702	31	Mauritania	1,113
16	Gambia, The	705	32	Sudan	1,120

a 2016   b 2012

Highest purchasing power

GDP per person in PPP (US = 100), 2017 or latest

1	Liechtenstein	232.2	35	South Korea	66.0
2	Qatar	213.3	36	Puerto Rico	65.8
3	Monaco	193.2	37	New Zealand	64.7
4	Macau	184.6	38	Italy	64.0
5	Luxembourg	172.5		Spain	64.0
6	Singapore	159.5	40	Cyprus	63.5
7	Brunei	131.8	41	Virgin Islands (US)	61.8
8	Ireland	122.2	42	Israel	61.2
9	Norway	120.5	43	Czech Republic	59.4
10	United Arab Emirates	114.6		Guam	59.4
11	Kuwait	110.5	45	Slovenia	57.5
12	Switzerland	103.7	46	Slovakia	55.2
13	Hong Kong	102.7	47	Lithuania	54.2
14	United States	100.0	48	Bahamas	54.1
15	Saudi Arabia	91.2	49	Estonia	53.6
16	Netherlands	90.0	50	Trinidad & Tobago	52.7
17	Iceland	89.9	51	New Caledonia	51.9
18	Bermuda	87.7	52	Portugal	51.1
19	Sweden	85.5	53	Poland	49.6
20	Germany	84.8	54	Hungary	49.5
21	Denmark	84.6	55	Malaysia	48.7
22	Australia	84.5	56	Russia	46.7
	Taiwan	84.5	57	Greece	46.4
24	Austria	83.5	58	Latvia	46.2
25	Andorra	83.3	59	Turkey	45.2
26	Bahrain	81.9	60	Kazakhstan	43.9
27	Canada	80.7	61	Croatia	41.4
28	Belgium	78.1	62	Chile	41.2
29	Oman	76.8		Romania	41.2
30	Finland	74.3	64	Panama	40.9
31	United Kingdom	74.1	65	Equatorial Guinea	40.8
32	France	73.7	66	Uruguay	37.4
33	Japan	71.5	67	Mauritius	37.3
34	Malta	71.0	68	Bulgaria	36.4

Lowest purchasing power

GDP per person in PPP (US = 100), 2017 or latest

1	Central African Rep.	1.14	15	Guinea-Bissau	3.11
2	Burundi	1.23	16	Burkina Faso	3.12
3	Congo-Kinshasa	1.24	17	Afghanistan	3.26
4	Malawi	1.95	18	Rwanda	3.49
	Niger	1.95	19	Ethiopia	3.59
6	Mozambique	2.10	20	Guinea	3.65
7	Liberia	2.34	21	Benin	3.82
8	South Sudan	2.56		Mali	3.82
9	Madagascar	2.60	23	Chad	3.92
10	Sierra Leone	2.61	24	Uganda	3.96
11	Eritrea	2.65	25	Yemen	4.10
12	Togo	2.79	26	Gambia, The	4.41
13	North Korea	2.84	27	Nepal	4.51
14	Haiti	3.04		Zimbabwe	4.51

The quality of life

Human development index[a]

Highest, 2017		Lowest, 2017	
1 Norway	95.3	1 Niger	35.4
2 Switzerland	94.4	2 Central African Rep.	36.7
3 Australia	93.9	3 South Sudan	38.8
4 Ireland	93.8	4 Chad	40.4
5 Germany	93.6	5 Burundi	41.7
6 Iceland	93.5	6 Sierra Leone	41.9
7 Hong Kong	93.3	7 Burkina Faso	42.3
Sweden	93.3	8 Mali	42.7
9 Singapore	93.2	9 Liberia	43.5
10 Netherlands	93.1	10 Mozambique	43.7
11 Denmark	92.9	11 Eritrea	44.0
12 Canada	92.6	12 Yemen	45.2
13 United States	92.4	13 Guinea-Bissau	45.5
14 United Kingdom	92.2	14 Congo-Kinshasa	45.7
15 Finland	92.0	15 Guinea	45.9
16 New Zealand	91.7	16 Gambia, The	46.0
17 Belgium	91.6	17 Ethiopia	46.3
Liechtenstein	91.6	18 Malawi	47.7
19 Japan	90.9	19 Ivory Coast	49.2
20 Austria	90.8	20 Afghanistan	49.8
21 Luxembourg	90.4	Haiti	49.8
22 Israel	90.3	22 Sudan	50.2
South Korea	90.3	23 Togo	50.3
24 France	90.1	24 Senegal	50.5

Gini coefficient[b]

Highest, 2010–17		Lowest, 2010–17	
1 South Africa	63.0	1 Azerbaijan	16.6
2 Namibia	61.0	2 Ukraine	25.0
3 Botswana	60.5	3 Slovenia	25.4
4 Zambia	57.1	4 Iceland	25.6
5 Central African Rep.	56.2	5 Czech Republic	25.9
6 Lesotho	54.2	6 Moldova	26.3
7 Mozambique	54.0	7 Slovakia	26.5
8 Swaziland	51.5	8 Kyrgyzstan	26.8
9 Brazil	51.3	9 Kazakhstan	26.9
10 Colombia	50.8	10 Belarus	27.0
11 Guinea-Bissau	50.7	11 Finland	27.1
12 Panama	50.4	12 Norway	27.5
Rwanda	50.4	13 Algeria	27.6
14 Honduras	50.0	14 Belgium	27.7
15 Congo-Brazzaville	48.9	15 Denmark	28.2
16 Costa Rica	48.7	16 Romania	28.3

a GDP or GDP per person is often taken as a measure of how developed a country is, but its usefulness is limited as it refers only to economic welfare. The UN Development Programme combines statistics on average and expected years of schooling and life expectancy with income levels (now GNI per person, valued in PPP US$). The HDI is shown here scaled from 0 to 100; countries scoring over 80 are considered to have very high human development, 70–79 high, 55–69 medium and those under 55 low.
b The lower its value, the more equally household income is distributed.

Household wealth

$trn, 2017

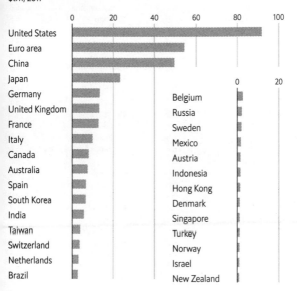

United States	
Euro area	
China	
Japan	
Germany	Belgium
United Kingdom	Russia
France	Sweden
Italy	Mexico
Canada	Austria
Australia	Indonesia
Spain	Hong Kong
South Korea	Denmark
India	Singapore
Taiwan	Turkey
Switzerland	Norway
Netherlands	Israel
Brazil	New Zealand

Number of millionaires

Persons with net worth above $1m, 2017, m

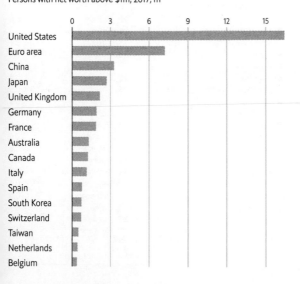

United States
Euro area
China
Japan
United Kingdom
Germany
France
Australia
Canada
Italy
Spain
South Korea
Switzerland
Taiwan
Netherlands
Belgium

Economic growth

Highest economic growth
Average annual % increase in real GDP, 2007–17

1	Ethiopia	10.1		Sri Lanka	5.6
2	Turkmenistan	9.5		Togo	5.6
3	China	8.3	28	Burkina Faso	5.5
4	Qatar	8.0		Indonesia	5.5
5	Myanmar	7.9		Ivory Coast	5.5
	Uzbekistan	7.9	31	West Bank & Gaza	5.4
7	Laos	7.7	32	Guinea	5.1
8	Rwanda	7.4		Maldives	5.1
9	Mongolia	7.1		Zimbabwe	5.1
10	India	7.0	35	Kenya	5.0
11	Ghana	6.9		Macau	5.0
12	Tajikistan	6.8		Malawi	5.0
13	Afghanistan	6.6		Papua New Guinea	5.0
	Panama	6.6		Turkey	5.0
	Tanzania	6.6	40	Bolivia	4.9
16	Bangladesh	6.3		Dominican Rep.	4.9
	Mozambique	6.3		Peru	4.9
18	Cambodia	6.2	43	Malaysia	4.7
19	Congo-Kinshasa	6.1		Nigeria	4.7
20	Iraq	6.0	45	Paraguay	4.6
	Vietnam	6.0	46	Nepal	4.5
	Zambia	6.0		Senegal	4.5
23	Niger	5.8		Sierra Leone	4.5
24	Uganda	5.7	49	Kyrgyzstan	4.4
25	Philippines	5.6		Liberia	4.4

Lowest economic growth
Average annual % change in real GDP, 2007–17

1	Libya	-11.3	20	Finland	0.0
2	Virgin Islands (US)	-3.7	21	Barbados	0.1
3	Venezuela	-3.2		Latvia	0.1
4	Yemen	-3.0	23	Martinique[a]	0.3
5	Greece	-2.9		Spain	0.3
6	Andorra	-1.7	25	Cyprus	0.4
	Central African Rep.	-1.7	26	Estonia	0.5
8	Ukraine	-1.6		Japan	0.5
9	Bermuda	-1.4		North Korea	0.5
10	Timor-Leste	-1.2	29	Denmark	0.6
11	Puerto Rico	-1.1		Euro area	0.6
12	Italy	-0.6		Slovenia	0.6
13	Equatorial Guinea	-0.5	32	France	0.7
14	Brunei	-0.3	33	Austria	0.9
	Trinidad & Tobago	-0.3		Belgium	0.9
16	Croatia	-0.2		Netherlands	0.9
17	Bahamas	-0.1		Serbia	0.9
	Jamaica	-0.1	37	Guadeloupe[a]	1.0
	Portugal	-0.1		Hungary	1.0

a 2007–15

Highest economic growth
Average annual % increase in real GDP, 1997–2007

1	Equatorial Guinea	23.4	11	Macau	8.2
2	Timor-Leste[a]	18.8	12	Angola	8.1
3	Azerbaijan	15.3		Kazakhstan	8.1
4	Myanmar	12.0		Trinidad & Tobago	8.1
5	Qatar	10.7	15	Afghanistan[b]	8.0
6	Armenia	10.4		Tajikistan	8.0
7	China	10.0	17	Rwanda	7.9
8	Cambodia	9.5	18	Latvia	7.7
9	Chad	9.1	19	Turkmenistan	7.6
10	Mozambique	8.3	20	Belarus	7.4

Lowest economic growth
Average annual % change in real GDP, 1997–2007

1	Zimbabwe	-4.6	11	Uruguay	1.2
2	Guinea-Bissau	-1.2	12	Jamaica	1.3
3	Liberia[a]	-0.7	13	Guyana	1.4
4	Eritrea	0.2	14	Italy	1.5
5	Gabon	0.3	15	North Korea	1.6
6	Ivory Coast	0.8		Paraguay	1.6
7	Channel Islands[c]	0.9	17	Congo-Kinshasa	1.7
	Haiti	0.9		Germany	1.7
9	Japan	1.0	19	Papua New Guinea	1.9
10	Togo	1.1			

Highest services growth
Average annual % increase in real terms, 2007–17

1	Liberia	13.7	10	Uzbekistan	8.1
2	Ethiopia	12.2	11	Mongolia	7.9
3	Zimbabwe	11.6	12	Kuwait[d]	7.7
4	Myanmar[d]	9.3		Mozambique	7.7
5	Afghanistan	9.2	14	Zambia	7.3
6	India	9.0	15	Burkina Faso	7.2
7	China	8.7		Tajikistan	7.2
8	Rwanda	8.6	17	Papua New Guinea	7.0
9	Qatar[e]	8.2			

Lowest services growth
Average annual % change in real terms, 2007–17

1	Libya	-4.2	10	Italy	0.0
2	Syria	-3.8		Jamaica	0.0
3	Greece	-2.5		Suriname	0.0
	Puerto Rico	-2.5	13	Japan[f]	0.3
5	Yemen	-2.0	14	Estonia	0.4
6	North Korea	-1.1		Portugal	0.4
7	Ukraine	-0.9	16	Croatia	0.5
8	Bermuda	-0.8		Finland	0.5
9	Bahamas	-0.3	18	Latvia	0.7

a 2000–07 b 2002–07 c 1998–2007 d 2010–17 e 2011–17 f 2007–16
Note: Rankings of highest and lowest industrial growth 2007–17 can be found on page 44.

Trading places

Biggest exporters

% of total world exports (goods, services and income), 2017

1	Euro area (19)	16.43		**22**	Luxembourg	1.37
2	United States	12.47		**23**	Australia	1.29
3	China	10.33		**24**	Thailand	1.21
4	Germany	7.52		**25**	Poland	1.14
5	Japan	4.39		**26**	Hong Kong	1.11
6	France	3.87		**27**	Sweden	1.09
	United Kingdom	3.87		**28**	Brazil	1.05
8	Netherlands	3.68		**29**	Saudi Arabia	0.98
9	South Korea	2.66		**30**	Austria	0.97
10	Italy	2.63		**31**	Malaysia	0.90
11	Canada	2.29		**32**	Vietnam	0.87
12	Switzerland	2.26		**33**	Turkey	0.82
13	Spain	1.96		**34**	Denmark	0.79
14	India	1.93		**35**	Indonesia	0.76
15	Ireland	1.85		**36**	Norway	0.71
16	Belgium	1.83		**37**	Czech Republic	0.70
17	Russia	1.74		**38**	Hungary	0.53
18	Singapore	1.72		**39**	Finland	0.44
19	Mexico	1.70			Israel	0.44
20	Taiwan	1.63		**41**	Iran	0.42
21	United Arab Emirates	1.54				

Trade dependency

Trade[a] as % of GDP, 2017

Most				Least		
1	Vietnam	93.1		**1**	Sudan	5.2
2	Slovakia	84.0		**2**	Cuba[b]	7.0
3	United Arab Emirates	73.2		**3**	Venezuela[b]	7.8
4	Hungary	68.3		**4**	Bermuda	8.9
5	Czech Republic	65.0		**5**	Brazil	9.0
6	Slovenia	64.1		**6**	Argentina	9.6
7	Lithuania	63.5		**7**	United States	10.0
8	Belgium	61.5			Yemen[b]	10.0
9	Cambodia	60.3		**9**	Nigeria	10.4
10	South Sudan	60.0		**10**	Ethiopia	10.7
11	Puerto Rico	58.1			Hong Kong	10.7
12	Netherlands	58.0		**12**	Tanzania	11.7
13	Belarus	55.4		**13**	Timor-Leste	11.8
	Malaysia	55.4		**14**	Pakistan	12.5
	Suriname	55.4		**15**	Burundi	12.6
16	Lesotho	55.3		**16**	Colombia	13.3
17	Taiwan	53.8		**17**	Cameroon	13.5
18	Bulgaria	53.1		**18**	Japan	13.7
19	Estonia	52.8			Kenya	13.7
20	Congo-Brazzaville[b]	52.2		**20**	Macau	13.9
21	Singapore	50.9		**21**	India	14.3

Notes: The figures are drawn wherever possible from balance of payment statistics, so have differing definitions from statistics taken from customs or similar sources. For Hong Kong and Singapore, only domestic exports and retained imports are used. Euro area data exclude intra-euro area trade.

a Average of imports plus exports of goods.   b 2016

Biggest traders of goods[a]

% of world, 2018

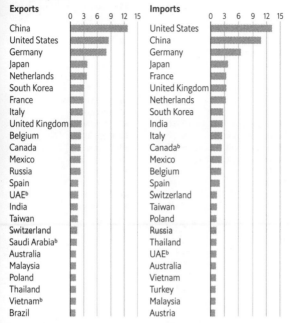

Exports

	0 3 6 9 12 15
China	
United States	
Germany	
Japan	
Netherlands	
South Korea	
France	
Italy	
United Kingdom	
Belgium	
Canada	
Mexico	
Russia	
Spain	
UAE[b]	
India	
Taiwan	
Switzerland	
Saudi Arabia[b]	
Australia	
Malaysia	
Poland	
Thailand	
Vietnam[b]	
Brazil	

Imports

	0 3 6 9 12 15
United States	
China	
Germany	
Japan	
France	
United Kingdom	
Netherlands	
South Korea	
India	
Italy	
Canada[b]	
Mexico	
Belgium	
Spain	
Switzerland	
Taiwan	
Poland	
Russia	
Thailand	
UAE[b]	
Australia	
Vietnam	
Turkey	
Malaysia	
Austria	

Biggest earners from services and income

% of world exports of services and income, 2017

1	Euro area (19)	18.58	19	Sweden	1.28
2	United States	18.06	20	South Korea	1.25
3	United Kingdom	6.09	21	Australia	1.13
4	Germany	5.85	22	Russia	1.09
5	China	5.24	23	Austria	1.03
6	Japan	4.87	24	Denmark	0.99
7	France	4.84	25	United Arab Emirates	0.96
8	Netherlands	4.65	26	Thailand	0.88
9	Luxembourg	3.56	27	Norway	0.87
10	Hong Kong	3.00	28	Taiwan	0.83
11	Switzerland	2.91	29	Poland	0.75
12	Ireland	2.82	30	Brazil	0.60
13	Singapore	2.77	31	Israel	0.59
14	India	2.13	32	Malaysia	0.52
15	Spain	2.10	33	Turkey	0.51
16	Italy	2.02	34	Finland	0.49
17	Canada	1.87	35	Greece	0.48
18	Belgium	1.86		Philippines	0.48

a Individual countries only.   b Estimate.

Balance of payments: current account

Largest surpluses
$m, 2017

1	Euro area (19)	415,252		26	Israel	9,968
2	Germany	296,172		27	Malaysia	9,450
3	Japan	201,639		28	Austria	7,996
4	China	195,117		29	Kuwait	7,757
5	Netherlands	87,394		30	Qatar	6,426
6	Taiwan	82,882		31	Vietnam	6,124
7	South Korea	75,231		32	Papua New Guinea	5,127
8	Singapore	53,913		33	Hungary	3,848
9	Italy	51,598		34	Belgium	3,567
10	Thailand	50,211		35	Slovenia	3,483
11	Switzerland	45,360		36	Czech Republic	3,148
12	Russia	33,156		37	Luxembourg	3,067
13	Ireland	29,099		38	Croatia	2,997
14	United Arab Emirates	27,465		39	Botswana	2,149
15	Denmark	26,270		40	Brunei	2,021
16	Spain	25,004		41	Cuba[a]	1,903
17	Norway	22,367		42	Bulgaria	1,847
18	Sweden	16,985		43	Azerbaijan	1,685
19	Macau	16,662		44	Uzbekistan	1,480
20	Hong Kong	15,885		45	Malta	1,337
21	Iran	15,816		46	Paraguay	1,206
22	Iraq	14,892		47	Guatemala	1,189
23	Puerto Rico	10,527		48	Portugal	1,170
24	Saudi Arabia	10,464		49	Trinidad & Tobago	1,089
25	Nigeria	10,381		50	Bermuda	940

Largest deficits
$m, 2017

1	United States	-449,137		22	New Zealand	-5,873
2	United Kingdom	-98,374		23	Ethiopia	-5,566
3	Turkey	-47,347		24	Kazakhstan	-5,102
4	Canada	-46,388		25	Kenya	-5,018
5	India	-38,168		26	Panama	-4,941
6	Australia	-35,758		27	Libya[a]	-4,705
7	Argentina	-31,598		28	Sudan	-4,611
8	Algeria	-22,059		29	Myanmar	-4,504
9	Mexico	-19,401		30	Jordan	-4,301
10	Pakistan	-16,251		31	Afghanistan	-4,227
11	Indonesia	-16,196		32	Tunisia	-4,080
12	France	-13,306		33	Morocco	-3,911
13	Lebanon	-12,396		34	Venezuela[a]	-3,870
14	Oman	-10,764		35	Congo-Brazzaville[a]	-3,594
15	Colombia	-10,296		36	Greece	-3,325
16	South Africa	-8,908		37	Peru	-2,720
17	Egypt	-7,940		38	Mozambique	-2,586
18	Brazil	-7,235		39	Ukraine	-2,442
19	Romania	-6,756		40	Yemen[a]	-2,421
20	Bangladesh	-6,365		41	Serbia	-2,322
21	Chile	-5,965		42	Sri Lanka	-2,309

Note: Euro area data exclude intra-euro area trade.
a 2016

Largest surpluses as % of GDP
$m, 2017

1	Macau	33.1	26	Luxembourg	4.9
2	Papua New Guinea	25.0		South Korea	4.9
3	Brunei	16.7		Trinidad & Tobago	4.9
4	Singapore	16.6	29	Hong Kong	4.7
5	Bermuda	15.0	30	Azerbaijan	4.1
6	Taiwan	14.4		Japan	4.1
7	Swaziland	12.5	32	Qatar	3.8
8	Botswana	12.3	33	Iceland	3.7
9	Thailand	11.0	34	Guyana[a]	3.6
10	Malta	10.7	35	Iran	3.5
11	Netherlands	10.5	36	Euro area (19)	3.3
12	Puerto Rico	10.1	37	Bulgaria	3.2
13	South Sudan	9.6		Estonia	3.2
14	Ireland	8.8		Sweden	3.2
15	Denmark	8.0	40	Malaysia	3.0
	Germany	8.0		Paraguay	3.0
17	Iraq	7.8		Uzbekistan	3.0
18	French Polynesia[a]	7.6	43	Hungary	2.8
19	United Arab Emirates	7.2		Israel	2.8
20	Slovenia	7.1		Nigeria	2.8
21	Switzerland	6.7	46	Italy	2.7
22	Kuwait	6.5		Vietnam	2.7
23	Norway	5.6	48	Tajikistan	2.2
24	Croatia	5.4	49	Cuba[a]	2.1
25	Guinea	5.0		Russia	2.1

Largest deficits as % of GDP
$m, 2017

1	Congo-Brazzaville[a]	-39.8	22	Benin	-10.0
2	Lebanon	-23.1	23	Georgia	-9.6
3	Maldives	-22.0	24	Central African Rep.	-8.9
4	Afghanistan	-21.6	25	Cyprus	-8.4
5	Mozambique	-20.4	26	Cambodia	-7.9
6	Sierra Leone	-19.5		Mali	-7.9
7	Libya[a]	-17.9		Panama	-7.9
8	Liberia	-17.2	29	Haiti	-7.7
9	Bahamas	-16.3	30	Albania	-7.5
10	Malawi	-16.2	31	Gambia, The	-7.4
11	Montenegro	-15.7		Moldova	-7.4
	Niger	-15.7	33	Burkina Faso	-7.3
13	Oman	-15.2		Fiji	-7.3
14	Mauritania	-14.1	35	Senegal	-7.2
15	Algeria	-13.2	36	Laos	-7.1
16	Timor-Leste	-11.5		Lesotho	-7.1
17	Burundi	-11.3	38	Ethiopia	-6.9
18	West Bank & Gaza	-10.8		Kyrgyzstan	-6.9
19	Jordan	-10.7		New Caledonia[a]	-6.9
20	Tunisia	-10.2	41	Rwanda	-6.8
21	Mongolia	-10.1	42	Myanmar	-6.7

a 2016

Official reserves[a]

$m, end-2018

1	China	3,168,059	16	Mexico	176,380
2	Japan	1,270,402	17	United Kingdom	172,631
3	Euro area (19)	821,608	18	France	166,276
4	Switzerland	786,933	19	Italy	152,153
5	Saudi Arabia	509,441	20	Czech Republic	142,511
6	Taiwan	479,204	21	Indonesia	120,654
7	Russia	468,465	22	Poland	116,946
8	United States	449,214	23	Israel	115,266
9	Hong Kong	424,620	24	Malaysia	101,449
10	South Korea	403,073	25	United Arab Emirates	99,503
11	India	399,116	26	Turkey	92,941
12	Brazil	374,704	27	Algeria	87,368
13	Singapore	292,705	28	Libya	85,326
14	Thailand	205,628	29	Canada	83,926
15	Germany	197,740	30	Philippines	79,179

Official gold reserves

Market prices, $m, end-2018

1	Euro area (19)	443,217	14	Portugal	15,729
2	United States	334,457	15	Kazakhstan	14,411
3	Germany	138,567	16	Saudi Arabia	13,285
4	Italy	100,822	17	United Kingdom	12,759
5	France	100,173	18	Lebanon	11,795
6	Russia	86,890	19	Spain	11,579
7	China	76,177	20	Austria	11,514
8	Switzerland	42,766	21	Belgium	9,351
9	Japan	31,467	22	Philippines	8,139
10	Netherlands	25,185	23	Algeria	7,140
11	India	24,691	24	Venezuela[b]	6,487
12	Turkey	20,074	25	Thailand	6,331
13	Taiwan	17,420	26	Poland	5,290

Workers' remittances

Inflows, $m, 2017

1	India	68,967	16	Indonesia	9,012
2	China	63,860	17	Guatemala	8,453
3	Philippines	32,810	18	Russia	8,235
4	Mexico	30,618	19	Lebanon	7,440
5	France	24,885	20	Sri Lanka	7,190
6	Egypt	22,524	21	Nepal	6,928
7	Nigeria	22,001	22	Poland	6,870
8	Pakistan	19,689	23	Morocco	6,847
9	Germany	16,778	24	Thailand	6,729
10	Vietnam	15,000	25	United States	6,301
11	Bangladesh	13,498	26	South Korea	6,224
12	Ukraine	12,208	27	Dominican Rep.	6,178
13	Spain	10,630	28	Colombia	5,525
14	Belgium	10,511	29	El Salvador	5,054
15	Italy	9,809	30	Hungary	4,638

a Foreign exchange, SDRs, IMF position and gold at market prices.   b June.

Exchange rates

The Economist's Big Mac index

Local currency under (-)/over (+) valuation against the $ᵃ, %
January 2019

Big Mac price, $ᵇ

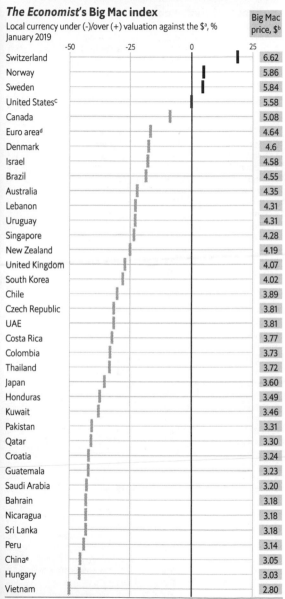

	Big Mac price, $ᵇ
Switzerland	6.62
Norway	5.86
Sweden	5.84
United Statesᶜ	5.58
Canada	5.08
Euro areaᵈ	4.64
Denmark	4.6
Israel	4.58
Brazil	4.55
Australia	4.35
Lebanon	4.31
Uruguay	4.31
Singapore	4.28
New Zealand	4.19
United Kingdom	4.07
South Korea	4.02
Chile	3.89
Czech Republic	3.81
UAE	3.81
Costa Rica	3.77
Colombia	3.73
Thailand	3.72
Japan	3.60
Honduras	3.49
Kuwait	3.46
Pakistan	3.31
Qatar	3.30
Croatia	3.24
Guatemala	3.23
Saudi Arabia	3.20
Bahrain	3.18
Nicaragua	3.18
Sri Lanka	3.18
Peru	3.14
Chinaᵉ	3.05
Hungary	3.03
Vietnam	2.80

a Based on purchasing-power parity: local price of a Big Mac burger divided by United States price. b At market exchange rates. c Average of four cities.
d Weighted average of prices in euro area. e Average of five cities.

Inflation

Consumer-price inflation

Highest, 2018, %

1	Venezuela[a]	929,789.5
2	South Sudan[a]	83.5
3	Sudan	63.3
4	Yemen[a]	41.8
5	Argentina	34.3
6	Iran	31.2
7	Congo-Kinshasa	29.3
8	Liberia[a]	23.4
9	Libya[a]	23.1
10	Egypt	20.9
11	Angola	19.6
12	Uzbekistan	17.9
13	Sierra Leone[a]	16.9
14	Turkey	16.3
15	Ethiopia[a]	13.8
16	Turkmenistan[a]	13.6
17	Haiti	13.5
18	Nigeria	12.1
19	Ukraine[a]	10.9
20	Zimbabwe	10.6
21	Ghana[a]	9.8

Lowest, 2018, %

1	Ecuador	-0.2
2	Brunei[a]	0.1
3	Qatar	0.2
4	Ivory Coast[a]	0.3
5	Iraq[a]	0.4
	Singapore[a]	0.4
7	Senegal	0.5
8	Afghanistan[a]	0.6
9	Denmark	0.7
	Ireland	0.7
	Kuwait	0.7
	Togo	0.7
13	Cyprus	0.8
	Greece	0.8
	Israel[a]	0.8
	Panama[a]	0.8
17	Cameroon	0.9
	Oman	0.9
	Switzerland[a]	0.9

Highest average annual consumer-price inflation, 2008–18, %

1	Venezuela[a]	332.8
2	South Sudan	78.2
3	Sudan	27.3
4	Belarus[a]	19.3
5	Iran	18.4
6	Argentina	17.7
7	Congo-Kinshasa	16.6
8	Malawi	15.9
9	Angola	15.5
10	Egypt	12.9
11	Ethiopia[a]	12.7
	Ukraine[a]	12.7
13	Yemen[a]	12.1
14	Nigeria	11.9
15	Ghana[a]	11.8
16	Suriname	11.7
17	Uzbekistan	11.6
18	Libya[a]	11.5
19	Guinea[a]	11.2
20	Eritrea[a]	10.4
21	Liberia[a]	9.9
22	Zambia	9.3
23	Sierra Leone[a]	9.0
24	Turkey	8.9

Lowest average annual consumer-price inflation, 2008–18, %

1	Switzerland[a]	-0.1
2	Brunei[a]	0.1
	Ireland	0.1
4	Japan	0.3
5	Senegal	0.6
6	Bosnia & Herz.	0.7
7	Cyprus	0.8
	Qatar	0.8
9	Greece	0.9
10	Burkina Faso[a]	1.0
11	Bulgaria	1.1
	Denmark	1.1
	Portugal	1.1
	Spain	1.1
15	Benin[a]	1.2
	Croatia	1.2
	El Salvador	1.2
	France	1.2
	Guinea-Bissau[a]	1.2
	Morocco[a]	1.2
	Puerto Rico[a]	1.2
	Slovenia	1.2

a Estimate.

Commodity prices

End 2018, % change on a year earlier		*2013–18, % change*	
1 Wheat	22.3	1 Wool (Aus)	64.2
2 Cocoa	21.5	2 Zinc	21.6
3 Corn	7.1	3 Lamb	18.1
4 Wool (Aus)	5.5	4 Aluminium	7.6
5 Beef (US)	3.7	5 Gold	4.8
6 Wool (NZ)	1.1	6 Beef (Aus)	0.5
7 Tin	0.0	7 Tea	0.0
8 Lamb	-1.2	8 Beef (US)	-0.2
9 Gold	-1.3	9 Rice	-1.8
10 Beef (Aus)	-1.5	10 Coffee	-5.2
11 Soya meal	-2.4	11 Timber	-6.9
12 Rice	-4.1	12 Lead	-9.5
13 Rubber	-4.8	13 Cotton	-10.2
14 Soyabeans	-7.8	14 Corn	-10.5
15 Cotton	-9.1	15 Tin	-13.9
16 Nickel	-10.4	16 Wheat	-14.7
17 Aluminium	-11.2	17 Cocoa	-18.5
18 Coffee	-12.2	18 Copper	-19.8
19 Tea	-12.9	19 Nickel	-22.7
20 Hides	-14.8	20 Sugar	-24.7
21 Sugar	-15.0	21 Soya oil	-28.5
22 Copper	-15.5	22 Rubber	-29.2
23 Soya oil	-16.4	23 Soya meal	-29.7
24 Lead	-19.3	24 Soyabeans	-32.6
25 Zinc	-21.6	25 Coconut oil	-33.3
26 Palm oil	-23.5	26 Wool (NZ)	-42.5

The Economist's house prices

Q4 2018ª, % change on a year earlier		*Q4 2013–Q4 2018ª, % change*	
1 Slovenia	11.1	1 Turkey	67.3
2 Czech Republic	7.6	2 Ireland	65.4
3 Latvia	7.3	3 Iceland	62.9
Netherlands	7.3	4 India	54.3
5 Mexico	6.7	5 Hungary	53.7
6 Portugal	6.5	6 Colombia	44.9
7 Ireland	6.4	7 New Zealand	43.8
8 Luxembourg	5.6	8 Canada	41.0
Turkey	5.6	9 Czech Republic	40.3
10 China	5.2	10 Mexico	38.0
Spain	5.2	11 Sweden	37.7
12 United States	5.0	12 Portugal	36.3
13 Poland	4.9	13 China	36.1
14 Lithuania	4.6	14 Lithuania	33.3
15 Iceland	4.5	15 Estonia	32.2
16 Hungary	4.1	16 Netherlands	31.4
17 Germany	3.6	17 United Kingdom	30.8
India	3.6	18 Chile	30.3
South Africa	3.6	19 Luxembourg	30.0
20 Switzerland	3.5	20 Austria	28.8

a Or latest.

Debt

Highest foreign debt[a]

$bn, 2017

1	China	1,710.2	26	Romania	109.4
2	Hong Kong	643.0	27	Venezuela	105.6
3	Singapore	566.1	28	Vietnam	104.1
4	Brazil	543.0	29	Panama	91.9
5	India	513.2	30	Israel	88.8
6	Russia	492.8	31	Pakistan	84.5
7	Mexico	455.1	32	Egypt	82.9
8	Turkey	454.7	33	Lebanon	73.5
9	South Korea	384.6	34	Philippines	73.1
10	Indonesia	354.4	35	Iraq	72.1
11	Poland	242.6	36	Peru	68.1
12	United Arab Emirates	237.6	37	Sudan	56.1
13	Argentina	229.0	38	Bahrain	52.1
14	Malaysia	215.9	39	Sri Lanka	50.1
15	Saudi Arabia	206.9	40	Morocco	49.8
16	Czech Republic	205.1	41	Kuwait	49.1
17	Chile	183.4	42	Croatia	48.1
18	Taiwan	181.9	43	Bangladesh	47.2
19	South Africa	176.3	44	Oman	46.3
20	Kazakhstan	167.5	45	Bulgaria	40.4
21	Qatar	165.0	46	Nigeria	40.2
22	Hungary	153.2	47	Belarus	39.6
23	Thailand	129.8	48	Ecuador	39.5
24	Colombia	124.4	49	Angola	37.2
25	Ukraine	113.3	50	Serbia	34.5

Highest foreign debt burden[a]

Total foreign debt as % of GDP, 2017

1	Mongolia	247.7	21	Moldova	85.8
2	Hong Kong	188.2	22	Mauritania	84.3
3	Singapore	168.1	23	Nicaragua	82.9
4	Mauritius	158.8	24	Tajikistan	82.3
5	Panama	148.6	25	Tunisia	80.5
6	Bahrain	147.2	26	Serbia	77.8
7	Lebanon	137.2	27	Bosnia & Herz.	77.4
8	Hungary	109.8	28	Macedonia	75.9
9	Kyrgyzstan	107.9	29	Jordan	73.8
10	Jamaica	106.1	30	Belarus	72.7
11	Kazakhstan	105.5	31	Albania	69.9
12	Georgia	104.5	32	Bulgaria	69.5
13	Ukraine	101.0	33	Malaysia	68.6
14	Qatar	98.9	34	El Salvador	67.3
15	Czech Republic	94.9	35	Chile	66.2
	Mozambique	94.9	36	Oman	65.4
17	Armenia	89.6	37	Montenegro	64.8
18	Papua New Guinea	88.1	38	Gambia, The	64.1
19	Croatia	87.2	39	Zambia	63.2
20	Laos	86.0	40	United Arab Emirates	62.1

a Foreign debt is debt owed to non-residents and repayable in foreign currency; the figures shown include liabilities of government, public and private sectors. Longer-established developed countries have been excluded.

Highest foreign debt[a]

As % of exports of goods and services, 2017

1	Sudan	962.5	15	Turkey	210.4
2	Mongolia	394.4	16	Mozambique	206.8
3	Ethiopia	375.6	17	Kenya	206.5
4	Venezuela	310.7	18	Mauritania	200.7
5	Panama	306.4	19	Sierra Leone	199.9
6	Argentina	293.8	20	Jamaica	196.9
7	Kazakhstan	285.3	21	Tanzania	196.7
8	Lebanon	256.9	22	Brazil	195.6
9	Yemen	245.2	23	Burundi	194.9
10	Laos	238.3	24	Sri Lanka	189.4
11	Central African Rep.	228.8	25	Zambia	178.4
12	Niger	214.9	26	Bahrain	176.1
13	Chile	211.9	27	Qatar	176.0
14	Colombia	210.6	28	Uganda	175.8

Highest debt service ratio[b]

Average, %, 2017

1	Syria	67.4	15	Papua New Guinea	30.3
2	Mongolia	54.1	16	Bahrain	29.1
3	Croatia	53.4	17	Jamaica	28.5
4	Lebanon	51.2	18	Ecuador	26.0
5	Kazakhstan	47.7	19	Russia	25.5
6	Turkey	40.0	20	Georgia	24.4
7	Venezuela	39.4	21	Zambia	24.3
8	Chile	38.5	22	Mauritius	23.9
9	Colombia	37.7	23	Romania	21.4
10	Hungary	37.3	24	Armenia	21.0
11	Sudan	35.4	25	Cuba	20.9
12	Brazil	34.4	26	Serbia	20.8
13	Indonesia	32.6	27	Bulgaria	20.5
14	Namibia	31.2	28	Ethiopia	19.6

Household debt[c]

As % of net disposable income, 2017

1	Denmark	281.2	14	New Zealand[e]	121.2
2	Netherlands	242.8	15	France	119.7
3	Norway	235.5	16	Belgium	117.4
4	Australia	216.3	17	Spain	116.2
5	Switzerland[d]	212.1	18	United States	108.8
6	Sweden	186.3	19	Japan[d]	105.6
7	South Korea	185.9	20	Greece	105.4
8	Luxembourg	182.9	21	Germany	93.3
9	Canada	181.4	22	Austria	92.2
10	Ireland	153.2	23	Italy	86.8
11	United Kingdom	148.9	24	Estonia	80.2
12	Finland	138.6	25	Slovakia	78.5
13	Portugal	136.3	26	Chile[e]	66.7

b Debt service is the sum of interest and principal repayments (amortisation) due on outstanding foreign debt. The debt service ratio is debt service as a percentage of exports of goods, non-factor services, primary income and workers' remittances.
c OECD countries.   d 2016   e 2015

Aid

Largest recipients of bilateral and multilateral aid
$bn, 2017

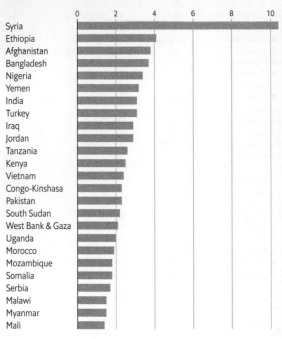

$ per person, 2017

1	Syria	567.1		**21**	Rwanda	100.4
2	West Bank & Gaza	450.7		**22**	Maldives	96.0
3	Jordan	301.0		**23**	Nicaragua	90.5
4	Mongolia	248.4		**24**	Haiti	89.3
5	Serbia	240.4		**25**	Armenia	87.2
6	Lebanon	214.6		**26**	Bolivia	85.7
7	Kosovo	214.3		**27**	Malawi	81.4
8	Montenegro	188.7		**28**	Iraq	76.0
9	Timor-Leste	178.9		**29**	Kyrgyzstan	74.3
10	South Sudan	173.6		**30**	Namibia	73.7
11	Fiji	161.1		**31**	Mali	73.2
12	Liberia	131.4		**32**	Macedonia	72.0
13	Gambia, The	128.4		**33**	Sierra Leone	71.1
14	Bosnia & Herz.	125.6		**34**	Laos	69.4
15	Georgia	120.1		**35**	Moldova	67.9
16	Somalia	119.4		**36**	Libya	67.7
17	Yemen	114.5		**37**	Tunisia	67.3
18	Central African Rep.	109.0		**38**	Guyana	65.7
19	Swaziland	107.3			Lesotho	65.7
20	Afghanistan	107.1		**40**	Papua New Guinea	64.5

Largest bilateral and multilateral donors[a]

2017

		$bn	As % of GNI				$bn	As % of GNI
1	United States	34.7	0.2		15	Australia	3.0	0.2
2	Germany	25.0	0.7		16	Spain	2.6	0.2
3	United Kingdom	18.1	0.7		17	Denmark	2.4	0.7
4	Japan	11.5	0.2		18	Belgium	2.2	0.4
5	France	11.3	0.4			South Korea	2.2	0.1
6	Turkey	8.1	1.0		20	Austria	1.3	0.3
7	Saudi Arabia[b]	6.8	1.1		21	Russia	1.2	0.1
8	Italy	5.9	0.3		22	Finland	1.1	0.4
9	Sweden	5.6	1.0		23	Ireland	0.8	0.3
10	Netherlands	5.0	0.6		24	Poland	0.7	0.1
11	Canada	4.3	0.3		25	Kuwait	0.6	0.4
12	Norway	4.1	1.0		26	Luxembourg	0.4	1.0
13	United Arab					New Zealand	0.4	0.2
	Emirates	4.0	1.0			Portugal	0.4	0.2
14	Switzerland	3.1	0.5					

Biggest changes to aid

2017 compared with 2013, $m

	Increases			Decreases	
1	Syria	6,722.9	1	Egypt	-5,626.2
2	Yemen	2,194.4	2	Myanmar	-2,393.3
3	Jordan	1,520.4	3	Vietnam	-1,709.2
4	Iraq	1,365.9	4	Afghanistan	-1,348.5
5	Bangladesh	1,106.4	5	Brazil	-890.7
6	Serbia	907.5	6	Tanzania	-849.1
7	Nigeria	843.1	7	Kenya	-832.1
8	South Sudan	783.9	8	Sudan	-667.0
9	Somalia	705.8	9	Mozambique	-537.0
10	Lebanon	683.9	10	West Bank & Gaza	-491.0
11	India	637.3	11	Ivory Coast	-446.0
12	Cuba	618.3	12	China	-388.5
13	Cameroon	460.6	13	Peru	-371.3
14	Niger	409.4	14	Belarus	-360.3
15	Nepal	385.1	15	Congo-Kinshasa	-303.8
16	Malawi	382.9	16	South Africa	-281.0
17	Ukraine	375.4	17	Georgia	-200.0
18	Uzbekistan	343.1	18	Honduras	-184.5
19	Mongolia	333.4	19	Kosovo	-176.2
20	Uganda	311.0	20	Lesotho	-173.9
21	Central African Rep.	305.0	21	Haiti	-171.9
22	Libya	303.0	22	Burkina Faso	-159.7
23	Turkey	293.8	23	Mauritius	-134.1
24	Madagascar	280.3	24	Burundi	-130.4
25	Bolivia	244.6	25	Guatemala	-130.1
26	Ethiopia	232.0	26	Papua New Guinea	-125.4
27	Thailand	221.2	27	Morocco	-123.8
28	Chad	188.5	28	Zambia	-121.8
29	Azerbaijan	186.3	29	Albania	-112.7

a China also provides aid, but does not disclose amounts. b 2015

Industry and services

Largest industrial output
$bn, 2017

1	China	4,950	23	Thailand	160
2	United States	3,516	24	Iran	158
3	Japan[a]	1,450	25	Poland	152
4	Germany	1,015	26	Netherlands	145
5	India	684	27	Argentina	139
6	South Korea	549	28	Malaysia	122
7	Canada[b]	495	29	Norway	119
8	United Kingdom	487		Sweden	119
9	Russia	474	31	Ireland	111
10	France	448	32	Austria	105
11	Italy	413	33	Belgium	97
12	Indonesia	400	34	Philippines	95
13	Brazil	380		Qatar	95
14	Mexico	346	36	South Africa	90
15	Saudi Arabia	312	37	Colombia	84
16	Australia	305		Nigeria	84
17	Spain	283	39	Chile	83
18	Turkey	248	40	Iraq	83
19	Taiwan	204	41	Egypt	79
20	Venezuela[b]	180	42	Singapore	75
21	Switzerland	171		Vietnam	75
28	United Arab Emirates	167	44	Czech Republic	72

Highest growth in industrial output
Average annual % increase in real terms, 2007–17

1	Liberia	21.1	11	Rwanda	9.0
2	Ethiopia	16.7	12	Bangladesh	8.8
3	Myanmar	13.8	13	China	8.6
4	Laos	12.1	14	Cambodia	8.3
5	Bahamas	12.0		Tanzania	8.3
6	Panama	11.0	16	Qatar	7.9
7	Ghana	10.3	17	Iraq	7.5
	Uzbekistan	10.3	18	Kosovo	7.0
9	Congo-Kinshasa	9.6		Tajikistan	7.0
10	Niger	9.3	20	Ireland	6.6

Lowest growth in industrial output
Average annual % change in real terms, 2007–17

1	Yemen	-5.6		Italy	-1.6
2	Greece	-5.2		Jamaica	-1.6
3	Ukraine	-4.8		Spain	-1.6
4	Cyprus	-4.1	15	Botswana	-1.5
5	Barbados[c]	-3.4		Finland	-1.5
	Macau	-3.4		Latvia	-1.5
7	Timor-Leste[c]	-3.2	18	Portugal	-1.3
8	Equatorial Guinea	-2.5	19	Luxembourg	-1.0
9	Trinidad & Tobago	-2.2	20	Sweden	-0.7
10	Brunei	-1.9	21	France	-0.6
11	Croatia	-1.6	22	Venezuela[d]	-0.5

a 2016   b 2014   c 2007–16   d 2007–14

Largest manufacturing output
$bn, 2017

1	China	3,591		21	Poland	93
2	United States[a]	2,161		22	Netherlands	91
3	Japan a	1,042		23	Saudi Arabia	88
4	Germany	778		24	Argentina	83
5	South Korea	422		25	Australia	76
6	India	394		26	Sweden	73
7	Italy	290		27	Malaysia	70
8	France	262		28	Austria	69
9	United Kingdom	237		29	Belgium	63
10	Brazil	216		30	Philippines	61
11	Indonesia	205		31	Algeria	59
12	Mexico	198		32	Singapore	58
13	Russia	193			Venezuela[c]	58
14	Taiwan	179		34	Iran	54
15	Spain	169		35	Czech Republic	52
16	Canada[b]	160		36	Puerto Rico[a]	50
17	Turkey	149		37	Israel	44
18	Thailand	123			Romania	44
19	Switzerland	122		39	Bangladesh	43
20	Ireland	106				

Largest services output
$bn, 2017

1	United States[a]	14,300		27	Thailand	256
2	China	6,320		28	Norway	230
3	Japan[a]	3,400		29	Singapore	228
4	Germany	2,270		30	Venezuela[c]	226
5	United Kingdom	1,860		31	Israel[a]	222
6	France	1,810		32	Denmark	216
7	Brazil	1,300		33	South Africa	215
8	Italy	1,290		34	Nigeria	210
9	India	1,270		35	Philippines	188
10	Canada[b]	1,160		36	Ireland	187
11	Australia	886		37	United Arab Emirates	179
	Russia	886		38	Colombia	172
13	Spain	869		39	Pakistan	162
14	South Korea	809		40	Chile	160
15	Mexico	701			Malaysia	160
16	Netherlands	584		42	Finland	150
17	Switzerland	485		43	Portugal	143
18	Turkey	454		44	Greece	139
19	Indonesia	443		45	Bangladesh	134
20	Argentina	363		46	Romania	119
21	Saudi Arabia	359		47	Czech Republic	118
22	Sweden	349		48	New Zealand[b]	117
23	Belgium	341		49	Kazakhstan	92
24	Poland	306		50	Vietnam[a]	84
25	Iran	287		51	Hungary	77
26	Austria	261		52	Algeria	75

a 2016   b 2015   c 2014

Agriculture and fisheries

Largest agricultural output
$bn, 2017

1	China	969		Italy	37
2	India	414	17	Argentina	36
3	United States[a]	189		Sudan	36
4	Indonesia	134	19	Spain	35
5	Brazil	95	20	Vietnam	34
6	Nigeria	78	21	Bangladesh	33
7	Pakistan	70	22	Philippines	30
8	Japan[a]	57		South Korea	30
9	Russia	56	24	Germany	29
10	Turkey	52	25	Malaysia	28
11	Iran	43	26	Canada[b]	27
12	France	39		Egypt	27
	Mexico	39		Ethiopia	27
	Thailand	39		Kenya	27
15	Australia	37	30	Venezuela[c]	24

Most economically dependent on agriculture
% of GDP from agriculture, 2017

1	Sierra Leone	60.3		Tanzania	28.7
2	Chad	49.1	16	Nepal	26.2
3	Guinea-Bissau	49.0	17	Malawi	26.1
4	Togo	41.8	18	Uganda	24.6
5	Niger	39.7	19	Cambodia	23.4
6	Central African Rep.	39.6	20	Myanmar	23.3
7	Mali	38.3	21	Mauritania	23.1
8	Liberia	37.1	22	Benin	23.0
9	Kenya	34.6		Gambia, The	23.0
10	Ethiopia	34.0	24	Pakistan	22.9
11	Rwanda	31.0	25	North Korea[a]	21.7
12	Burundi[b]	30.6	26	Ivory Coast	21.6
13	Sudan	30.5	27	Mozambique	21.3
14	Burkina Faso	28.7	28	Nigeria	20.8

Least economically dependent on agriculture
% of GDP from agriculture, 2017

1	Macau	0.0		Puerto Rico[a]	0.8
	Singapore	0.0		United Arab Emirates	0.8
3	Hong Kong	0.1	16	Bahamas	1.0
4	Qatar	0.2		Malta	1.0
5	Bahrain	0.3		United States	1.0
	Luxembourg	0.3	19	Brunei	1.1
7	Kuwait	0.5		Sweden	1.1
	Andorra[a]	0.5	21	Austria	1.2
	Trinidad & Tobago	0.5		Ireland	1.2
10	United Kingdom	0.6		Israel	1.2
11	Belgium	0.7		Japan[a]	1.2
	Switzerland	0.7	25	Barbados[a]	1.4
13	Germany	0.8		Denmark	1.4

a 2016 b 2015 c 2014

Fisheries and aquaculture production

Fish, crustaceans and molluscs, million tonnes, 2017

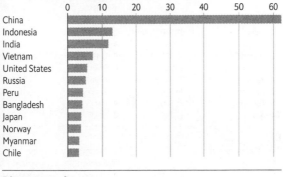

Biggest producers

'000 tonnes, 2016

Cereals

1	China	616,251	6	Brazil	84,129
2	United States	475,959	7	Ukraine	65,218
3	India	297,850	8	Argentina	61,148
4	Russia	117,744	9	Canada	58,793
5	Indonesia	102,933	10	France	54,652

Meat

1	China	87,745	6	India	7,204
2	United States	44,634	7	Mexico	6,553
3	Brazil	26,978	8	Spain	6,547
4	Russia	9,899	9	France	5,656
5	Germany	8,436	10	Argentina	5,398

Fruit

1	China	257,720	6	Mexico	21,422
2	India	89,919	7	Spain	19,208
3	Brazil	39,350	8	Iran	18,641
4	United States	27,987	9	Indonesia	18,531
5	Turkey	21,781	10	Italy	17,931

Vegetables

1	China	556,909	6	Russia	16,291
2	India	123,205	7	Nigeria	16,195
3	Turkey	26,276	8	Iran	15,211
4	Ukraine	16,517	9	Vietnam	15,205
5	Egypt	16,352	10	Mexico	14,915

Roots and tubers

1	China	174,499	5	Thailand	31,688
2	Nigeria	117,358	6	Russia	31,108
3	India	49,215	7	Ghana	26,683
4	Congo-Kinshasa	35,748	8	Brazil	25,856

Commodities

Wheat

Top 10 producers, 2017–18 '000 tonnes		Top 10 consumers, 2017–18 '000 tonnes	
1 EU28	151,363	1 EU28	127,030
2 China	134,334	2 China	123,450
3 India	98,510	3 India	95,700
4 Russia	85,132	4 Russia	43,110
5 United States	47,380	5 United States	29,320
6 Canada	29,984	6 Pakistan	24,370
7 Pakistan	26,981	7 Egypt	20,020
8 Ukraine	26,600	8 Turkey	18,960
9 Turkey	21,500	9 Iran	15,800
10 Australia	21,244	10 Brazil	11,780

Rice[a]

Top 10 producers, 2017–18 '000 tonnes		Top 10 consumers, 2017–18 '000 tonnes	
1 China	148,873	1 China	142,487
2 India	112,910	2 India	98,819
3 Indonesia	37,000	3 Indonesia	38,100
4 Bangladesh	32,650	4 Bangladesh	35,200
5 Vietnam	28,471	5 Vietnam	22,100
6 Thailand	20,370	6 Philippines	13,250
7 Myanmar	13,200	7 Thailand	10,600
8 Philippines	12,235	8 Myanmar	10,200
9 Brazil	8,204	9 Japan	8,600
10 Japan	7,787	10 Brazil	7,800

Sugar[b]

Top 10 producers, 2017 '000 tonnes		Top 10 consumers, 2017 '000 tonnes	
1 Brazil	38,100	1 India	24,520
2 India	22,450	2 EU28	18,000
3 EU28	17,520	3 China	16,090
4 Thailand	10,780	4 Brazil	10,920
5 China	9,310	5 United States	10,090
6 United States	7,510	6 Indonesia	6,750
7 Russia	6,590	7 Russia	5,800
8 Pakistan	6,550	8 Pakistan	5,070
9 Mexico	6,050	9 Mexico	4,440
10 Australia	4,480	10 Egypt	3,600

Coarse grains[c]

Top 5 producers, 2017–18 '000 tonnes		Top 5 consumers, 2017–18 '000 tonnes	
1 United States	384,884	1 United States	325,290
2 China	268,046	2 China	300,680
3 EU28	154,737	3 EU28	161,810
4 Brazil	83,903	4 Brazil	67,620
5 Argentina	49,200	5 Mexico	50,070

a Milled. b Raw. c Includes: maize (corn), barley, sorghum, oats, rye, millet, triticale and other. d Tonnes at 65 degrees brix.

Tea

Top 10 producers, 2017		*Top 10 consumers, 2017*	
'000 tonnes		*'000 tonnes*	
1 China	2,460	1 China	2,135
2 India	1,325	2 India	1,083
3 Kenya	440	3 Turkey	327
4 Sri Lanka	350	4 Pakistan	175
5 Vietnam	260	5 Russia	156
6 Turkey	234	6 United States	123
7 Indonesia	139	7 United Kingdom	110
8 Myanmar	105	8 Japan	105
9 Iran	101	9 Egypt	94
10 Bangladesh	82	10 Indonesia	89

Coffee

Top 10 producers, 2018		*Top 10 consumers, 2017–18*	
'000 tonnes		*'000 tonnes*	
1 Brazil	3,750	1 EU28	2,641
2 Vietnam	1,770	2 United States	1,567
3 Colombia	852	3 Brazil	1,274
4 Indonesia	612	4 Japan	465
5 Ethiopia	450	5 Indonesia	282
6 Honduras	447	6 Russia	259
7 India	312	7 Canada	230
8 Uganda	294	8 Ethiopia	225
9 Mexico	270	9 Philippines	180
10 Peru	264	10 Vietnam	150

Cocoa

Top 10 producers, 2017–18		*Top 10 consumers, 2017–18*	
'000 tonnes		*'000 tonnes*	
1 Ivory Coast	1,964	1 Netherlands	595
2 Ghana	906	2 Ivory Coast	559
3 Ecuador	285	3 Indonesia	483
4 Nigeria	255	4 Germany	448
5 Cameroon	250	5 United States	385
6 Indonesia	240	6 Ghana	311
7 Brazil	204	7 Malaysia	236
8 Peru	134	8 Brazil	230
9 Dominican Rep.	70	9 France	152
10 Colombia	60	10 Spain	100

Orange juice[d]

Top 5 producers, 2017–18		*Top 5 consumers, 2017–18*	
'000 tonnes		*'000 tonnes*	
1 Brazil	1,041	1 EU28	741
2 United States	187	2 United States	575
3 Mexico	195	3 China	96
4 EU28	97	4 Canada	84
5 China	44	5 Japan	72

Copper

Top 10 producers[a], 2017		*Top 10 consumers[b], 2017*	
'000 tonnes		*'000 tonnes*	
1 Chile	5,504	1 China	11,790
2 Peru	2,445	2 EU28	2,755
3 China	1,656	3 United States	1,771
4 United States	1,258	4 Germany	1,180
5 Congo-Kinshasa	1,095	5 Japan	998
6 EU28	965	6 South Korea	656
7 Zambia	942	7 Italy	635
8 Australia	860	8 Taiwan	498
9 Kazakhstan	745	9 India	486
10 Mexico	742	10 Turkey	445

Lead

Top 10 producers[a], 2017		*Top 10 consumers[b], 2017*	
'000 tonnes		*'000 tonnes*	
1 China	2,332	1 China	4,795
2 Australia	460	2 EU28	1,871
3 United States	313	3 United States	1,640
4 Peru	307	4 South Korea	622
5 Mexico	241	5 India	551
6 Russia	202	6 Germany	414
7 India	176	7 United Kingdom	295
8 EU28	170	8 Japan	287
9 Kazakhstan	112	9 Spain	261
10 Bolivia	111	10 Brazil	251

Zinc

Top 10 producers[a], 2017		*Top 10 consumers[c], 2017*	
'000 tonnes		*'000 tonnes*	
1 China	4,997	1 China	6,965
2 Peru	1,473	2 EU28	1,981
3 Australia	849	3 United States	829
4 India	835	4 South Korea	716
5 United States	774	5 India	653
6 EU28	674	6 Japan	482
Mexico	674	7 Germany	452
8 Bolivia	504	8 Belgium	306
9 Turkey	365	9 Turkey	267
10 Kazakhstan	347	10 Taiwan	225

Tin

Top 5 producers[a], 2017		*Top 5 consumers[b], 2017*	
'000 tonnes		*'000 tonnes*	
1 China	93.4	1 China	183.4
2 Indonesia	82.8	2 EU28	55.6
3 Myanmar	58.9	3 United States	31.5
4 Bolivia	18.3	4 Japan	29.1
5 Peru	17.8	5 Germany	20.0

Nickel

Top 10 producers[a], 2017
'000 tonnes

1	Philippines	389.4
2	Indonesia	358.0
3	New Caledonia	215.4
4	Canada	211.2
5	Russia	206.9
6	Australia	178.9
7	China	94.4
8	Brazil	68.8
9	EU28	56.0
10	Guatemala	55.7

Top 10 consumers[b], 2017
'000 tonnes

1	China	982
2	EU28	334
3	Japan	163
4	United States	145
5	South Korea	109
6	Taiwan	84
7	India	82
8	Germany	65
9	Italy	60
10	South Africa	48

Aluminium

Top 10 producers[d], 2017
'000 tonnes

1	China	32,273
2	Russia	3,741
3	Canada	3,212
4	United Arab Emirates	2,677
5	EU28	2,264
6	India	2,028
7	Australia	1,487
8	Norway	1,253
9	Bahrain	981
10	Saudi Arabia	914

Top 10 consumers[e], 2017
'000 tonnes

1	China	31,908
2	EU28	7,281
3	United States	5,615
4	Germany	2,160
5	Japan	1,950
6	South Korea	1,420
7	India	1,220
8	Turkey	961
9	Italy	924
10	Brazil	868

Precious metals

Gold[a]
Top 10 producers, 2017
tonnes

1	China	420.5
2	Australia	292.3
3	Russia	270.0
4	United States	236.8
5	Canada	171.3
6	Peru	166.7
7	South Africa	137.1
8	Mexico	130.5
9	Ghana	129.7
10	Sudan	103.0

Silver[a]
Top 10 producers, 2017
tonnes

1	Mexico	5,394
2	Peru	4,304
3	China	3,502
4	EU28	2,110
5	Poland	1,438
6	Russia	1,305
7	Chile	1,260
8	Bolivia	1,196
9	Australia	1,120
10	Kazakhstan	1,029

Platinum
Top 3 producers, 2017
tonnes

1	South Africa	143.0
2	Russia	21.8
3	Zimbabwe	14.0

Palladium
Top 3 producers, 2017
tonnes

1	South Africa	86.5
2	Russia	85.2
3	Canada	17.0

a Mine production. b Refined consumption. c Slab consumption.
d Primary refined production. e Primary refined consumption.

Rubber (natural and synthetic)

Top 10 producers, 2017
'000 tonnes

1	Thailand	5,031
2	China	3,820
3	Indonesia	3,499
4	EU28	2,408
5	United States	2,306
6	South Korea	1,624
7	Japan	1,621
8	Russia	1,542
9	Vietnam	1,094
10	Malaysia	741

Top 10 consumers, 2017
'000 tonnes

1	China	9,639
2	EU28	3,811
3	United States	2,819
4	India	1,698
5	Japan	1,560
6	Thailand	1,259
7	Malaysia	978
8	Brazil	940
9	Indonesia	608
10	Russia	603

Cotton

Top 10 producers, 2017–18
'000 tonnes

1	India	6,350
2	China	5,890
3	United States	4,555
4	Brazil	2,006
5	Pakistan	1,795
6	Australia	1,044
7	Uzbekistan	800
8	Turkey	792
9	Mexico	335
10	Turkmenistan	304

Top 10 consumers, 2017–18
'000 tonnes

1	China	8,500
2	India	5,423
3	Pakistan	2,346
4	Bangladesh	1,662
5	Vietnam	1,530
6	Turkey	1,481
7	Indonesia	778
8	United States	768
9	Brazil	680
10	Uzbekistan	464

Major oil seeds[a]

Top 5 producers, 2017–18
'000 tonnes

1	United States	133,766
2	Brazil	121,116
3	Argentina	60,002
4	China	61,473
5	India	34,534

Top 5 consumers, 2017–18
'000 tonnes

1	China	154,047
2	United States	70,614
3	EU28	53,713
4	Argentina	53,316
5	Brazil	49,297

Major vegetable oils[b]

Top 5 producers, 2017–18
'000 tonnes

1	Indonesia	41,500
2	China	23,468
3	Malaysia	20,593
4	EU28	16,528
5	United States	12,149

Top 5 consumers, 2017–18
'000 tonnes

1	China	32,750
2	EU28	23,270
3	India	20,280
4	United States	14,469
5	Indonesia	12,094

a Soyabeans, rapeseed (canola), cottonseed, sunflowerseed and groundnuts
(peanuts).   b Palm, soyabean, rapeseed and sunflowerseed oil.
c Includes crude oil, shale oil, oil sands and natural gas liquids.   d Opec member.
e Opec membership suspended 30 November 2016.

Oil[c]

Top 10 producers, 2018		*Top 10 consumers, 2018*	
'000 barrels per day		*'000 barrels per day*	
1 United States	15,311	1 United States	20,456
2 Saudi Arabia[d]	12,287	2 China	13,525
3 Russia	11,438	3 India	5,156
4 Canada	5,208	4 Japan	3,854
5 Iran[d]	4,715	5 Saudi Arabia[d]	3,724
6 Iraq[d]	4,614	6 Russia	3,228
7 United Arab Emirates[d]	3,942	7 Brazil	3,081
8 China	3,798	8 South Korea	2,793
9 Kuwait[d]	3,049	9 Canada	2,447
10 Brazil	2,683	10 Germany	2,321

Natural gas

Top 10 producers, 2018		*Top 10 consumers, 2018*	
Billion cubic metres		*Billion cubic metres*	
1 United States	831.8	1 United States	817.1
2 Russia	669.5	2 Russia	454.5
3 Iran[d]	239.5	3 China	283.0
4 Canada	184.7	4 Iran[d]	225.6
5 Qatar[d]	175.5	5 Canada	115.7
6 China	161.5	Japan	115.7
7 Australia	130.1	7 Saudi Arabia[d]	112.1
8 Norway	120.6	8 Mexico	89.5
9 Saudi Arabia[d]	112.1	9 Germany	88.3
10 Algeria[d]	92.3	10 United Kingdom	78.9

Coal

Top 10 producers, 2018		*Top 10 consumers, 2018*	
Million tonnes oil equivalent		*Million tonnes oil equivalent*	
1 China	1,828.8	1 China	1,906.7
2 United States	364.5	2 India	452.2
3 Indonesia[e]	323.3	3 United States	317.0
4 India	308.0	4 Japan	117.5
5 Australia	301.1	5 South Korea	88.2
6 Russia	220.2	6 Russia	88.0
7 South Africa	143.2	7 South Africa	86.0
8 Colombia	57.9	8 Germany	66.4
9 Kazakhstan	50.6	9 Indonesia[e]	61.6
10 Poland	47.5	10 Poland	50.5

Oil reserves[c]

Top proved reserves, end 2018
% of world total

1 Venezuela[d]	17.5	6 Russia	6.1
2 Saudi Arabia[d]	17.2	7 Kuwait	5.9
3 Canada	9.7	8 United Arab Emirates[d]	5.7
4 Iran[d]	9.0	9 United States	3.5
5 Iraq[d]	8.5	10 Libya[d]	2.8

Energy

Largest producers
Million tonnes of oil equivalent, 2016

1	China	2,701		16	Mexico	185
2	United States	2,125		17	Kuwait	178
3	Russia	1,492		18	Algeria	174
4	Saudi Arabia	742			Venezuela	174
5	Canada	534		20	South Africa	158
6	Iran	429		21	Nigeria	144
7	India	411		22	Colombia	131
8	Australia	401			United Kingdom	131
9	Indonesia	382		24	France	128
10	Brazil	293		25	Germany	121
11	Qatar	256		26	Malaysia	103
12	United Arab Emirates	252		27	Angola	99
13	Norway	243		28	Turkmenistan	85
14	Iraq	241		29	Oman	82
15	Kazakhstan	186		30	Argentina	81

Largest consumers
Million tonnes of oil equivalent, 2016

1	China	3,510		16	Italy	170
2	United States	2,501		17	South Africa	153
3	Russia	794		18	Australia	151
4	India	732			Turkey	151
5	Japan	496		20	Spain	145
6	Canada	370		21	Thailand	137
7	Germany	350		22	Taiwan	120
8	South Korea	327		23	United Arab Emirates	119
9	Brazil	315		24	Poland	104
10	Iran	284		25	Netherlands	100
11	Saudi Arabia	273		26	Ukraine	98
12	France	256		27	Egypt	96
13	United Kingdom	221		28	Argentina	93
14	Mexico	200		29	Singapore	89
15	Indonesia	183		30	Kazakhstan	88

Energy efficiency[a]
GDP per unit of energy use, 2014

Most efficient			Least efficient		
1	South Sudan	31.9	1	Congo-Kinshasa	2.0
2	Hong Kong	26.8	2	Trinidad & Tobago	2.2
3	Ireland[b]	21.5	3	Iceland[b]	2.5
4	Sri Lanka	20.7		Mozambique	2.5
5	Switzerland[b]	19.4	5	Ethiopia	2.9
6	Panama	18.6		Turkmenistan	2.9
7	Malta	17.9	7	Togo	3.1
8	Colombia	17.8	8	Ukraine	3.4
9	Dominican Rep.	17.2	9	Bahrain	4.1
10	Mauritius	16.4	10	Haiti	4.2
11	Denmark[b]	16.3	11	South Africa	4.6

a 2011 PPP $ per kg of oil equivalent.   b 2015   c 2014

Net energy importers
% of commercial energy use, 2014

Highest			Lowest		
1	Hong Kong	98.7	1	South Sudan	-1,058.1
2	Malta	98.4	2	Norway[b]	-581.3
3	Lebanon	97.9	3	Angola	-541.0
4	Singapore	97.7	4	Congo-Brazzaville	-496.6
5	Jordan	96.8	5	Qatar	-399.0
6	Luxembourg[b]	96.3	6	Kuwait	-391.1
7	Cyprus	94.0	7	Brunei	-357.4
8	Japan[b]	93.0	8	Azerbaijan	-310.4
9	Morocco	90.7	9	Colombia	-274.1
10	Moldova	90.0	10	Iraq	-229.4
11	Belarus	86.8	11	Gabon	-213.4
12	Dominican Rep.	86.7	12	Oman	-206.2

Largest consumption per person
Kg of oil equivalent, 2015

1	Qatar[c]	18,562.7	12	Oman[c]	6,141.8
2	Iceland	17,478.9	13	Finland	5,924.7
3	Trinidad & Tobago[c]	14,446.7	14	Norway	5,817.6
4	Bahrain[c]	10,594.0	15	Australia	5,483.8
5	Kuwait[c]	8,956.8	16	South Korea	5,413.3
6	Brunei[c]	8,632.3	17	Singapore[c]	5,121.8
7	United Arab Emirates[c]	7,769.2	18	Sweden	5,102.8
8	Canada	7,603.7	19	Russia[c]	4,942.9
9	Saudi Arabia[c]	6,937.2	20	Turkmenistan[c]	4,893.5
10	United States	6,803.9	21	Belgium	4,687.8
11	Luxembourg	6,548.4	22	New Zealand	4,444.7

Sources of electricity
% of total, 2015

Oil			Gas		
1	Eritrea	99.5	1	Bahrain	100.0
2	South Sudan	99.4		Qatar	100.0
3	Lebanon	97.4		Turkmenistan	100.0
4	Benin	94.4	4	Trinidad & Tobago	99.8
5	Malta	92.3	5	Brunei	99.0

Hydropower			Nuclear power		
1	Albania	100	1	France	77.6
	Paraguay	100	2	Slovakia	56.9
3	Nepal	99.8	3	Hungary	52.2
4	Congo-Kinshasa	99.7	4	Ukraine	48.6
5	Tajikistan	98.5	5	Slovenia	38.1

Coal			Renewables excl. hydropower		
1	Kosovo	97.5	1	Denmark	65.4
2	Botswana	96.4	2	Kenya	48.3
3	Mongolia	92.7	3	Nicaragua	43.6
	South Africa	92.7	4	El Salvador	35.2
5	Poland	80.9	5	Lithuania	31.2

Labour markets

Labour-force participation
% of working-age population[a] working or looking for work, 2018 or latest

Highest			Lowest		
1	Qatar	86.9	1	Yemen	38.5
2	Madagascar	86.4	2	Timor-Leste	39.0
3	Rwanda	83.9	3	Jordan	39.3
4	Zimbabwe	83.6	4	Puerto Rico	41.2
5	Tanzania	83.2		Syria	41.2
6	Nepal	83.0	6	Algeria	41.3
	United Arab Emirates	83.0	7	Moldova	42.1
8	Cambodia	81.1	8	Iraq	42.6
9	Eritrea	80.6	9	Tajikistan	43.6
	North Korea	80.6	10	Iran	44.1
11	Ethiopia	80.3	11	Morocco	45.4
12	Burundi	79.0	12	Mauritania	46.3
13	Niger	78.7	13	Senegal	46.4
14	Mozambique	78.5		Somalia	46.4
15	Laos	78.2	15	Tunisia	46.5
16	Angola	77.7	16	Bosnia & Herz.	46.8
	Togo	77.7		Papua New Guinea	46.8
18	Vietnam	77.4	18	Sudan	47.2
19	Malawi	77.3	19	Lebanon	47.3
20	Peru	77.2	20	Egypt	48.1
21	Cameroon	76.3	21	Italy	48.9
	Iceland	76.3	22	Montenegro	50.7
23	Zambia	75.2	23	Suriname	51.6
24	Bahamas	74.6	24	Croatia	51.7
25	Kuwait	73.9	25	India	51.9
26	Guinea-Bissau	73.0	26	Gabon	52.1
	South Sudan	73.0	27	Libya	52.4
28	Bahrain	72.8			

Modern slavery[b]
Prevalence per 1,000 pop., 2018

Highest			Lowest		
1	North Korea	104.6	1	Japan	0.3
2	Eritrea	93.0	2	Canada	0.5
3	Burundi	40.0		Taiwan	0.5
4	Central African Rep.	22.3	4	Australia	0.6
5	Afghanistan	22.2		New Zealand	0.6
6	Mauritania	21.4	6	Chile	0.8
7	South Sudan	20.5	7	Mauritius	1.0
8	Cambodia	16.8		Uruguay	1.0
	Pakistan	16.8	9	Argentina	1.3
10	Iran	16.2		Costa Rica	1.3
11	Somalia	15.5		United States	1.3
12	Congo-Kinshasa	13.7	12	Hong Kong	1.4
13	Mongolia	12.3	13	Kuwait	1.5
14	Chad	12.0		Luxembourg	1.5
	Sudan	12.0		Qatar	1.5
16	Rwanda	11.6			

a Aged 15 and over.   b Involuntary servitude or forced work.

Highest rate of unemployment
% of labour force[a], 2018

1	South Africa	27.0	**18**	Somalia	14.0
2	West Bank & Gaza	26.8	**19**	Albania	13.9
3	Lesotho	23.6	**20**	New Caledonia	13.6
4	Namibia	23.1	**21**	Haiti	13.5
5	Swaziland	22.5		Serbia	13.5
6	Macedonia	21.6	**23**	Sudan	12.9
7	Bosnia & Herz.	20.8		Yemen	12.9
8	Gabon	19.5	**25**	South Sudan	12.7
9	Greece	19.2	**26**	Brazil	12.5
10	Botswana	17.9	**27**	Algeria	12.2
11	Armenia	17.7		Guyana	12.2
12	Libya	17.3	**29**	French Polynesia	12.0
13	Montenegro	15.5		Iran	12.0
	Spain	15.5	**31**	Bahamas	11.9
	Tunisia	15.5	**32**	Egypt	11.4
16	Jordan	15.0		Puerto Rico	11.4
17	Georgia	14.1			

Highest rate of youth unemployment
% of labour force[a] aged 15–24, 2018

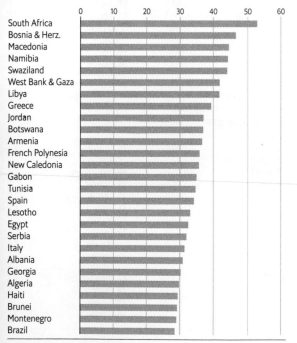

a ILO definition.

Unpaid work[a]

Average minutes per day, 2017 or latest

1	Portugal	328	16	Germany	196
2	Mexico	270		Latvia	196
3	Australia	243		Norway	196
4	Slovenia	231		Sweden	196
5	Hungary	229		United States	196
6	Poland	226	21	United Kingdom	195
7	Lithuania	224	22	Belgium	192
8	Italy	219	23	India	191
9	Denmark	217	24	Canada	186
	Spain	217		Netherlands	186
11	Ireland	213		Turkey	186
12	Estonia	208	27	South Africa	182
13	New Zealand	204	28	France	181
14	Austria	202	29	Greece	180
15	Finland	197	30	Luxembourg	179

Average hours worked

Per employed person per week, 2017

1	Nepal[b]	53.6	12	Malaysia[c]	45.5
2	Qatar	49.0		Namibia[c]	45.5
3	Maldives[c]	48.5	14	Iran	45.1
4	Myanmar	48.3	15	Egypt	44.2
5	Mongolia	48.0		Sri Lanka[c]	44.2
6	Pakistan[c]	47.4	17	Saudi Arabia[b]	44.1
7	Bangladesh	46.9	18	Thailand	44.0
8	Brunei	46.6	19	Algeria	43.7
9	Mexico	46.3	20	Colombia	43.4
10	Turkey	45.9	21	Cambodia[c]	43.3
11	Ivory Coast[c]	45.7		Guatemala[c]	43.3

Gender pay gap[d]

2017 or latest

1	South Korea	34.6	16	Australia	14.3
2	Estonia	28.3		Portugal	14.3
3	Japan	24.5	18	Netherlands	14.1
4	Israel	21.6	19	Sweden	13.4
5	Chile	21.1	20	Lithuania	12.5
	Latvia	21.1	21	Mexico	11.1
7	Canada	18.2	22	Ireland	10.6
	United States	18.2	23	France	9.9
9	Finland	16.5		Iceland	9.9
	United Kingdom	16.5	25	Hungary	9.4
11	Austria	15.7		Poland	9.4
12	Czech Republic	15.6	27	New Zealand	7.2
13	Germany	15.5	28	Norway	7.1
14	Slovakia	15.0	29	Turkey	6.9
15	Switzerland	14.8	30	Denmark	5.7

a OECD countries.   b 2015   c 2016
d Difference between male and female median wages divided by the male median wages.

Business costs and foreign direct investment

Office rents

Rent, taxes and operating expenses, Q1 2018, $ per sq. ft.

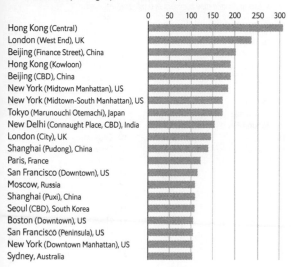

	0	50	100	150	200	250	300
Hong Kong (Central)							
London (West End), UK							
Beijing (Finance Street), China							
Hong Kong (Kowloon)							
Beijing (CBD), China							
New York (Midtown Manhattan), US							
New York (Midtown-South Manhattan), US							
Tokyo (Marunouchi Otemachi), Japan							
New Delhi (Connaught Place, CBD), India							
London (City), UK							
Shanghai (Pudong), China							
Paris, France							
San Francisco (Downtown), US							
Moscow, Russia							
Shanghai (Puxi), China							
Seoul (CBD), South Korea							
Boston (Downtown), US							
San Francisco (Peninsula), US							
New York (Downtown Manhattan), US							
Sydney, Australia							

Foreign direct investment[a]

Inflows, $m, 2017

1	United States	275,381
2	China	136,320
3	Hong Kong	104,333
4	Brazil	62,713
5	Singapore	62,006
6	Netherlands	57,957
7	France	49,795
8	Australia	46,368
9	Switzerland	40,986
10	India	39,916
11	Germany	34,726
12	Mexico	29,695
13	Ireland	28,975
14	Russia	25,284
15	Canada	24,244
16	Indonesia	23,063
17	Spain	19,086
18	Israel	18,954
19	Italy	17,077
20	South Korea	17,053
21	Sweden	15,396
22	United Kingdom	15,090

Outflows, $m, 2017

1	United States	342,269
2	Japan	160,449
3	China	124,630
4	United Kingdom	99,614
5	Hong Kong	82,843
6	Germany	82,336
7	Canada	76,988
8	France	58,116
9	Luxembourg	41,155
10	Spain	40,786
11	Russia	36,032
12	South Korea	31,676
13	Singapore	24,682
14	Sweden	24,303
15	Netherlands	23,318
16	Belgium	20,926
17	Thailand	19,283
18	Ireland	18,614
19	United Arab Emirates	13,956
20	Taiwan	11,357
21	India	11,304
22	Austria	10,892

Note: CBD is Central Business District.
a Investment in companies in a foreign country.

Business creativity and research

Entrepreneurial activity

Percentage of population aged 18–64 who are either a nascent entrepreneur[a] or owner-manager of a new business, average 2013–18

Highest		Lowest	
1 Nigeria	39.9	1 Suriname	3.6
Zambia	39.9	2 Kosovo	4.0
3 Senegal	38.6	3 Italy	4.3
4 Namibia	33.3	4 Japan	4.4
5 Ecuador	32.7	Morocco	4.4
6 Uganda	30.4	6 Bulgaria	4.5
7 Cameroon	30.1	7 Algeria	4.9
8 Botswana	29.0	8 Germany	5.0
9 Burkina Faso	28.3	9 France	5.1
10 Angola	28.2	10 Belgium	5.5
11 Malawi	28.1	Denmark	5.5
12 Bolivia	27.4	12 Russia	5.6
13 Ghana	25.8	13 Spain	5.7
14 Chile	25.0	14 Norway	5.9
15 Lebanon	24.9	15 Finland	6.1
16 Peru	24.4	16 Greece	6.2
17 Sudan	22.2	17 Macedonia	6.4
18 Colombia	22.0	Morocco	6.4
19 Madagascar	21.3	19 Slovenia	6.7
20 Guatemala	20.5	20 Bosnia & Herz.	7.2
21 Brazil	18.9	21 Czech Republic	7.3
Thailand	18.9	Sweden	7.3
23 Barbados	18.5	23 Cyprus	7.7
24 Philippines	18.0	24 Switzerland	7.8
25 Mexico	17.2	25 Georgia	7.9
26 Trinidad & Tobago	17.1	26 Jordan	8.2

Brain drains[b]

Highest, 2018		Lowest, 2018	
1 Haiti	1.7	1 Switzerland	5.9
Venezuela	1.7	2 United States	5.8
3 Bosnia & Herz.	1.8	3 Singapore	5.5
4 Croatia	1.9	United Arab Emirates	5.5
Romania	1.9	5 Luxembourg	5.4
Yemen	1.9	6 Hong Kong	5.3
7 Moldova	2.0	Netherlands	5.3
8 Macedonia	2.1	United Kingdom	5.3
9 Benin	2.3	9 Germany	5.2
Serbia	2.3	10 Iceland	5.1
11 El Salvador	2.4	Malaysia	5.1
Greece	2.4	Norway	5.1
Mauritania	2.4	13 Canada	5.0
Mongolia	2.4	Finland	5.0
Slovakia	2.4	Oman	5.0
Zimbabwe	2.4	Sweden	5.0

a An individual who has started a new firm which has not paid wages for over three months.
b Scores: 1 = talented people leave for other countries; 7 = they stay and pursue opportunities in the country.

Total spending on R&D

$bn, 2017		
1	United States	543.2
2	China	260.5
3	Japan	156.1
4	Germany	111.6
5	South Korea	69.7
6	France	56.5
7	United Kingdom	43.9
8	Canada[a]	26.6
9	Italy	26.3
10	Australia[c]	23.4
11	Switzerland[c]	22.9
12	Brazil[b]	22.7
13	Taiwan	18.9
14	Sweden	17.8
15	Netherlands	16.5
16	Israel	16.1

% of GDP, 2017		
1	South Korea	4.55
2	Israel	4.54
3	Switzerland[c]	3.37
4	Sweden	3.33
5	Taiwan	3.30
6	Japan	3.21
7	Austria	3.16
8	Denmark	3.06
9	Germany	3.02
10	United States	2.79
11	Finland	2.76
12	Belgium	2.60
13	France	2.19
14	China	2.13
	Iceland	2.13
16	Norway	2.11

Innovation index[d]

100=maximum score, 2018

■ Outputs   ■ Overall   ■ Inputs

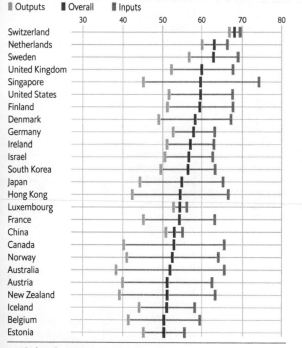

a 2018   b 2016   c 2015
d The innovation index averages countries' capacity for innovation (inputs) and success
in innovation (outputs), based on 79 indicators.

Businesses and banks

Largest non-financial companies
By market capitalisation, $bn, end-December 2018

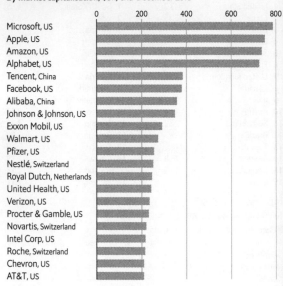

Microsoft, US	
Apple, US	
Amazon, US	
Alphabet, US	
Tencent, China	
Facebook, US	
Alibaba, China	
Johnson & Johnson, US	
Exxon Mobil, US	
Walmart, US	
Pfizer, US	
Nestlé, Switzerland	
Royal Dutch, Netherlands	
United Health, US	
Verizon, US	
Procter & Gamble, US	
Novartis, Switzerland	
Intel Corp, US	
Roche, Switzerland	
Chevron, US	
AT&T, US	

By net profit, $bn, 2018

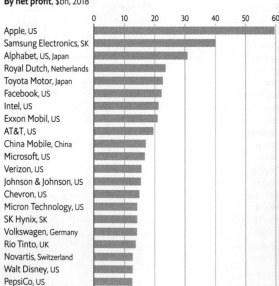

Apple, US	
Samsung Electronics, SK	
Alphabet, US, Japan	
Royal Dutch, Netherlands	
Toyota Motor, Japan	
Facebook, US	
Intel, US	
Exxon Mobil, US	
AT&T, US	
China Mobile, China	
Microsoft, US	
Verizon, US	
Johnson & Johnson, US	
Chevron, US	
Micron Technology, US	
SK Hynix, SK	
Volkswagen, Germany	
Rio Tinto, UK	
Novartis, Switzerland	
Walt Disney, US	
PepsiCo, US	

Largest banks

By market capitalisation, $bn, end December 2018

1	JPMorgan Chase	United States	324.6
2	Industrial & Commercial Bank of China	China	267.9
3	Bank of America	United States	241.8
4	Wells Fargo	United States	216.9
5	China Construction Bank	China	207.2
6	Agricultural Bank of China	China	180.5
7	HSBC	United Kingdom	165.2
8	Bank of China	China	146.7
9	Citigroup	United States	127.1
10	Royal Bank of Canada	Canada	98.7
11	China Merchants Bank	China	92.4
12	TD Bank Group	Canada	91.4
13	Commonwealth Bank of Australia	Australia	90.3
14	HDFC	India	82.8
15	Itaú Unibanco	Italy	82.7

By assets, $bn, end December 2018

1	Industrial & Commercial Bank of China	China	4,027
2	China Construction Bank	China	3,376
3	Agricultural Bank of China	China	3,287
4	Bank of China	China	3,092
5	Mitsubishi UFJ	Japan	2,890
6	JPMorgan Chase	United States	2,623
7	HSBC	United Kingdom	2,558
8	Bank of America	United States	2,355
9	BNP Paribas	France	2,337
10	Japan Post	Japan	1,983
11	Mizuho Financial	Japan	1,930
12	Citigroup	United States	1,917
13	Wells Fargo	United States	1,896
14	Sumitomo Mitsui Financial	Japan	1,874
15	Crédit Agricole	France	1,860

Largest sovereign-wealth funds

By assets, $bn, April 2019

1	Government Pension Fund, Norway	990
2	China Investment Corporation	941
3	Abu Dhabi Investment Authority, UAE	697
4	Kuwait Investment Authority	592
5	Hong Kong Monetary Authority Investment Portfolio	509
6	SAFE Investment Company, China	440
7	Government of Singapore Investment Corporation	390
8	Temasek Holdings, Singapore	375
9	National Council for Social Security Fund, China	341
10	Qatar Investment Authority	320
11	Public Investment Fund of Saudi Arabia	290
12	Investment Corporation of Dubai	234
13	Mubadala Investment Company, UAE	227
14	Korea Investment Corporation	134

Note: Countries listed refer to the company's domicile.

Stockmarkets

Largest market capitalisation
$bn, end 2018

1	NYSE	20,679	21	Singapore Exchange	687
2	Nasdaq – US	9,757	22	Moscow Exchange	576
3	Japan Exchange Group	5,297	23	Stock Exchange of	
4	Shanghai SE	3,919		Thailand	501
5	Hong Kong Exchanges	3,819	24	Saudi SE (Tadawul)	496
6	Euronext	3,730	25	Indonesia SE	487
7	London SE Group[a]	3,638	26	Bursa Malaysia	398
8	Shenzhen SE	2,405	27	Bolsa Mexicana de	
9	BSE India	2,083		Valores	385
10	National Stock		28	Oslo Bors	267
	Exchange of India	2,056	29	Philippine SE	258
11	TMX Group	1,938	30	Bolsa de Comercio de	
12	Deutsche Börse	1,755		Santiago	251
13	SIX Swiss Exchange	1,441	31	Tel-Aviv SE	187
14	Korea Exchange[b]	1,414	32	Qatar SE	163
15	Nasdaq OMX Nordic		33	Warsaw SE	160
	Exchanges[c]	1,323	34	Borsa Istanbul	149
16	Australian Securities		35	Tehran SE	144
	Exchange	1,263	36	Abu Dhabi Securities	
17	Taiwan SE	959		Exchange	138
18	BM&FBOVESPA	917	37	Ho Chi Minh SE	124
19	Johannesburg SE	865	38	Wiener Börse	117
20	BME Spanish Exchanges	724	39	Irish SE	110

Stockmarket gains and losses
$ terms, % change December 29th 2017 to December 31st 2018

Best performance

1	Saudi Arabia (TASI)	8.3
2	Brazil (BVSP)	-1.6
3	India BSE (SENSEX) 30	-3.2
4	United States (NAScomp)	-3.9
5	United States (DJIA)	-5.6
6	Norway (OSEAX)	-6.0
7	United States (S&P 500)	-6.2
8	Malaysia (KLSE)	-7.9
9	Indonesia (IDX)	-8.0
10	Hungary (BUX)	-8.5
11	Israel (TA 125)	-9.2
12	Japan (NIKKEI 225)	-9.7
13	Thailand (SET)	-10.7
14	Colombia (IGBC)	-10.8
15	Switzerland (SMI)	-11.2
16	Taiwan (TWI)	-11.5
17	Singapore (STI)	-11.6
18	Czech Republic (PX)	-13.6
19	Hong Kong (Hang Seng)	-13.8
20	Egypt (EGX 30)	-13.9

Worst performance

1	Argentina (MERV)	-49.6
2	Turkey (BIST)	-43.6
3	China (SSEA)	-28.5
4	Greece (Athex composite)	-27.2
	Pakistan (KSE)	-27.2
6	China (SSEB)	-24.8
7	South Africa (FTSE JSE)	-23.7
8	Austria (ATX)	-23.6
9	Russia (RTS)	-23.4
10	Belgium (BEL 20)	-22.4
11	Germany (DAX) d	-22.2
12	South Korea (KOSPI)	-20.6
13	Italy (FTSE MIB)	-20.2
14	Spain (IGBM)	-19.1
15	Canada (S&P TSX)	-18.9
16	Euro area (FTSE	
	EURO 100)	-18.6
17	Euro area (EURO	
	STOXX 50)	-18.5
18	Chile (IGPA)	-17.8

a Includes Borsa Italiana.   b Includes Kosdaq.   c Armenia, Copenhagen, Helsinki, Iceland, Riga, Stockholm, Tallinn and Vilnius stock exchanges.   d Total return index.

Value traded[a]

$bn, 2018

1	Nasdaq – US	43,656
2	NYSE	22,941
3	BATS Global Markets – US	16,036
4	BATS Chi-x Europe	13,306
5	Shenzhen SE	7,600
6	Japan Exchange Group	7,207
7	Shanghai SE	6,140
8	London SE Group[b]	4,768
9	Korea Exchange[c]	2,559
10	Hong Kong Exchanges	2,483
11	Deutsche Börse	2,349
12	Euronext	2,263
13	TMX Group	1,448
14	National Stock Exchange of India	1,166
15	SIX Swiss Exchange	1,100
16	Taiwan SE	983
17	Australian Securities Exchange	982
18	Nasdaq OMX Nordic Exchanges[d]	921
19	BM&FBOVESPA	817
20	BME Spanish Exchanges	692
21	Johannesburg SE	422
22	Borsa Istanbul	419
23	Stock Exchange of Thailand	405
24	Taipei Exchange	271
25	Saudi SE (Tadawul)	232
26	Moscow Exchange	231
27	Singapore Exchange	222
28	Oslo Bors	160
29	Bursa Malaysia	154
30	Indonesia SE	144
31	BSE India	121
32	Bolsa Mexicana de Valores	112
33	Tel-Aviv SE	77
34	Warsaw SE	60

Number of listed companies[e]

End 2018

1	BSE India	5,066
2	Japan Exchange Group	3,657
3	TMX Group	3,383
4	Nasdaq – US	3,058
5	BME Spanish Exchanges	3,006
6	London SE Group[b]	2,479
7	Hong Kong Exchanges	2,315
8	NYSE	2,285
9	Korea Exchange[c]	2,207
10	Australian Securities Exchange	2,146
11	Shenzhen SE	2,134
12	National Stock Exchange of India	1,923
13	Shanghai SE	1,450
14	Euronext	1,208
15	Nasdaq OMX Nordic Exchanges[d]	1,019
16	Taiwan SE	945
17	Bursa Malaysia	912
18	Warsaw SE	851
19	Taipei Exchange	766
20	Singapore Exchange	741
21	Stock Exchange of Thailand	704
22	Wiener Börse	677
23	Indonesia SE	619
24	Deutsche Börse	514
25	Tel-Aviv SE	448
26	Borsa Istanbul	378
27	Hanoi SE	376
28	Ho Chi Minh SE	373
29	Johannesburg SE	360
30	BM&FBOVESPA	339
31	Tehran SE	323
32	Dhaka SE	311
33	Colombo SE	297
34	Bolsa de Comerclo de Santiago	285
35	Chittagong SE	282
36	SIX Swiss Exchange	270
37	Philippine SE	267
38	The Egyptian Exchange	252
39	Moscow Exchange	225
40	Bolsa de Valores de Lima	223

Note: Figures are not entirely comparable due to different reporting rules and calculations.
a Includes electronic and negotiated deals.   b Includes Borsa Italiana.
c Includes Kosdaq.   d Armenia, Copenhagen, Helsinki, Iceland, Riga, Stockholm, Tallinn and Vilnius stock exchanges.   e Domestic and foreign.

Public finance

Government debt
As % of GDP, 2018

1	Japan	226.4	16	Germany	68.1
2	Greece	187.6	17	Netherlands	67.2
3	Italy	153.3	18	Poland	66.8
4	Portugal	144.0	19	Iceland	62.1
5	France	125.0	20	Israel	61.6
6	Belgium	120.2	21	Norway	59.1
7	United Kingdom	115.6	22	Slovakia	57.0
8	Spain	114.6	23	Denmark	48.4
9	United States	106.8	24	Latvia	47.4
10	Austria	97.3	25	Sweden	46.7
11	Canada	93.0	26	South Korea	43.3
12	Hungary	91.3	27	Lithuania	43.1
13	Slovenia	86.9	28	Czech Republic	42.1
14	Ireland	75.7	29	Australia	42.0
15	Finland	72.4	30	Switzerland	40.0

Government spending
As % of GDP, 2018

1	France	56.2		New Zealand	41.6
2	Finland	52.7	17	Poland	41.4
3	Belgium	51.6	18	Spain	41.2
4	Denmark	51.5	19	Iceland	40.8
5	Sweden	49.0	20	Canada	40.3
6	Italy	48.8	21	Israel	40.0
7	Norway	48.6		United Kingdom	40.0
8	Austria	48.0	23	Estonia	39.8
9	Hungary	46.6		Slovakia	39.8
10	Greece	46.5	25	Czech Republic	39.3
11	Portugal	44.4	26	Japan	38.4
12	Germany	43.9	27	United States	37.8
13	Luxembourg	42.8	28	Latvia	37.6
14	Slovenia	42.7	29	Australia	35.4
15	Netherlands	41.6	30	Lithuania	34.0

Tax revenue
As % of GDP, 2017

1	France	46.2	14	Germany	37.5
2	Denmark	46.0	15	Slovenia	36.0
3	Belgium	44.6	16	Czech Republic	34.9
4	Sweden	44.0	17	Portugal	34.7
5	Finland	43.3	18	Poland	33.9
6	Italy	42.4	19	Spain	33.7
7	Austria	41.8	20	United Kingdom	33.3
8	Greece	39.4	21	Estonia	33.0
9	Netherlands	38.8	22	Slovakia	32.9
10	Luxembourg	38.7	23	Israel	32.7
11	Norway	38.2	24	Canada	32.2
12	Hungary	37.7	25	New Zealand	32.0
	Iceland	37.7	26	Latvia	30.4

Note: Includes only OECD countries.

Democracy

Democracy index

Most democratic = 10, 2018

Most			Least		
1	Norway	9.87	1	North Korea	1.08
2	Iceland	9.58	2	Syria	1.43
3	Sweden	9.39	3	Central African Rep.	1.49
4	New Zealand	9.26	4	Congo-Kinshasa	1.52
5	Denmark	9.22	5	Chad	1.61
6	Canada	9.15	6	Turkmenistan	1.72
	Ireland	9.15	7	Equatorial Guinea	1.92
8	Finland	9.14	8	Saudi Arabia	1.93
9	Australia	9.09		Tajikistan	1.93
10	Switzerland	9.03	10	Yemen	1.95
11	Netherlands	8.89	11	Guinea-Bissau	1.98
12	Luxembourg	8.81	12	Uzbekistan	2.01
13	Germany	8.68	13	Sudan	2.15
14	United Kingdom	8.53	14	Libya	2.19
15	Uruguay	8.38	15	Burundi	2.33
16	Austria	8.29	16	Eritrea	2.37
17	Mauritius	8.22		Laos	2.37
18	Malta	8.21	18	Iran	2.45
19	Costa Rica	8.08	19	Azerbaijan	2.65
20	Spain	8.07	20	Bahrain	2.71

Parliamentary seats

Lower or single house, seats per 100,000 population, May 2019

Most			Fewest		
1	Liechtenstein	62.5	1	India	0.06
2	Monaco	60.0	2	United States	0.16
3	Andorra	28.0	3	Bangladesh	0.21
4	Maldives	21.8		China	0.21
5	Iceland	21.0	5	Indonesia	0.22
6	Barbados	17.0	6	Pakistan	0.23
7	Malta	16.3	7	Nigeria	0.25
8	Bahamas	13.8	8	Brazil	0.28
9	Montenegro	13.5	9	Philippines	0.31
10	Equatorial Guinea	13.1			

Women in parliament

Lower or single house, women as % of total seats, May 2019

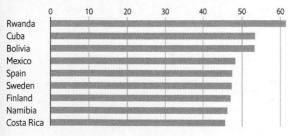

Education

Primary enrolment
Number enrolled as % of relevant age group

Highest			Lowest		
1	Madagascar	144	1	Eritrea	49
2	Malawi	140	2	Equatorial Guinea	62
3	Nepal	134	3	South Sudan	67
4	Rwanda	133	4	Niger	75
5	Suriname	131	5	Sudan	76
6	Benin	127	6	Mali	80
7	Burundi	126	7	Senegal	84
8	Sweden	125	8	Nigeria	85
9	Togo	123		Tanzania	85
10	Sierra Leone	121	10	Puerto Rico	87
11	Namibia	119	11	Chad	88
12	Saudi Arabia	116		North Korea	88
13	India	115	13	Romania	89
	Tunisia	115	14	Bermuda	90
15	Brazil	114	15	Moldova	91
				Paraguay	91

Highest secondary enrolment
Number enrolled as % of relevant age group

1	Belgium	161	12	Ireland	117
2	Australia	154		Thailand	117
3	Finland	152	14	Liechtenstein	116
	United Kingdom	152		Norway	116
5	Sweden	145	16	Estonia	115
6	Netherlands	133		Slovenia	115
7	Denmark	129		Uruguay	115
8	Spain	128	19	New Zealand	114
9	Costa Rica	126	20	Canada	113
10	Iceland	118		Kazakhstan	113
	Portugal	118	22	Latvia	111

Highest tertiary enrolment[a]
Number enrolled as % of relevant age group

1	Greece	126	11	Macau	85
2	Australia	122		Puerto Rico	85
3	Turkey	104	13	Austria	84
4	South Korea	94		Singapore	84
5	Spain	91	15	New Zealand	82
6	Chile	90		Russia	82
7	Argentina	89	17	Denmark	81
	United States	89		Latvia	81
9	Belarus	87		Norway	81
	Finland	87	20	Netherlands	80

Notes: Latest available year 2014–18. The gross enrolment ratios shown are the actual number enrolled as a percentage of the number of children in the official primary age group. They may exceed 100 when children outside the primary age group are receiving primary education.

a Tertiary education includes all levels of post-secondary education including courses leading to awards not equivalent to a university degree, courses leading to a first university degree and postgraduate courses.

Literacy rate
% adult population[a]

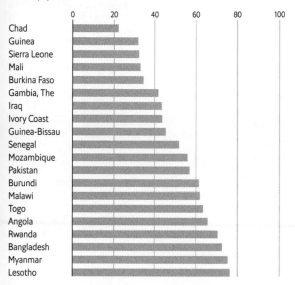

Chad	
Guinea	
Sierra Leone	
Mali	
Burkina Faso	
Gambia, The	
Iraq	
Ivory Coast	
Guinea-Bissau	
Senegal	
Mozambique	
Pakistan	
Burundi	
Malawi	
Togo	
Angola	
Rwanda	
Bangladesh	
Myanmar	
Lesotho	

Education spending
% of GDP[b]

Highest			Lowest		
1	Iceland	7.7	**1**	Monaco	1.4
2	Denmark	7.6	**2**	Bermuda	1.5
	Norway	7.6	**3**	South Sudan	1.8
	Sweden	7.6	**4**	Cambodia	1.9
5	Zimbabwe	7.5	**5**	Guinea-Bissau	2.1
6	Costa Rica	7.4		Madagascar	2.1
7	Bolivia	7.3	**7**	Myanmar	2.2
8	Kyrgyzstan	7.2	**8**	Congo-Kinshasa	2.3
9	Finland	7.1		Uganda	2.3
	Swaziland	7.1	**10**	Guinea	2.4
11	Moldova	6.7	**11**	Bangladesh	2.5
	Oman	6.7		Lebanon	2.5
13	Belgium	6.6	**13**	Mauritania	2.6
	Tunisia	6.6	**14**	Bahrain	2.7
15	Cyprus	6.4		Gabon	2.7
	Lesotho	6.4	**16**	Armenia	2.8
	Uzbekistan	6.4		Cameroon	2.8
18	Guyana	6.3		Gambia, The	2.8
	New Zealand	6.3		Guatemala	2.8
20	Brazil	6.2		Pakistan	2.8
	Senegal	6.2			

a Latest year 2013–17. b Latest year 2014–18.

Marriage and divorce

Highest marriage rates
Number of marriages per 1,000 population, 2017 or latest

1	West Bank & Gaza	10.4	21	Belarus	7.0
2	Fiji	9.8		Hong Kong	7.0
3	Egypt	9.6		Kyrgyzstan	7.0
4	Bahamas	9.5	24	United States	6.9
	Uzbekistan	9.5	25	Azerbaijan	6.8
6	Iran	8.8		Latvia	6.8
7	Moldova	8.5	27	Barbados	6.7
	Russia	8.5		Malta	6.7
9	Tajikistan	8.4	29	Macedonia	6.6
10	Albania	8.2	30	Mongolia	6.5
11	Kazakhstan	7.9	31	Georgia	6.4
12	Jordan	7.7		Jamaica	6.4
	Mauritius	7.7	33	Israel	6.2
14	Guam	7.6	34	Brunei	6.1
15	Cyprus	7.5	35	Liechtenstein	6.0
	Lithuania	7.5		Trinidad & Tobago	6.0
17	Turkey	7.4	37	Macau	5.9
18	Bermuda	7.3	38	Slovakia	5.8
	Romania	7.3	39	Bosnia & Herz.	5.6
20	Singapore	7.1	40	Denmark	5.5

Lowest marriage rates
Number of marriages per 1,000 population, 2017 or latest

1	Qatar	1.4	24	Bulgaria	4.0
2	French Guiana	2.4		Japan	4.0
3	Peru	2.5	26	Andorra	4.1
	Venezuela	2.5	27	New Zealand	4.3
5	Argentina	2.7		Norway	4.3
6	Martinique	2.8	29	Mexico	4.4
	Uruguay	2.8		United Kingdom	4.4
8	Guadeloupe	3.0	31	Finland	4.5
9	Slovenia	3.1	32	Ireland	4.6
10	Luxembourg	3.2	33	Greece	4.7
11	New Caledonia	3.3	34	Cuba	4.8
	Portugal	3.3		Switzerland	4.8
13	Chile	3.4	36	Australia	4.9
	Italy	3.4		Croatia	4.9
	Réunion	3.4		Estonia	4.9
16	France	3.5		Germany	4.9
	Kuwait	3.5		Guatemala	4.9
	Panama	3.5	41	Czech Republic	5.0
19	Spain	3.7	42	Austria	5.1
	Suriname	3.7		Montenegro	5.1
21	Netherlands	3.8		Poland	5.1
	Puerto Rico	3.8		Serbia	5.1
23	Belgium	3.9		South Korea	5.1

Note: The data are based on latest available figures (no earlier than 2013) and hence will be affected by the population age structure at the time. Marriage rates refer to registered marriages only and, therefore, reflect the customs surrounding registry and efficiency of administration.

Highest divorce rates
Number of divorces per 1,000 population, 2017 or latest[a]

1	Russia	4.7		Puerto Rico	2.6
2	Guam	4.2	14	Estonia	2.5
3	Moldova	3.7		Finland	2.5
4	Belarus	3.4		United States	2.5
5	Latvia	3.1	17	Czech Republic	2.4
	Ukraine	3.1		Liechtenstein	2.4
7	Kazakhstan	3.0		Sweden	2.4
	Lithuania	3.0	20	Cyprus	2.3
9	Cuba	2.9		Iran	2.3
10	Georgia	2.7		Macau	2.3
11	Costa Rica	2.6	23	Dominican Rep.	2.2
	Denmark	2.6			

Lowest divorce rates
Number of divorces per 1,000 population, 2017 or latest[a]

1	Guatemala	0.4		Suriname	1.1
	Qatar	0.4	17	Armenia	1.2
3	Peru	0.5		Jamaica	1.2
4	Bosnia & Herz.	0.6		Slovenia	1.2
	Ireland	0.6	20	Azerbaijan	1.3
6	French Guiana	0.8		Mongolia	1.3
	Malta	0.8		Serbia	1.3
8	Greece	1.0	23	Brunei	1.4
	Macedonia	1.0	24	Bulgaria	1.5
	Martinique	1.0		Kyrgyzstan	1.5
	Tajikistan	1.0	26	Barbados	1.6
	Uzbekistan	1.0		Italy	1.6
13	Mexico	1.1		Mauritius	1.6
	Montenegro	1.1		Romania	1.6
	Panama	1.1		Turkey	1.6

Mean age of women at first marriage
Years, 2016 or latest[b]

Youngest			Oldest		
1	South Sudan	14.6	1	Barbados	35.3
2	Central African Rep.	17.3	2	Slovenia	34.1
3	Niger	17.4	3	French Polynesia	33.8
4	Mali	18.5	4	Martinique	33.3
5	Bangladesh	18.8	5	Estonia	32.8
	Chad	18.8		Hungary	32.8
7	Mozambique	19.3		New Caledonia	32.8
8	Burkina Faso	19.9	8	Ireland	32.4
9	Madagascar	20.0	9	Bulgaria	32.3
	Malawi	20.0		Netherlands	32.3
11	Uganda	20.1	11	Czech Republic	32.0
12	Somalia	20.4		French Guiana	32.0
13	Equatorial Guinea	20.5	13	Norway	31.9
14	Eritrea	20.6			

a No earlier than 2013.   b No earlier than 2000.

Households, living costs and giving

Number of households

Biggest, m, 2017 or latest

1	China	466.8		21	Turkey	23.1
2	India	278.2		22	Ethiopia	21.9
3	United States	126.2		23	South Korea	20.5
4	Indonesia	66.9		24	Spain	18.5
5	Brazil	64.8		25	South Africa	16.9
6	Russia	57.2		26	Ukraine	16.7
7	Japan	53.4		27	Poland	14.5
8	Germany	40.7		28	Colombia	14.4
9	Nigeria	40.6		29	Canada	14.1
10	Mexico	33.8		30	Argentina	13.8
11	Bangladesh	33.3		31	Congo-Kinshasa	11.5
12	Pakistan	29.4		32	Tanzania	11.2
13	France	29.3		33	Myanmar	11.1
14	Vietnam	28.9		34	Kenya	11.0
15	United Kingdom	28.8		35	Australia	9.9
16	Italy	25.9		36	North Korea	9.6
17	Iran	24.7		37	Taiwan	8.6
18	Philippines	23.9			Venezuela	8.6
19	Thailand	23.8		39	Peru	8.4
20	Egypt	23.5		40	Uganda	8.2

Average household size, people

Biggest, 2017 or latest			*Smallest, 2017 or latest*		
1	Angola	8.5	1	Germany	2
2	Senegal	8.3	2	Denmark	2.1
3	Gambia, The	8.2		Finland	2.1
4	Afghanistan	8.0	4	Austria	2.2
5	Equatorial Guinea	7.9		Estonia	2.2
6	Gabon	7.8		France	2.2
	Guinea-Bissau	7.8		Latvia	2.2
8	Congo-Kinshasa	7.1		Netherlands	2.2
9	Oman	6.9		Norway	2.2
10	Mauritania	6.7		Sweden	2.2
	Pakistan	6.7	11	Bulgaria	2.3
	Yemen	6.7		Italy	2.3
13	Guinea	6.3		Slovenia	2.3
	Iraq	6.3		Switzerland	2.3
	Papua New Guinea	6.3		United Kingdom	2.3
	Tajikistan	6.3	16	Belarus	2.4
	Turkmenistan	6.3		Belgium	2.4
18	Maldives	6.2		Czech Republic	2.4
19	Libya	6.1		Japan	2.4
20	Benin	6.0		Lithuania	2.4
	Niger	6.0			

a The cost of living index shown is compiled by the Economist Intelligence Unit for use by companies in determining expatriate compensation: it is a comparison of the cost of maintaining a typical international lifestyle in the country rather than a comparison of the purchasing power of a citizen of the country. The index is based on typical urban prices an international executive and family will face abroad. The prices

Cost of living[a]

December 2018, US=100

Highest

	0 20 40 60 80 100
France	
Hong Kong	
Singapore	
Switzerland	
Denmark	
South Korea	
Israel	
Norway	
Japan	
Austria	
Iceland	
Australia	
Finland	
Ireland	
New Caledonia	
United Kingdom	
Jordan	
Italy	
Belgium	
Spain	
Netherlands	
New Zealand	
Thailand	

Lowest

	0 20 40 60
Venezuela	
Syria	
Uzbekistan	
Kazakhstan	
Nigeria	
Pakistan	
Argentina	
Algeria	
India	
Iran	
Turkey	
Romania	
Nepal	
Egypt	
Paraguay	
Zambia	
South Africa	
Sri Lanka	
Brazil	
Panama	
Ukraine	
Hungary	
Saudi Arabia	

World Giving Index[b]

Top givers, % of population, 2018

1	Australia	59	16	Iceland	48
	Indonesia	59		Nigeria	48
3	New Zealand	58	18	Liberia	47
	United States	58		Malta	47
5	Ireland	56		Sierra Leone	47
6	United Kingdom	55	21	Denmark	46
7	Kenya	54		Germany	46
	Myanmar	54		Mauritius	46
	Singapore	54		Trinidad & Tobago	46
10	Bahrain	53		Zambia	46
11	Netherlands	51	26	Iran	45
	United Arab Emirates	51		Libya	45
13	Norway	50		Sri Lanka	45
14	Canada	49		Switzerland	45
	Haiti	49			

---

a are for products of international comparable quality found in a supermarket or department store. Prices found in local markets and bazaars are not used unless the available merchandise is of the specified quality and the shopping area itself is safe for executive and family members. New York City prices are used as the base, so United States = 100.
b Three criteria are used to assess giving: in the previous month those surveyed either gave money to charity, gave time to those in need or helped a stranger.

Transport: roads and cars

Longest road networks
Km, 2017 or latest

1	United States	6,853,024	25	Argentina	230,923
2	India	5,903,293	26	Vietnam	228,645
3	China	4,846,500	27	Colombia	219,159
4	Brazil	1,751,868	28	Philippines	217,456
5	Russia	1,452,200	29	Malaysia	216,604
6	Canada	1,409,008	30	Hungary	206,632
7	Japan	1,226,559	31	Nigeria	198,233
8	France	1,079,398	32	Peru	173,209
9	South Africa	891,932	33	Egypt	167,774
10	Australia	872,848	34	Ukraine	163,028
11	Spain	683,175	35	Belgium	155,357
12	Germany	644,480	36	Congo-Kinshasa	154,633
13	Indonesia	537,838	37	Netherlands	139,448
14	Italy	494,844	38	Czech Republic	130,671
15	Sweden	432,009	39	Austria	124,591
16	Poland	423,997	40	Algeria	119,386
17	United Kingdom	422,310	41	Greece	116,986
18	Thailand	396,721	42	Ghana	109,515
19	Turkey	394,390	43	South Korea	105,758
20	Mexico	393,473	44	Belarus	99,606
21	Iran	312,761	45	Zimbabwe	97,724
22	Saudi Arabia	274,861	46	Kazakhstan	96,643
23	Bangladesh	266,216	47	Venezuela	96,156
24	Pakistan	263,775	48	Ireland	96,115

Densest road networks
Km of road per km² land area, 2017 or latest

1	Monaco	35.0		Denmark	1.8
2	Macau	13.6	26	Czech Republic	1.7
3	Malta	9.7		Italy	1.7
4	Bermuda	8.3		United Kingdom	1.7
5	Bahrain	5.3	29	Austria	1.5
6	Belgium	5.1		Finland	1.5
7	Singapore	4.9	31	Cyprus	1.4
8	Netherlands	4.1		Ireland	1.4
9	Barbados	3.7		Poland	1.4
10	Japan	3.4		Spain	1.4
11	Puerto Rico	3.0		Estonia	1.4
12	Liechtenstein	2.5	36	Lithuania	1.3
13	Hungary	2.3	37	Taiwan	1.1
14	Slovenia	2.2		Latvia	1.1
15	Luxembourg	2.2		South Korea	1.1
16	Bangladesh	2.0		Sweden	1.1
	Jamaica	2.0		Mauritius	1.1
	Hong Kong	2.0	42	Portugal	0.9
	India	2.0		Qatar	0.9
	France	2.0		Greece	0.9
21	Guam	1.9		Israel	0.9
22	Germany	1.8		West Bank & Gaza	0.9
	Sri Lanka	1.8	47	Costa Rica	0.8
	Switzerland	1.8			

Most crowded road networks

Number of vehicles per km of road network, 2017 or latest

1	United Arab Emirates	523.0	26	Liechtenstein	77.3
2	Monaco	427.3	27	Germany	75.1
3	Hong Kong	322.1	28	Tunisia	72.8
4	Kuwait	273.3	29	Armenia	72.5
5	Macau	238.0	30	Dominican Rep.	71.6
6	Singapore	235.5	31	Romania	69.5
7	South Korea	198.5	32	Portugal	69.2
8	Taiwan	185.1	33	Barbados	68.8
9	Israel	157.2		Switzerland	68.8
10	Jordan	156.6	35	Netherlands	67.4
11	Bahrain	140.3	36	Iraq	66.6
12	Puerto Rico	123.6	37	Japan	63.1
13	Guatemala	113.8	38	Malaysia	61.4
14	Guam	112.9	39	Slovakia	61.0
15	Mauritius	110.2	40	Morocco	60.6
16	Malta	104.8	41	Argentina	59.5
17	Brunei	99.3	42	Chile	57.4
18	Syria	98.8	43	Poland	57.2
19	Qatar	96.4	44	Croatia	56.5
20	Mexico	94.9	45	Ukraine	55.8
21	Lebanon	94.8	46	Moldova	53.9
22	United Kingdom	90.5	47	Bermuda	53.7
23	Bulgaria	89.5	48	Greece	53.0
24	Italy	85.4	49	Ecuador	51.3
25	Luxembourg	80.8	50	Georgia	51.1

Most road deaths

Fatalities per 100,000 population, 2016

1	Liberia	35.9	24	Chad	27.6
2	Burundi	34.7	25	Benin	27.5
	Zimbabwe	34.7	26	Congo-Brazzaville	27.4
4	Congo-Kinshasa	33.7	27	Somalia	27.1
	Venezuela	33.7	28	Ethiopia	26.7
6	Central African Rep.	33.6	29	Syria	26.5
7	Thailand	32.7	30	Vietnam	26.4
8	Guinea-Bissau	31.1	31	Niger	26.2
9	Malawi	31.0	32	Libya	26.1
10	Burkina Faso	30.5	33	South Africa	25.9
11	Namibia	30.4	34	Sudan	25.7
12	Cameroon	30.1	35	Eritrea	25.3
	Mozambique	30.1	36	Ghana	24.9
14	South Sudan	29.9	37	Mauritania	24.7
15	Rwanda	29.7	38	Equatorial Guinea	24.6
16	Tanzania	29.2		Guyana	24.6
	Togo	29.2	40	Jordan	24.4
18	Uganda	29.0	41	Botswana	23.8
19	Lesotho	28.9	42	Angola	23.6
20	Saudi Arabia	28.8		Ivory Coast	23.6
21	Madagascar	28.6		Malaysia	23.6
22	Guinea	28.2	45	Senegal	23.4
23	Kenya	27.8	46	Gabon	23.2

Fastest-growing ownership
% increase in number of cars, 2006–15

1	Tanzania	500.0	26	Senegal	102.4
2	China	418.4	27	Syria	100.9
3	Kyrgyzstan	301.8	28	Iraq	98.4
4	Vietnam	275.9	29	Mali	97.7
5	Brunei	268.3	30	Egypt	95.8
6	Botswana	212.4	31	Argentina	95.6
7	Qatar	178.9	32	Oman	94.9
8	Angola	168.1	33	Panama	92.4
9	India	162.1	34	Saudi Arabia	92.1
10	Madagascar	159.7	35	Iran	86.8
11	Uganda	154.2	36	Pakistan	84.1
12	United Arab Emirates	147.8	37	Chile	83.6
13	Afghanistan	138.4	38	Sri Lanka	81.8
14	Georgia	134.2	39	Bahrain	81.3
15	Kenya	127.6	40	Algeria	81.1
16	Burkina Faso	127.3	41	Albania	79.3
17	Indonesia	123.4	42	Bulgaria	78.8
18	Kazakhstan	121.0	43	Brazil	78.3
19	Thailand	120.3	44	Paraguay	77.0
20	Mozambique	112.8	45	Bolivia	74.9
21	Suriname	111.3	46	Colombia	74.1
22	Jordan	107.5	47	Guatemala	74.0
23	Azerbaijan	105.8	48	Costa Rica	73.0
24	Mauritius	104.9		Ecuador	73.0
25	Ghana	103.6	50	Turkey	72.4

Slowest-growing car ownership
% change in number of cars, 2006–15

1	Lithuania	-21.9	23	Nicaragua	13.2
2	Zambia	-17.5	24	Tunisia	13.3
3	Latvia	-17.4	25	Belgium	13.4
4	United States	-9.4	26	Trinidad & Tobago	13.6
5	Bermuda	-9.1	27	Switzerland	14.1
6	Germany	-3.2	28	Iceland	14.9
7	Croatia	4.4	29	Netherlands	15.3
8	Finland	5.0	30	Taiwan	15.4
9	France	5.3	31	Bahamas	16.3
10	Liberia	5.3	32	Cuba	16.8
11	Italy	5.8	33	Canada	17.8
12	Japan	6.0	34	Denmark	18.1
13	Spain	6.2		Jamaica	18.1
14	Portugal	7.1	36	New Caledonia	18.6
15	Haiti	8.1	37	Barbados	20.0
16	Hungary	8.2	38	Serbia	20.1
17	United Kingdom	8.8	39	Australia	20.2
18	Slovenia	10.4	40	Luxembourg	20.9
19	Sweden	11.1	41	Congo-Kinshasa	21.8
20	Ireland	11.6	42	Estonia	22.1
21	Greece	12.4	43	Ethiopia	23.3
22	Austria	12.9	44	Norway	24.3

Car production

Number of cars produced, m, 2017

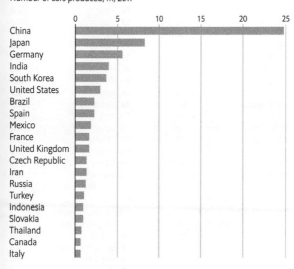

China	
Japan	
Germany	
India	
South Korea	
United States	
Brazil	
Spain	
Mexico	
France	
United Kingdom	
Czech Republic	
Iran	
Russia	
Turkey	
Indonesia	
Slovakia	
Thailand	
Canada	
Italy	

Cars sold

New car registrations[a], change 2016–17, %

1	Ecuador	84.9	**24**	Portugal	7.1
2	Argentina	26.1	**25**	Kazakhstan	6.5
3	Ukraine	24.5	**26**	Japan	5.9
4	Thailand	22.4		Peru	5.9
5	Iran	20.6	**28**	New Zealand	5.8
6	Hungary	20.4	**29**	Czech Republic	4.7
7	Chile	18.0		France	4.7
8	Philippines	17.4	**31**	Luxembourg	4.4
9	Poland	16.6	**32**	Singapore	3.7
10	Croatia	15.1	**33**	Germany	2.7
11	Pakistan	14.7	**34**	Norway	2.6
12	Puerto Rico	13.5	**35**	China	2.4
13	Romania	13.4	**36**	South Africa	2.3
14	Russia	12.4	**37**	Morocco	1.9
15	Greece	11.7		Sweden	1.9
16	Slovenia	11.3	**39**	Belgium	1.3
17	Brazil	10.0	**40**	Malaysia	1.0
18	Slovakia	9.0		Taiwan	1.0
19	India	8.8	**42**	Finland	-0.3
20	Netherlands	8.3	**43**	Denmark	-0.6
21	Italy	7.9	**44**	Switzerland	-1.0
22	Spain	7.7	**45**	Indonesia	-1.2
23	Austria	7.2	**46**	Australia	-1.3

a Countries registering over 50,000 new cars.

Transport: planes and trains

Most air travel
Passengers carried, m, 2017

1	United States	849.4	16	Spain	71.9
2	China	551.2	17	Thailand	71.2
3	Ireland	153.5	18	France	68.3
4	United Kingdom	151.9	19	Mexico	58.5
5	India	139.8	20	Malaysia	58.2
6	Japan	123.9	21	Hong Kong	45.6
7	Germany	116.8	22	Philippines	44.1
8	Indonesia	110.3	23	Netherlands	42.8
9	Turkey	107.9	24	Vietnam	42.6
10	Brazil	96.4	25	Singapore	37.7
11	United Arab Emirates	95.3	26	Saudi Arabia	37.5
12	Canada	91.4	27	Colombia	32.5
13	Russia	89.4	28	Qatar	29.9
14	South Korea	84.0	29	Italy	27.8
15	Australia	74.3	30	Switzerland	26.7

Busiest airports
Total passengers, m, 2018

1	Atlanta, Hartsfield	107.4
2	Beijing, Capital	101.0
3	Dubai, Intl.	89.1
4	Los Angeles, Intl.	87.5
5	Tokyo, Haneda	87.1
6	Chicago, O'Hare	83.2
7	London, Heathrow	80.1
8	Hong Kong, Intl.	74.7
9	Shanghai, Pudong Intl.	74.0
10	Paris, Charles de Gaulle	72.2
11	Amsterdam, Schiphol	71.1
12	Indira Gandhi Intl.	69.9
13	Guangzhou Baiyun, Intl	69.7
14	Frankfurt, Main	69.5
15	Dallas, Ft Worth	69.1

Total cargo, m tonnes, 2018

1	Hong Kong, Intl.	5.1
2	Memphis, Intl.	4.5
3	Shanghai, Pudong Intl.	3.8
4	Seoul, Incheon	3.0
5	Dubai, Intl.	2.6
	Louisville, Standiford Field	2.6
7	Miami, Intl.	2.3
	Taiwan, Taoyuan Intl.	2.3
9	Singapore, Changi	2.2
	Tokyo, Narita	2.2
11	Beijing, Capital	2.1
	Frankfurt, Main	2.1
13	Chicago, O'Hare	1.9
	Guangzhou Baiyun, Intl	1.9
15	Amsterdam, Schiphol	1.7

Average daily aircraft movements, take-offs and landings, 2018

1	Chicago, O'Hare	2,476
2	Atlanta, Hartsfield	2,454
3	Los Angeles, Intl.	1,939
4	Dallas, Ft Worth	1,828
5	Beijing, Capital	1,682
6	Denver, Intl.	1,653
7	Charlotte/Douglas, Intl.	1,507
8	Las Vegas, McCarran Intl.	1,479
9	Frankfurt, Main	1,403
10	Shanghai, Pudong Intl.	1,383
11	Amsterdam, Schiphol	1,368
12	Indira Gandhi Intl.	1,353
13	Paris, Charles de Gaulle	1,318
14	London, Heathrow	1,316
15	Guangzhou Baiyun, Intl.	1,308
16	San Francisco, Intl.	1,288
17	Houston, George Bush Intl.	1,279
18	New York, JFK	1,248
19	Indonesia Soekarno-Hatta Intl.	1,226
20	Phoenix, Skyharbor Intl.	1,190
21	Hong Kong, Intl.	1,172
22	Miami, Intl.	1,140
23	Munich	1,133
24	Madrid Barajas	1,123
25	Dubai, Intl.	1,118

Longest railway networks

'000 km, 2017 or latest

1	United States	151.0		21	Turkey	10.2
2	Russia	85.5		22	Sweden	9.7
3	India	67.4		23	Czech Republic	9.4
4	China	67.3		24	Iran	9.0
5	Canada	48.2		25	Pakistan	7.8
6	Germany	33.5		26	Hungary	7.2
7	Australia	32.8		27	Finland	5.9
8	Brazil	29.8		28	Belarus	5.5
9	France	29.2			Chile	5.5
10	Ukraine	21.6		30	Egypt	5.2
11	South Africa	21.0		31	Austria	5.0
12	Poland	18.5		32	Indonesia	4.7
13	Argentina	17.6		33	Uzbekistan	4.6
14	Japan	17.0		34	Thailand	4.5
15	Italy	16.8		35	Sudan	4.3
16	United Kingdom	16.3		36	South Korea	4.2
17	Kazakhstan	16.0		37	Norway	4.1
18	Spain	15.6		38	Algeria	4.0
19	Mexico	14.3			Bulgaria	4.0
20	Romania	10.8			Switzerland	4.0

Most rail passengers

Km per person per year, 2017 or latest

1	Switzerland	2,193		13	Russia	854
2	Japan	1,547		14	Finland	777
3	Austria	1,382		15	Czech Republic	696
4	France	1,303			Slovakia	696
5	Netherlands	1,058		17	Belarus	663
6	Kazakhstan	1,057		18	Italy	657
7	Denmark	1,023		19	Sweden	636
8	Germany	944		20	Ukraine	634
9	Belgium	907		21	Luxembourg	622
10	United Kingdom	985		22	Norway	582
11	Taiwan	909			Spain	582
12	India	859		24	Hungary	564

Most rail freight

Million tonne-km per year, 2017 or latest

1	Russia	2,491,876		13	Poland	28,720
2	United States	2,445,132		14	France	24,598
3	China	2,146,466		15	Uzbekistan	22,940
4	India	620,175		16	Japan	21,265
5	Canada	540,141		17	Austria	16,052
6	Kazakhstan	206,258		18	Lithuania	15,414
7	Ukraine	191,914		19	Mongolia	13,493
8	Mexico	73,879		20	Turkmenistan	13,327
9	Germany	70,614		21	Czech Republic	11,819
10	Australia	59,649		22	Turkey	10,773
11	Belarus	48,538		23	Finland	10,319
12	Iran	30,299		24	Latvia	9,971

Transport: shipping

Merchant fleets
Number of vessels, by country of domicile, January 2019

1	China	5,512	16	Vietnam	991
2	Greece	4,371	17	Taiwan	987
3	Japan	3,841	18	Denmark	944
4	Germany	2,869	19	United Arab Emirates	895
5	Singapore	2,629	20	France	859
6	United States	2,073	21	Italy	746
7	Norway	1,982	22	Malaysia	662
8	Indonesia	1,948	23	Bermuda	494
9	Russia	1,707	24	Philippines	449
10	South Korea	1,626	25	Switzerland	412
11	Hong Kong	1,592	26	Thailand	402
12	Turkey	1,522	27	Brazil	390
13	United Kingdom	1,363	28	Ukraine	371
14	Netherlands	1,228	29	Canada	369
15	India	1,011	30	Cyprus	295

Ships' flags
Registered fleet, 2018

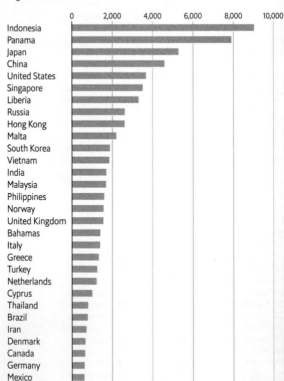

Crime and punishment

Murders

Homicides per 100,000 pop., 2016 or latest

1	El Salvador	82.8
2	Honduras	56.5
3	Venezuela	56.3
4	Virgin Islands (US)	49.3
5	Jamaica	47.0
6	Lesotho	41.2
7	South Africa	34.0
8	Trinidad & Tobago	30.9
9	Brazil	29.5
10	Bahamas	28.4
11	Guatemala	27.3
12	Colombia	25.5
13	Central African Rep.	19.8
14	Mexico	19.3
15	Puerto Rico	18.5
16	Guyana	18.4
17	Swaziland	17.3
18	Namibia	17.1
19	Dominican Rep.	15.2
20	Congo-Kinshasa	13.5

Robberies

Per 100,000 pop., 2016 or latest

1	Costa Rica	1,096
2	Argentina	989
3	Chile	647
4	Uruguay	546
5	Ecuador	503
6	Brazil	500
7	Paraguay	331
8	Swaziland	310
9	Colombia	302
10	Guatemala	274
11	Peru	242
12	Belgium	196
13	Panama	191
14	Maldives	183
15	Honduras	183
16	Trinidad & Tobago	182
17	Guyana	167
18	France	153
19	Spain	152
20	Bolivia	141

Prisoners

Total prison pop., 2019 or latest

1	United States	2,121,600
2	China	1,649,804
3	Brazil	712,305
4	Russia	554,995
5	India	433,003
6	Thailand	382,895
7	Indonesia	265,079
8	Turkey	260,000
9	Iran	240,000
10	Mexico	203,364
11	Philippines	188,278
12	South Africa	164,129
13	Vietnam	130,002
14	Colombia	120,022
15	Ethiopia	113,727
16	Egypt[a]	106,000
17	Argentina	92,161
18	Myanmar	92,000
19	Peru	90,934
20	Bangladesh	88,371
21	Pakistan	83,718
22	United Kingdom	82,538
23	Morocco	82,512
24	Poland	74,352
25	Nigeria	73,241
26	France	70,059

Per 100,000 pop., 2019 or latest

1	United States	655
2	El Salvador	618
3	Thailand	553
4	Turkmenistan	552
5	Virgin Islands (US)	542
6	Cuba	510
7	Maldives	499
8	Rwanda	464
9	Bahamas	438
10	Russia	383
11	Guam	381
12	Costa Rica	374
13	Belarus	343
14	Brazil	333
15	Uruguay	321
16	Bermuda	319
17	Turkey	318
18	Puerto Rico	313
19	Barbados	300
20	Namibia	295
21	Iran	294
22	Trinidad & Tobago	292
23	Dominica	289
24	South Africa	286
25	Guyana	283
26	Peru	278

a Estimate.

War and terrorism

Defence spending
As % of GDP, 2018

1	Oman	11.0		Jordan	3.9
2	Saudi Arabia	10.8	14	Bahrain	3.8
3	Afghanistan	10.1	15	Lebanon	3.7
4	Iraq	7.5		Pakistan	3.7
5	Algeria	5.3	17	Azerbaijan	3.5
6	Israel	5.1	18	Namibia	3.4
7	Iran	4.6	19	Colombia	3.2
8	Kuwait	4.3		Singapore	3.2
9	Mali	4.1	21	Botswana	3.1
10	Armenia	4.0		Morocco	3.1
	Trinidad & Tobago	4.0		United States	3.1
12	Cambodia	3.9			

Defence spending
$bn, 2018

1	United States	643.3		*Per person, $, 2018*	
2	China	168.2	1	Oman	2,561
3	Saudi Arabia	82.9	2	Saudi Arabia	2,506
4	India	57.9	3	Israel[b]	2,200
5	United Kingdom	56.1	4	Kuwait	2,119
6	France	53.4	5	United States	1,954
7	Japan	47.3	6	Singapore	1,835
8	Germany	45.7	7	Norway	1,265
9	Russia[a]	45.3	8	Australia	1,131
10	South Korea	39.2	9	Bahrain	1,026
11	Brazil	28.0	10	United Kingdom	862
12	Australia	26.6	11	Brunei	815
13	Italy	24.9	12	France	792
14	Iran	19.6	13	South Korea	763
15	Israel[b]	18.5	14	Trinidad & Tobago	757
			15	Denmark	731

Armed forces
'000, 2018

		Regulars	Reserves			Regulars	Reserves
1	China	2,035	510	16	Colombia	293	35
2	India	1,445	1,155	17	Mexico	277	82
3	United States	1,359	846	18	Sri Lanka	255	6
4	North Korea	1,280	600	19	Japan	247	56
5	Russia	900	2,000	20	Saudi Arabia	227	0
6	Pakistan	654	0	21	Ukraine	209	900
7	South Korea	625	3,100	22	France	204	36
8	Iran	523	350	23	Eritrea	202	120
9	Vietnam	482	5,000	24	Morocco	196	150
10	Egypt	439	479	25	South Sudan	185	0
11	Myanmar	406	0	26	Germany	180	28
12	Indonesia	396	400	27	Afghanistan	174	0
13	Thailand	361	200	28	Italy	171	18
14	Turkey	355	379	29	Israel	170	465
15	Brazil	335	1,340	30	Taiwan	163	1,657

a National defence budget only.   b Includes US Foreign Military Assistance.

Arms exporters

$m, 2018

1	United States	10,508
2	Russia	6,409
3	France	1,768
4	Germany	1,277
5	Spain	1,188
6	South Korea	1,083
7	China	1,040
8	United Kingdom	741
9	Israel	707
10	Italy	611
11	Netherlands	369
12	Turkey	364
13	Switzerland	243
14	Ukraine	224
15	South Africa	149

Arms importers

$m, 2018

1	Saudi Arabia	3,810
2	Australia	1,572
3	China	1,566
4	India	1,539
5	Egypt	1,484
6	Algeria	1,318
7	South Korea	1,317
8	UAE	1,101
9	Qatar	816
10	Pakistan	777
11	Japan	696
12	Turkey	685
13	United States	613
14	Iraq	596
15	Thailand	578

Terrorist attacks

Number of incidents, 2017

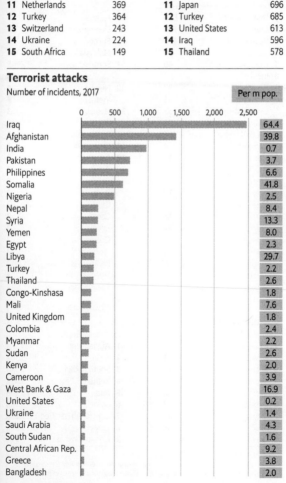

Country	Per m pop.
Iraq	64.4
Afghanistan	39.8
India	0.7
Pakistan	3.7
Philippines	6.6
Somalia	41.8
Nigeria	2.5
Nepal	8.4
Syria	13.3
Yemen	8.0
Egypt	2.3
Libya	29.7
Turkey	2.2
Thailand	2.6
Congo-Kinshasa	1.8
Mali	7.6
United Kingdom	1.8
Colombia	2.4
Myanmar	2.2
Sudan	2.6
Kenya	2.0
Cameroon	3.9
West Bank & Gaza	16.9
United States	0.2
Ukraine	1.4
Saudi Arabia	4.3
South Sudan	1.6
Central African Rep.	9.2
Greece	3.8
Bangladesh	2.0

Space and peace

Orbital launches

2018	Low-earth orbit[a]	Greater than low-earth orbit	Total
1 China	24	15	39
2 United States	12	14	26
3 Russia	15	5	20
4 Europe	2	5	7
5 India	3	4	7
6 Japan	6	0	6
7 New Zealand	3	0	3
8 Ukraine	2	0	2

Satellites in space

By country of ownership[b], 2018

1 United States	883		26 Algeria	5
2 China	296		Denmark	5
3 Russia	150		Finland	5
4 Japan	79		Malaysia	5
5 United Kingdom	60		South Africa	5
6 India	57		Thailand	5
7 Canada	37		32 Nigeria	4
8 Germany	33		Vietnam	4
Luxembourg	33		34 Mexico	3
10 Spain	19		Pakistan	3
11 South Korea	15		Switzerland	3
12 Argentina	14		37 Venezuela	3
13 France	13		38 Azerbaijan	2
Saudi Arabia	13		Bangladesh	2
15 Australia	12		Belarus	2
Israel	12		Bulgaria	2
Netherlands	12		Chile	2
18 Brazil	11		Czech Republic	2
Italy	11		Egypt	2
20 Indonesia	9		Greece	2
21 Norway	8		Morocco	2
Singapore	8		Philippines	2
Turkey	8		Sweden	2
United Arab Emirates	8		Taiwan	2
25 Kazakhstan	7			

Global Peace Index[c]

Most peaceful, 2019		Least peaceful, 2019	
1 Iceland	1.072	1 Afghanistan	3.574
2 New Zealand	1.221	2 Syria	3.566
3 Portugal	1.274	3 South Sudan	3.526
4 Austria	1.291	4 Yemen	3.412
5 Denmark	1.316	5 Iraq	3.369
6 Canada	1.327	6 Somalia	3.300
7 Singapore	1.347	7 Central African Rep.	3.296
8 Slovenia	1.355	8 Libya	3.285
9 Japan	1.369	9 Congo-Kinshasa	3.218

a Up to 2,000km.   b Excludes multi-country/agency.
c Ranks 163 countries using 23 indicators which gauge the level of safety and security in society, the extent of domestic or international conflict and the degree of militarisation.

Environment

Biggest emitters of carbon dioxide
Million tonnes, 2015

1	China	10,603.7	31	Argentina	200.2
2	United States	5,414.6	32	Vietnam	194.7
3	India	2,151.1	33	Venezuela	179.2
4	Russia	1,801.9	34	Pakistan	165.1
5	Japan	1,199.7	35	Iraq	153.7
6	Germany	826.3	36	Algeria	144.8
7	South Korea	732.0	37	Belgium	135.6
8	Saudi Arabia	662.1	38	Qatar	118.0
9	Iran	642.1	39	Philippines	109.3
10	Canada	641.7	40	Uzbekistan	107.5
11	Brazil	541.1	41	Czech Republic	105.7
12	Indonesia	504.3	42	Kuwait	105.3
13	South Africa	502.7	43	Turkmenistan	102.1
14	United Kingdom	459.0	44	Nigeria	100.6
15	Mexico	454.2	45	Hong Kong	94.8
16	Australia	403.5	46	Colombia	83.9
17	Italy	358.7	47	Chile	79.1
18	France	354.9	48	Bangladesh	73.2
19	Turkey	351.9	49	Romania	72.8
20	Thailand	338.5	50	Greece	71.5
21	Taiwan	318.3	51	Israel	71.2
22	Poland	299.6	52	Oman	70.9
23	Spain	290.1	53	Austria	67.6
24	United Arab Emirates	285.6	54	Belarus	56.7
25	Kazakhstan	268.9	55	Portugal	55.7
26	Netherlands	245.4	56	Trinidad & Tobago	54.3
27	Singapore	240.9	57	Libya	53.4
28	Egypt	227.9	58	Morocco	52.8
29	Malaysia	218.6	59	Peru	52.4
30	Ukraine	216.0	60	Sweden	49.9

Largest amount of carbon dioxide emitted per person
Tonnes, 2015

1	Qatar	53.6	18	Kazakhstan	15.3
2	Singapore	43.0	19	South Korea	14.6
3	Trinidad & Tobago	38.8	20	Netherlands	14.5
4	United Arab Emirates	31.0	21	Taiwan	13.6
5	Virgin Islands (US)	29.3	22	Hong Kong	13.0
6	Bahrain	27.4	23	Russia	12.6
7	Kuwait	27.0	24	Belgium	12.0
8	Brunei	24.1	25	Guam	10.8
9	Saudi Arabia	21.0	26	Germany	10.2
10	Turkmenistan	18.9	27	Czech Republic	10.1
11	Canada	17.9	28	Iceland	9.8
12	Malta	17.8	29	Japan	9.5
13	Luxembourg	17.2	30	South Africa	9.2
14	Australia	16.8	31	Israel	8.8
	New Caledonia	16.8	32	Libya	8.5
	United States	16.8		New Zealand	8.5
17	Oman	15.8	34	Norway	8.4

Change in carbon emissions

Million tonnes, 2015 compared with 2000

Biggest increases		Biggest decreases	
1 China	7,080.5	1 United States	-471.0
2 India	1,233.5	2 Ukraine	-132.5
3 Saudi Arabia	371.3	3 United Kingdom	-115.0
4 Iran	320.2	4 Italy	-87.5
5 South Korea	267.6	5 North Korea	-61.7
6 Russia	236.1	6 France	-54.7
7 Indonesia	231.3	7 Spain	-29.2
8 Brazil	186.6	8 Greece	-24.8
9 Thailand	180.4	9 Syria	-20.7
10 United Arab Emirates	169.6	10 Romania	-19.6
11 Turkey	146.9	11 Denmark	-17.8
12 Vietnam	144.4	12 Czech Republic	-15.9

Most polluted capital cities

Annual mean particulate matter concentration[a], micrograms per cubic metre, 2017 or latest

1 Delhi, India	292	14 Tunis, Tunisia	90
2 Cairo, Egypt	284	15 La Paz, Bolivia	82
3 Riyadh, Saudi Arabia	251	Muscat, Oman	82
4 Baghdad, Iraq	179	17 Tehran, Iran	72
5 Accra, Ghana	172	18 Skopje, Macedonia	69
6 Kampala, Uganda	170	19 Amman, Jordan	68
7 Abu Dhabi, UAE	150	Ankara, Turkey	68
8 Dakar, Senegal	149	21 Santiago, Chile	67
9 Dhaka, Bangladesh	146	22 Jerusalem, Israel	66
10 Ulaanbaatar, Mongolia	124	23 Yaoundé, Cameroon	65
11 Brasília, Brazil	118	24 Colombo, Sri Lanka	64
Manila, Philippines	118	25 Pretoria, South Africa	63
13 Beijing, China	92	26 Antananarivo, Madagascar	60

Lowest access to basic sanitation

% of rural population, 2015

1 Chad	2.9	17 Mozambique	12.3
2 Ethiopia	4.3	18 Ivory Coast	12.7
3 Togo	4.5	19 Papua New Guinea	13.1
4 Benin	5.4	20 Guinea	14.7
5 Congo-Brazzaville	5.6	21 Namibia	15.4
6 Liberia	5.9	22 Mauritania	17.1
Niger	5.9	23 Tanzania	17.2
8 Eritrea	6.1	24 Uganda	17.4
9 Madagascar	6.2	25 Congo-Kinshasa	17.5
10 South Sudan	6.4	26 Zambia	18.7
11 Somalia	8.2	27 Cameroon	18.9
12 Guinea-Bissau	8.4	28 Angola	21.4
Sierra Leone	8.4	29 Mali	21.5
14 Ghana	9.0	30 Haiti	21.8
15 Central African Rep.	9.1	31 Sudan	22.9
16 Burkina Faso	11.8	32 Bolivia	26.8

a Particulates less than 10 microns in diameter.

Largest forested land

Sq km, 2016

1	Russia	8,148,895
2	Brazil	4,925,540
3	Canada	3,470,224
4	United States	3,103,700
5	China	2,098,635
6	Congo-Kinshasa	1,522,666
7	Australia	1,250,590
8	Indonesia	903,256
9	Peru	738,054
10	India	708,604
11	Mexico	659,484
12	Colombia	584,750
13	Angola	577,312
14	Bolivia	544,750
15	Zambia	484,684
16	Venezuela	465,186
17	Tanzania	456,880
18	Mozambique	377,336
19	Papua New Guinea	335,562
20	Myanmar	284,946
21	Sweden	280,730
22	Argentina	268,152
23	Japan	249,564
24	Gabon	232,000
25	Congo-Brazzaville	223,186
26	Finland	222,180
27	Malaysia	222,092
28	Central African Rep.	221,544
29	Sudan	190,355
30	Laos	189,506

Most forested

% of land area, 2016

1	Suriname	98.3
2	Gabon	90.0
3	Guyana	83.9
4	Laos	82.1
5	Papua New Guinea	74.1
6	Finland	73.1
7	Brunei	72.1
8	Guinea-Bissau	69.8
9	Sweden	68.9
10	Japan	68.5
11	Malaysia	67.6
12	Congo-Kinshasa	67.2
13	Congo-Brazzaville	65.4
14	Zambia	65.2
15	South Korea	63.4
16	Slovenia	62.0
17	Panama	61.9
18	Montenegro	61.5
19	Brazil	58.9
20	Peru	57.7
21	Puerto Rico	56.3
22	Fiji	55.9
23	Equatorial Guinea	55.5
24	Costa Rica	54.6
25	Latvia	54.0
26	Cambodia	52.9
27	Colombia	52.7
	Venezuela	52.7
29	Tanzania	51.6
30	Bahamas	51.4

Forestation

Biggest % change in forested land, 2000–16

Decrease			Increase		
1	Togo	-65.4	1	Iceland	75.3
2	Nigeria	-49.9	2	Bahrain	64.9
3	Uganda	-49.8	3	French Polynesia	47.6
4	Pakistan	-32.5	4	Burundi	41.7
5	Mauritania	-30.3	5	Rwanda	41.5
6	Honduras	-30.0	6	Uruguay	36.4
7	North Korea	-29.3	7	Dominican Rep.	35.7
8	Zimbabwe	-27.2	8	Azerbaijan	33.7
9	Kyrgyzstan	-26.7	9	Cuba	33.6
10	Chad	-24.9	10	Montenegro	32.1
11	Paraguay	-22.6	11	Kuwait	28.9
12	El Salvador	-21.5	12	Moldova	27.7
13	Mali	-21.4	13	Vietnam	27.1
14	Timor-Leste	-21.0	14	Tunisia	25.6
15	Cambodia	-19.2	15	Kenya	25.1
16	Nicaragua	-18.4	16	Egypt	24.7
17	Myanmar	-18.3	17	Algeria	24.4

Protected land and water area[a]
As % of total territorial area, 2016

1	Slovenia	55.1	11	Tanzania	30.8
2	Hong Kong	41.9	12	New Zealand	30.5
3	Germany	38.7	13	Botswana	29.1
4	Poland	38.0	14	Benin	28.9
	Zambia	38.0	15	Australia	28.6
6	Slovakia	37.3	16	Austria	28.4
7	Venezuela	36.9	17	Bulgaria	28.3
8	Congo-Brazzaville	36.7	18	Zimbabwe	27.2
9	Luxembourg	32.3	19	United States	26.3
10	Bolivia	30.9	20	France	26.1

Number of species under threat
Mammals, 2018

1	Indonesia	191	12	Peru	53
2	Madagascar	121	13	Myanmar	49
3	Mexico	96	14	Ecuador	47
4	India	93	15	Cameroon	46
5	Brazil	80	16	Laos	45
6	China	73	17	Papua New Guinea	41
7	Malaysia	71		Tanzania	41
8	Australia	63	19	United States	40
9	Thailand	59	20	Cambodia	39
10	Colombia	58	21	Argentina	38
11	Vietnam	56		Philippines	38

Plants, 2018

1	Ecuador	1,859	12	New Caledonia	350
2	Madagascar	1,111	13	Peru	328
3	Malaysia	727	14	Sri Lanka	297
4	Tanzania	644	15	Colombia	268
5	China	593	16	Philippines	254
6	Brazil	558	17	Spain	247
7	Cameroon	555	18	Kenya	243
8	United States	510	19	Vietnam	231
9	Mexico	484	20	Jamaica	215
10	Indonesia	458	21	Panama	212
11	India	396	22	Nigeria	205

Birds, 2018

1	Brazil	175	12	Malaysia	63
2	Indonesia	160	13	Thailand	62
3	Colombia	126	14	Russia	57
4	Peru	119	15	Myanmar	56
5	Ecuador	106	16	Bolivia	55
6	China	96	17	South Africa	54
7	India	93	18	Argentina	52
	Philippines	93		Australia	52
9	United States	91		Venezuela	52
10	Mexico	71		Vietnam	52
11	New Zealand	69			

a Countries with pop. of at least 300,000. Includes national parks and science reserves.

Worst natural catastrophes

2017

	Country/region	Type of disaster	Deaths[a]
1	Puerto Rico/Caribbean/US	Hurricane Maria	3,057
2	Sierra Leone	Flood/landslide	1,141
3	Iran, Iraq	Earthquake	630
4	India (Bihar)	Floods	514
5	Mexico	Earthquake	369
6	Colombia	Landslide caused by rain	336
7	Philippines	Tropical Storm Tembin	331
8	Sri Lanka	Floods	293
9	India	Heatwave	264
10	Zimbabwe	Floods	251
11	India (Gujarat)	Monsoon floods	224
12	Congo-Kinshasa	Landslide	200
13	Peru	Floods	184
14	Pakistan	Monsoon floods	172
15	Afghanistan, Pakistan	Snow, avalanches	165
16	Bangladesh	Rains/landslides	160
17	India	Monsoon floods	156
18	Nepal	Monsoon floods	134
19	US, Caribbean	Hurricane Irma	126
20	East Europe	Cold spell	123
	Vietnam, Philippines, Malaysia	Typhoon Damrey	123
22	Bangladesh	Monsoon floods	117
23	Congo-Kinshasa	Flood	105
24	Madagascar	Cyclone Enawo	99
25	Mexico, Guatemala	Earthquake	98

Most rainfall

Average precipitation in depth, cm, 2014

1	Colombia	324.0	21	Puerto Rico	205.4
2	Papua New Guinea	314.2	22	Jamaica	205.1
3	Panama	292.8	23	Venezuela	204.4
4	Costa Rica	292.6	24	Mauritius	204.1
5	Malaysia	287.5	25	Guatemala	199.6
6	Brunei	272.2	26	Honduras	197.6
7	Indonesia	270.2	27	Maldives	197.2
8	Bangladesh	266.6	28	Iceland	194.0
9	Fiji	259.2	29	Cambodia	190.4
10	Sierra Leone	252.6	30	Laos	183.4
11	Singapore	249.7	31	Gabon	183.1
12	Liberia	239.1	32	Vietnam	182.1
13	Guyana	238.7	33	El Salvador	178.4
14	Philippines	234.8	34	Brazil	176.1
15	Suriname	233.1	35	Peru	173.8
16	Nicaragua	228.0	36	New Zealand	173.2
17	Ecuador	227.4	37	Sri Lanka	171.2
18	Trinidad & Tobago	220.0	38	Japan	166.8
19	Equatorial Guinea	215.6	39	Guinea	165.1
20	Myanmar	209.1	40	Congo-Brazzaville	164.6

a Includes "missing".

Life expectancy

Highest life expectancy
Years, 2020–25

1	Monaco[a]	89.4		United Kingdom	82.6
2	Hong Kong	84.9	26	Finland	82.5
3	Macau	84.8		Portugal	82.5
4	Japan	84.7	28	Greece	82.4
5	Switzerland	84.3	29	Belgium	82.2
6	Singapore	84.1	30	Channel Islands	82.1
	Spain	84.1		Germany	82.1
8	Australia	84.0	32	Liechtenstein[a]	82.0
	Italy	84.0		Slovenia	82.0
10	Iceland	83.8	34	Malta	81.9
11	Israel	83.6	35	Denmark	81.7
12	Canada	83.5		Réunion	81.7
	France	83.5	37	Cyprus	81.6
	Sweden	83.5	38	Bermuda[a]	81.5
15	South Korea	83.4	39	French Guiana	81.3
16	Martinique	83.3	40	Puerto Rico	81.2
17	Norway	83.2	41	Costa Rica	81.1
18	Andorra[a]	82.9		Taiwan	81.1
	Luxembourg	82.9	43	Cuba	80.9
	Netherlands	82.9		Virgin Islands (US)	80.9
	New Zealand	82.9	45	Chile	80.8
22	Austria	82.8		Guam	80.8
23	Guadeloupe	82.7	47	Lebanon	80.7
24	Ireland	82.6	48	United States	80.4

Highest male life expectancy
Years, 2020–25

1	Monaco[a]	85.5		Macau	81.8
2	Iceland	82.6	12	Norway	81.6
3	Switzerland	82.5	13	Japan	81.4
4	Australia	82.3		New Zealand	81.4
5	Singapore	82.2	15	Netherlands	81.3
6	Israel	82.1		Spain	81.3
7	Italy	82.0	17	United Kingdom	81.0
	Sweden	82.0	18	Luxembourg	80.9
9	Hong Kong	81.9	19	Ireland	80.8
10	Canada	81.8			

Highest female life expectancy
Years, 2020–25

1	Monaco[a]	93.4		Switzerland	86.1
2	Hong Kong	87.9	10	Martinique	86.0
	Japan	87.9		Singapore	86.0
4	Macau	87.7	12	Australia	85.7
5	Spain	86.7		Guadeloupe	85.7
6	France	86.4	14	Andorra[a]	85.3
7	South Korea	86.2	15	Canada	85.1
8	Italy	86.1			

a 2018 estimate.

Lowest life expectancy

Years, 2020–25

1	Sierra Leone	54.3	26	Zambia	64.0
2	Chad	54.9	27	Mauritania	64.2
3	Central African Rep.	55.9	28	Ghana	64.5
4	Nigeria	56.3	29	Haiti	64.9
5	Lesotho	56.6	30	South Africa	65.0
6	Ivory Coast	56.7	31	Liberia	65.6
7	Somalia	58.9		Malawi	65.6
8	South Sudan	59.8	33	Afghanistan	65.8
9	Burundi	59.9		Sudan	65.8
	Guinea-Bissau	59.9	35	Yemen	66.2
	Swaziland	59.9	36	Namibia	66.3
12	Equatorial Guinea	60.0	37	Papua New Guinea	66.5
13	Mali	60.9	38	Congo-Brazzaville	67.2
14	Mozambique	61.1	39	Guyana	67.4
15	Cameroon	61.3		Pakistan	67.4
16	Togo	61.8	41	Myanmar	67.5
17	Uganda	61.9	42	Eritrea	67.8
18	Congo-Kinshasa	62.2	43	Ethiopia	68.0
19	Niger	62.4	44	Gabon	68.1
20	Benin	62.5		Tanzania	68.1
21	Gambia, The	62.6	46	Madagascar	68.2
22	Zimbabwe	62.8	47	Kenya	68.5
23	Burkina Faso	62.9	48	Turkmenistan	68.6
24	Angola	63.3	49	Laos	68.8
25	Guinea	63.7		Rwanda	68.8

Lowest male life expectancy

Years, 2020–25

1	Chad	53.6	10	Guinea-Bissau	58.1
	Sierra Leone	53.6	11	Equatorial Guinea	58.6
3	Central African Rep.	53.8	12	South Sudan	58.7
4	Lesotho	54.6	13	Mozambique	58.9
5	Ivory Coast	55.2	14	Uganda	59.8
6	Nigeria	55.4	15	Cameroon	60.0
7	Swaziland	56.9		Mali	60.0
8	Somalia	57.2	17	Angola	60.4
9	Burundi	57.9	18	Congo-Kinshasa	60.6

Lowest female life expectancy

Years, 2020–25

1	Sierra Leone	55.1	10	Guinea-Bissau	61.8
2	Chad	56.3		Mali	61.8
3	Nigeria	57.3	12	Burundi	62.0
4	Central African Rep.	58.2	13	Cameroon	62.5
5	Ivory Coast	58.3	14	Swaziland	62.7
	Lesotho	58.3		Togo	62.7
7	Somalia	60.7	16	Mozambique	63.2
8	South Sudan	61.0	17	Niger	63.6
9	Equatorial Guinea	61.4	18	Burkina Faso	63.7

Death rates and infant mortality

Highest death rates
Number of deaths per 1,000 population, 2020–25

#	Country	Rate	#	Country	Rate
1	Bulgaria	15.5	50	France	9.2
2	Latvia	15.4	51	Guinea-Bissau	9.1
3	Ukraine	14.9	52	Martinique	9.1
4	Lithuania	14.6		Netherlands	9.1
5	Russia	13.7		United Kingdom	9.1
6	Belarus	13.4	55	Mauritius	9.0
	Hungary	13.4		Sweden	9.0
8	Romania	13.3	57	Equatorial Guinea	8.9
9	Croatia	13.2		Swaziland	8.9
10	Serbia	13.0	59	Thailand	8.8
11	Georgia	12.7	60	Bermuda[a]	8.7
12	Estonia	12.4		Cuba	8.7
13	Moldova	11.9		Guadeloupe	8.7
14	Bosnia & Herz.	11.7		Mozambique	8.7
	Germany	11.7	64	Guyana	8.6
	Japan	11.7		Kazakhstan	8.6
17	Lesotho	11.6		Myanmar	8.6
18	Chad	11.5	67	Cameroon	8.5
19	Barbados	11.4		Mali	8.5
	Central African Rep.	11.4		United States	8.5
21	Sierra Leone	11.3	70	Albania	8.4
22	Portugal	11.2		Benin	8.4
23	Greece	11.1		Congo-Kinshasa	8.4
	Italy	11.1	73	Haiti	8.3
25	Czech Republic	11.0		Niger	8.3
	Poland	11.0		Puerto Rico	8.3
27	Nigeria	10.7	76	Switzerland	8.2
28	Ivory Coast	10.6	77	China	8.1
	Trinidad & Tobago	10.6		Togo	8.1
30	Slovakia	10.5	79	Taiwan	8.0
31	Macedonia	10.3	80	Canada	7.8
	Montenegro	10.3		Fiji	7.8
	Slovenia	10.3		Suriname	7.8
34	Monaco[a]	10.1	83	Angola	7.7
35	Finland	10.0		Norway	7.7
36	Armenia	9.8	85	Argentina	7.6
	Austria	9.8		Liechtenstein[a]	7.6
	Denmark	9.8		Sri Lanka	7.6
	Somalia	9.8		Uganda	7.6
40	Belgium	9.7	89	Guinea	7.5
	Virgin Islands (US)	9.7		India	7.5
42	Spain	9.6		Indonesia	7.5
43	Malta	9.5		Mauritania	7.5
	North Korea	9.5	93	Andorra[a]	7.4
	South Sudan	9.5		Cyprus	7.4
46	South Africa	9.4		Gambia, The	7.4
	Uruguay	9.4		Hong Kong	7.4
48	Burundi	9.3		Zimbabwe	7.4
	Channel Islands	9.3			

Note: Both death and, in particular, infant mortality rates can be underestimated in certain countries where not all deaths are officially recorded.   a 2018 estimate.

Highest infant mortality
Number of deaths per 1,000 live births, 2020–25

1	Central African Rep.	73	23	Afghanistan	45
2	Chad	72		Togo	45
3	Sierra Leone	68	25	Gambia, The	41
4	Somalia	63		Lesotho	41
5	Burundi	61		Papua New Guinea	41
	Guinea-Bissau	61	28	Guinea	40
7	Mauritania	59		Sudan	40
8	Pakistan	58		Zambia	40
9	Congo-Kinshasa	57	31	Myanmar	39
	Mozambique	57		Turkmenistan	39
	South Sudan	57	33	Haiti	38
12	Benin	56		Swaziland	38
	Mali	56		Yemen	38
14	Nigeria	55		Zimbabwe	38
15	Angola	54	37	Liberia	37
	Equatorial Guinea	54	38	Ghana	36
	Malawi	54	39	Congo-Brazzaville	35
18	Cameroon	52		Tanzania	35
19	Ivory Coast	49	41	Laos	34
	Niger	49		Rwanda	34
	Uganda	49	43	Gabon	31
22	Burkina Faso	46		Kenya	31

Lowest death rates
No. of deaths per 1,000 pop., 2020–25

1	Qatar	1.8
2	United Arab Emirates	2.0
3	Oman	2.5
4	Bahrain	2.6
5	French Guiana	3.1
6	Maldives	3.3
7	Kuwait	3.4
	West Bank & Gaza	3.4
9	Jordan	3.9
	Saudi Arabia	3.9
11	Syria	4.0
12	Brunei	4.1
13	Macau	4.3
14	Iran	4.6
15	Guatemala	4.7
	Iraq	4.7
17	Algeria	4.8
18	Honduras	4.9
	Nicaragua	4.9
20	Tajikistan	5.0
	Timor-Leste	5.0
22	Mexico	5.1
	Senegal	5.1

Lowest infant mortality
No. of deaths per 1,000 live births, 2020–25

1	Finland	1
	Hong Kong	1
	Iceland	1
	Norway	1
	Portugal	1
6	Austria	2
	Belgium	2
	Czech Republic	2
	France	2
	Germany	2
	Ireland	2
	Israel	2
	Italy	2
	Japan	2
	Luxembourg	2
	Macau	2
	Monaco[a]	2
	Netherlands	2
	Singapore	2
	Slovenia	2
	South Korea	2
	Spain	2
	Sweden	2

a 2016 estimate.

Death and disease

Diabetes

Prevalence in pop. aged 20–79, %
2017 age-standardised estimate[a]

1	New Caledonia	22.6
2	French Polynesia	22.0
3	Mauritius	21.3
4	Guam	20.9
5	Papua New Guinea	17.7
	Saudi Arabia	17.7
7	United Arab Emirates	17.2
8	Egypt	16.8
9	Malaysia	16.4
10	Bahrain	16.3
	Qatar	16.3
12	Kuwait	15.5
13	Sudan	15.2
14	Fiji	13.9
15	Réunion	13.4
16	Barbados	13.3

Cardiovascular disease

No. of deaths per 100,000 pop.,
2017

1	Ukraine	956.2
2	Bulgaria	930.5
3	Georgia	812.4
4	Latvia	794.9
5	Lithuania	781.4
6	Belarus	769.3
7	Serbia	756.3
8	Romania	745.3
9	Russia	684.2
10	Moldova	623.2
11	Montenegro	596.7
12	Estonia	589.1
13	Hungary	588.2
14	Croatia	547.9
15	Bosnia & Herz.	532.7
16	Greece	489.3

Cancer

Deaths per 100,000 pop., 2017

1	Hungary	330.4
2	Japan	323.1
3	Croatia	316.9
4	Netherlands	304.5
5	Serbia	303.9
6	Denmark	303.6
7	Germany	303.5
8	Greece	300.4
9	Italy	298.0
10	Virgin Islands (US)	293.8
11	Latvia	288.9
12	Slovenia	285.5
13	Poland	284.6
14	Lithuania	283.6
15	Uruguay	279.9
16	France	277.3
17	Portugal	277.1
18	Czech Republic	273.1
19	Belgium	271.9
20	United Kingdom	269.9
21	Bulgaria	265.6
22	Romania	263.6
23	Bosnia & Herz.	263.3
	Estonia	263.3
25	Spain	249.3
26	Austria	247.3

Suicide

Deaths per 100,000 pop., 2016

1	Lithuania	31.9
2	Russia	31.0
3	Guyana	29.2
4	South Korea	26.9
5	Belarus	26.2
6	Suriname	22.8
7	Kazakhstan	22.5
8	Ukraine	22.4
9	Latvia	21.2
	Lesotho	21.2
11	Belgium	20.7
12	Hungary	19.1
13	Slovenia	18.6
14	Japan	18.5
15	Uruguay	18.4
16	Estonia	17.8
17	France	17.7
18	Switzerland	17.2
19	Croatia	16.5
20	Equatorial Guinea	16.4
21	India	16.3
22	Poland	16.2
23	Finland	15.9
	Moldova	15.9
25	Austria	15.6
	Serbia	15.6

a Assumes that every country and region has the same age profile.
Note: Statistics are not available for all countries. The number of cases diagnosed and reported depends on the quality of medical practice and administration and can be under-reported in a number of countries.

Measles immunisation
Lowest % of children aged 12–23 months, 2017

1	South Sudan	20
2	Equatorial Guinea	30
3	Chad	37
4	Angola	42
	Nigeria	42
6	Somalia	46
7	Guinea	48
8	Central African Rep.	49
9	Haiti	53
10	Madagascar	58
	Montenegro	58
12	South Africa	60
13	Mali	61
14	Afghanistan	62
	Papua New Guinea	62
16	Gabon	63

DPT[a] immunisation
Lowest % of children aged 12–23 months, 2015

1	Equatorial Guinea	25
2	South Sudan	26
3	Chad	41
4	Nigeria	42
	Somalia	42
6	Guinea	45
7	Central African Rep.	47
8	Syria	48
9	Ukraine	50
10	Angola	52
11	Haiti	60
12	Papua New Guinea	62
13	Iraq	63
14	Afghanistan	65
15	Mali	66
	South Africa	66
17	Yemen	68

HIV/AIDS prevalence
Prevalence in adults aged 15–49, %, 2017

1	Swaziland	27.4
2	Lesotho	23.8
3	Botswana	22.8
4	South Africa	18.8
5	Zimbabwe	13.3
6	Mozambique	12.5
7	Namibia	12.1
8	Zambia	11.5
9	Malawi	9.6
10	Equatorial Guinea	6.5
11	Uganda	5.9
12	Kenya	4.8
13	Tanzania	4.5
14	Gabon	4.2
15	Central African Rep.	4.0
	Guatemala	4.0
17	Cameroon	3.7
18	Guinea-Bissau	3.4
19	Congo-Brazzaville	3.1
20	Ivory Coast	2.8
21	Rwanda	2.7
22	South Sudan	2.4
23	Togo	2.1
24	Angola	1.9
	Bahamas	1.9
	Haiti	1.9
27	Jamaica	1.8

AIDS
Deaths per 100,000 population, 2017

1	Lesotho	325
2	South Africa	246
3	Swaziland	223
4	Mozambique	207
5	Botswana	180
6	Namibia	168
7	Equatorial Guinea	130
8	Malawi	128
9	Zambia	126
10	Central African Rep.	115
11	Congo-Brazzaville	113
12	Zimbabwe	109
13	Kenya	100
14	Cameroon	82
	Nigeria	82
16	Guinea-Bissau	78
17	Ivory Coast	75
18	Uganda	66
19	Angola	52
	Tanzania	52
	Togo	52
22	Ghana	46
23	Gambia, The	41
24	Liberia	39
25	Gabon	38
26	South Sudan	37
27	Haiti	33

a Diphtheria, pertussis and tetanus.

Health

Highest health spending
As % of GDP, 2016

1	United States	17.1
2	Sierra Leone	16.5
3	Cuba	12.2
	Switzerland	12.2
5	Brazil	11.8
6	France	11.5
7	Germany	11.1
8	Japan	10.9
	Sweden	10.9
10	Maldives	10.6
11	Canada	10.5
	Norway	10.5
13	Andorra	10.4
	Austria	10.4
	Denmark	10.4
	Netherlands	10.4
17	Afghanistan	10.2
18	Belgium	10.0
19	Armenia	9.9
20	Malawi	9.8
	United Kingdom	9.8
22	Liberia	9.6
23	Finland	9.5

Lowest health spending
As % of GDP, 2016

1	Monaco	1.7
2	Papua New Guinea	2.0
3	Brunei	2.3
4	Bangladesh	2.4
	Laos	2.4
6	South Sudan	2.5
7	Pakistan	2.8
8	Angola	2.9
9	Eritrea	3.0
10	Gabon	3.1
	Indonesia	3.1
	Qatar	3.1
13	Venezuela	3.2
14	Iraq	3.3
15	Equatorial Guinea	3.4
16	Fiji	3.5
	Kazakhstan	3.5
	United Arab Emirates	3.5
19	Nigeria	3.6
20	India	3.7
	Thailand	3.7

Out-of-pocket spending
$ per person at PPP, 2015

Highest

1	Andorra	2,165
2	Switzerland	2,149
3	Malta	1,288
4	Singapore	1,161
5	United States	1,057
6	South Korea	940
7	Cyprus	938
8	Azerbaijan	937
9	Austria	921
10	Norway	888
11	Belgium	840
12	Trinidad & Tobago	823
13	Ireland	809
14	Sweden	805
15	Finland	795
16	Greece	782
17	Spain	771
18	Italy	765
19	Portugal	736
20	Armenia	721
21	Turkmenistan	713
22	Bulgaria	711

Lowest

1	Mozambique	4
2	Papua New Guinea	6
3	Burundi	12
	Malawi	12
5	Central African Rep.	13
	Congo-Kinshasa	13
7	Timor-Leste	14
8	Madagascar	17
9	Gambia, The	23
10	Ethiopia	25
	Liberia	25
	Tanzania	25
13	Eritrea	29
14	Guinea	31
15	Benin	34
16	Burkina Faso	35
17	Niger	36
18	Guinea-Bissau	37
	Rwanda	37
20	Lesotho	42
21	Senegal	43

Obesity[a]

% of adult population aged 18 and over, 2016

		Overall	Men	Women
1	Kuwait	37.9	33.3	45.6
2	United States	36.2	35.5	37.0
3	Jordan	35.5	28.2	43.1
4	Saudi Arabia	35.4	30.8	42.3
5	Qatar	35.1	32.5	43.1
6	Libya	32.5	25.0	39.6
7	Turkey	32.1	24.4	39.2
8	Egypt	32.0	22.7	41.1
	Lebanon	32.0	27.4	37.0
10	United Arab Emirates	31.7	27.5	41.0
11	Bahamas	31.6	24.4	38.1
12	New Zealand	30.8	30.1	31.4
13	Iraq	30.4	23.4	37.0
14	Fiji	30.2	25.1	35.3
15	Bahrain	29.8	25.5	36.8
16	Canada	29.4	29.5	29.3
17	Australia	29.0	29.6	28.4
18	Malta	28.9	29.2	28.5
	Mexico	28.9	24.3	32.8
20	Chile	28.0	24.9	31.0
21	Uruguay	27.9	24.9	30.6
22	United Kingdom	27.8	26.9	28.6
23	Israel	26.1	25.9	26.2
24	Andorra	25.6	25.9	25.3
	Venezuela	25.6	22.4	28.6

Underweight[b]

Adult population 18 years or over, 2016

		Overall	Men	Women
1	India	23.6	23.1	24.2
2	Bangladesh	21.5	20.0	23.0
3	Vietnam	17.7	17.3	18.2
4	Eritrea	17.3	17.9	16.9
5	Nepal	16.8	16.0	17.4
6	Afghanistan	16.4	17.1	15.8
7	Timor-Leste	16.1	14.5	17.9
8	Congo-Kinshasa	15.9	18.8	13.1
9	Ethiopia	15.8	17.2	14.5
10	Pakistan	15.0	15.2	14.7
11	Central African Rep.	14.8	17.5	12.3
12	Myanmar	14.6	14.9	14.4
13	Madagascar	14.5	14.3	14.7
14	Sri Lanka	14.0	15.3	12.9
15	Cambodia	13.6	13.0	14.1
16	Angola	13.5	16.3	10.9
17	Chad	13.3	13.4	13.3
18	Niger	13.2	13.7	12.5

a Defined as body mass index of 30 or more – see page 248.
b Defined as body mass index of less than 18 – see page 248.

Telephones and the internet

Mobile telephones
Subscribers per 100 population, 2017

1	Macau	328.8		26	Italy	141.3
2	Hong Kong	249.8			Suriname	141.3
3	United Arab Emirates	210.9		28	Gambia, The	141.2
4	Maldives	206.3		29	Georgia	140.7
5	Costa Rica	180.2		30	Malta	140.4
6	Thailand	176.0		31	Argentina	139.8
7	Kuwait	172.6		32	Cyprus	138.5
8	Austria	170.9		33	Luxembourg	136.1
9	Montenegro	166.1		34	New Zealand	136.0
10	Indonesia	164.9		35	Japan	135.5
11	Turkmenistan	162.9		36	Sri Lanka	135.1
12	Bahrain	158.4		37	Malaysia	133.9
13	Russia	157.9		38	Germany	133.6
14	El Salvador	156.5		39	Ukraine	133.5
15	South Africa	156.0		40	Finland	132.3
16	Qatar	151.1		41	Poland	132.2
17	Lithuania	150.9		42	Nicaragua	131.6
18	Oman	149.8		43	Gabon	131.5
19	Trinidad & Tobago	148.3		44	Switzerland	130.8
20	Uruguay	147.5		45	Ivory Coast	130.7
21	Singapore	146.8			Slovakia	130.7
22	Kazakhstan	146.6		47	Chile	127.5
23	Estonia	145.4			Ghana	127.5
	Mauritius	145.4		49	Brunei	127.1
25	Botswana	141.4		50	Colombia	126.8

Landline telephones
Per 100 population, 2017

1	Monaco	121.5		16	Iceland	43.6
2	Virgin Islands (US)	72.4		17	Austria	43.1
3	France	59.5			Switzerland	43.1
4	Hong Kong	57.7		19	Spain	42.5
5	Taiwan	57.4		20	Barbados	42.2
6	Malta	55.6		21	Liechtenstein	40.5
7	Germany	54.1		22	Canada	39.5
8	South Korea	52.7		23	Israel	38.9
9	Japan	50.2		24	Ireland	38.7
10	United Kingdom	50.1		25	Netherlands	38.5
11	Andorra	49.9		26	New Zealand	38.0
12	Belarus	47.5		27	Serbia	37.5
13	Luxembourg	47.2		28	Cyprus	37.3
14	Portugal	46.8		29	Belgium	37.2
15	Greece	46.4		30	United States	37.0

Broadband

Fixed-broadband subscribers per 100 population, 2017

1	Monaco	49.8	26	Australia	32.4
2	Switzerland	46.1	27	Japan	31.8
3	Andorra	44.5	28	Spain	31.6
4	Denmark	43.7	29	Finland	31.0
	France	43.7	30	Estonia	30.9
6	Liechtenstein	42.9	31	Hungary	30.5
7	Netherlands	42.3	32	Macau	29.9
8	Malta	42.1	33	Czech Republic	29.6
9	South Korea	41.6	34	Ireland	29.4
10	Norway	40.6		United Arab Emirates	29.4
11	Germany	40.5	36	Slovenia	28.9
12	Iceland	39.9	37	Austria	28.8
13	United Kingdom	39.3	38	Israel	28.1
14	Sweden	39.0	39	China	28.0
15	Belgium	38.3	40	Italy	27.9
16	Canada	38.0	41	Lithuania	27.6
17	Bermuda	37.2		Uruguay	27.6
18	Luxembourg	36.8	43	Latvia	27.0
19	Hong Kong	36.1	44	Croatia	26.2
20	Cyprus	34.8	45	Singapore	25.9
21	Portugal	34.6	46	Slovakia	25.8
22	Greece	33.9	47	Bulgaria	25.4
	United States	33.9	48	Romania	24.3
24	New Zealand	33.6	49	Barbados	24.2
25	Belarus	33.4		Taiwan	24.2

Broadband speeds

Average download speed, Mbps, 2017

1	Singapore	55.1	23	Germany	18.8
2	Sweden	40.2	24	Canada	18.4
3	Taiwan	34.4		Slovenia	18.4
4	Denmark	33.5	26	Bulgaria	17.5
	Netherlands	33.5	27	Czech Republic	17.3
6	Latvia	30.4	28	New Zealand	16.9
7	Norway	29.1		Thailand	16.9
8	Belgium	27.4	30	United Kingdom	16.5
9	Hong Kong	27.2	31	Monaco	16.1
10	Switzerland	26.9	32	Luxembourg	15.5
11	Lithuania	25.1	33	Austria	15.3
12	Japan	24.5	34	Poland	14.9
13	Estonia	24.1	35	Ireland	13.9
14	Hungary	23.2	36	France	13.4
15	South Korea	22.9	37	Croatia	12.6
16	Portugal	21.7	38	Serbia	12.3
17	Romania	21.3	39	Andorra	12.1
18	Finland	20.9	40	Russia	11.6
19	Macau	20.5	41	Liechtenstein	11.4
20	United States	20.0	42	Moldova	10.8
21	Spain	19.6	43	Italy	10.7
22	Slovakia	18.9	44	Iceland	10.6

Arts and entertainment

Music sales
Total including downloads, $bn, 2017

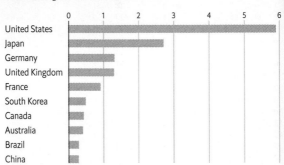

Revenue share, by type, %, 2017

■ Physical   ■ Digital   ▨ Performance rights   ■ Synchronisation rights

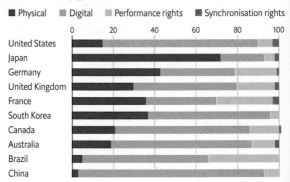

Book publishing
New titles per million population, 2016

1	Japan	10,125	15	Spain	1,109
2	China	7,533	16	Italy[a]	1,078
3	South Korea	7,491	17	Germany	1,044
4	Denmark	4,154	18	United States[a]	1,043
5	Iceland	3,110	19	Norway	1,029
6	United Kingdom[a]	2,710	20	Bosnia & Herz.[a]	731
7	Slovenia	2,640	21	Moldova	704
8	Greece[a]	2,240	22	Turkey	702
9	Serbia	1,686	23	Argentina[a]	687
10	Czech Republic[a]	1,509	24	Australia	572
11	Netherlands[a]	1,482	25	Poland[a]	547
12	Latvia	1,318	26	Georgia[a]	396
13	Finland	1,139	27	Colombia	364
14	France	1,111	28	Sweden	321

a 2015

Cinema attendances

Total visits, m, 2017

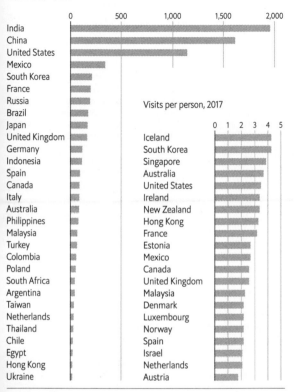

Visits per person, 2017

Feature films

Total number produced, 2017 or latest[a]

1	India	1,986	14	Turkey	148
2	China	874	15	Russia	128
3	United States	660	16	Switzerland	118
4	Japan	594	17	Iran	98
5	South Korea	339	18	Canada	92
6	France	300		Netherlands	92
7	United Kingdom	285		Uzbekistan	92
8	Spain	241	21	Belgium	87
9	Germany	233	22	Greece	85
10	Argentina	220		Malaysia	85
11	Mexico	176		United Arab Emirates	85
12	Italy	173	25	Kazakhstan	74
13	Brazil	160	26	Sweden	68

a 2015–17

The press

Press freedom[a]

Scores, 1 = best, 100 = worst, 2018

Most free		Least free	
1 Norway	7.6	**1** North Korea	88.9
2 Sweden	8.3	**2** Eritrea	84.2
3 Netherlands	10.0	Turkmenistan	84.2
4 Finland	10.3	**4** Syria	79.2
5 Jamaica	11.3	**5** China	78.3
Switzerland	11.3	**6** Vietnam	75.1
7 Belgium	13.2	**7** Sudan	71.1
8 New Zealand	13.6	**8** Cuba	68.9
9 Austria	14.0	**9** Equatorial Guinea	66.5
Costa Rica	14.0	**10** Laos	66.4
Denmark	14.0	**11** Saudi Arabia	63.1
12 Estonia	14.1	**12** Somalia	63.0
Iceland	14.1	**13** Yemen	62.2
14 Portugal	14.2	**14** Bahrain	60.9
15 Germany	14.4	**15** Uzbekistan	60.8
16 Ireland	14.6	**16** Iran	60.7
17 Luxembourg	14.7	**17** Azerbaijan	59.7
18 Canada	15.3	**18** Libya	56.8

Index of abuse against journalists[b]

2018, 100=worst

1 China	81.7	**13** Saudi Arabia	63.1
2 Syria	81.6	**14** Somalia	60.9
3 Eritrea	71.4	**15** Bahrain	60.8
4 Mexico	69.5	**16** India	60.1
5 Afghanistan	68.3	**17** Azerbaijan	59.6
Uzbekistan	68.3	**18** Philippines	58.9
7 Iraq	68.0	**19** Yemen	57.9
8 Iran	67.6	**20** Laos	56.0
9 Vietnam	66.0	**21** Russia	55.8
10 Ethiopia	65.4	**22** Bangladesh	54.3
11 Egypt	63.9	**23** North Korea	51.9
12 Turkey	63.7	**24** Libya	50.4

Number of journalists in prison

As of end 2017

1 Turkey	74	**11** Cameroon	5
2 China	42	Congo-Kinshasa	5
3 Egypt	20	Ethiopia	5
4 Eritrea	16	Russia	5
5 Saudi Arabia	11	**15** Bangladesh	4
6 Azerbaijan	10	Iran	4
Vietnam	10	Israel[c]	4
8 Uganda	8	Morocco	4
9 Syria	7	Uzbekistan	4
10 Bahrain	6		

a Based on 87 questions on topics such as media independence, censorship and transparency. b Based on the intensity of abuse and violence against the media.
c Includes West Bank & Gaza.

Nobel prize winners: 1901–2018

Peace

1	United States	19
2	United Kingdom	12
3	France	9
4	Sweden	5
5	Belgium	4
	Germany	4

Medicine

1	United States	58
2	United Kingdom	25
3	Germany	15
4	France	8
5	Sweden	7

Literature

1	France	16
2	United States	13
3	United Kingdom	11
4	Germany	8
5	Sweden	7

Economics[a]

1	United States	41
2	United Kingdom	9
3	France	2
	Sweden	2
	Norway	2

Physics

1	United States	56
2	United Kingdom	21
3	Germany	19
4	France	11
5	Japan	7

Chemistry

1	United States	52
2	United Kingdom	26
3	Germany	16
4	France	8
5	Switzerland	7

Nobel prize winners: 1901–2018

By country of birth

1	United States	271		Egypt	6
2	United Kingdom	101		Israel	6
3	Germany	82	26	Finland	5
4	France	55		Ireland	5
5	Sweden	29		Ukraine	5
6	Japan	26	29	Argentina	4
	Poland	26		Belarus	4
	Russia	26		Romania	4
9	Canada	19	32	Lithuania	3
	Italy	19		Mexico	3
11	Netherlands	18		New Zealand	3
12	Austria	17		Pakistan	3
	Switzerland	17	36	Algeria	2
14	China	12		Bosnia & Herz.	2
	Norway	12		Chile	2
16	Denmark	11		Colombia	2
17	Australia	10		Guatemala	2
18	Belgium	9		Iran	2
	Hungary	9		Liberia	2
	South Africa	9		Luxembourg	2
21	India	8		Portugal	2
22	Spain	7		South Korea	2
23	Czech Republic	6		Turkey	2

Notes: Prizes by country of residence at time awarded. When prizes have been shared in the same field, one credit given to each country.   a Since 1969.

Sports champions and cheats

World Cup winners and finalists

Men's football (since 1930)	Winner	Runner-up
1 Brazil	5	2
2 Germany[a]	4	4
3 Italy	4	2
4 Argentina	2	3
5 France	2	1
6 Uruguay	2	0
7 England	1	0
Spain	1	0
9 Netherlands	0	3
10 Czechoslovakia[b]	0	2
Hungary	0	2

Women's football (since 1991)	Winner	Runner-up
1 United States	3	1
2 Germany	2	1
3 Japan	1	1
Norway	1	1
5 Brazil	0	1
China	0	1
Sweden	0	1

Men's cricket (since 1975)	Winner	Runner-up
1 Australia	5	2
2 India	2	1
West Indies	2	1
4 Sri Lanka	1	2
5 Pakistan	1	1
6 England	0	3
7 New Zealand	0	1

Women's cricket (since 1973)	Winner	Runner-up
1 Australia	6	2
2 England	4	3
3 New Zealand	1	3
4 India	0	2
5 West Indies	0	1

Davis Cup, tennis (since 1900)[c]	Winner	Runner-up
1 United States	32	29
2 Australia	28	19
3 France	10	9
4 Great Britain	10	8
5 Sweden	7	5
6 Spain	5	4
7 Czech Republic[d]	3	2
Germany[a]	3	2
9 Russia	2	3
10 Croatia	2	1
11 Italy	1	6

Note: Data as of May 2019.   a Including West Germany.   b Until 1993.
c Excludes finalists who have never won.   d Including Czechoslovakia.

Olympic games
Summer: 1896–2016

■ Gold   ▓ Silver   ▓ Bronze

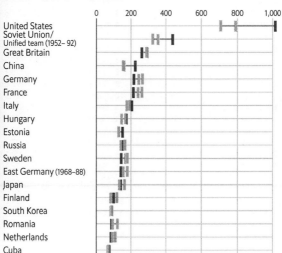

United States
Soviet Union/
Unified team (1952–92)
Great Britain
China
Germany
France
Italy
Hungary
Estonia
Russia
Sweden
East Germany (1968–88)
Japan
Finland
South Korea
Romania
Netherlands
Cuba
Poland
Canada

Winter: 1924–2018

Norway
United States
Germany
Soviet Union/
Unified team (1952–92)
Canada
Austria
Sweden
Switzerland
Russia
Netherlands
Finland
Italy
East Germany (1968–88)
France
South Korea
Japan
China
West Germany (1968–88)
United Kingdom
Czech Republic

Vices

Beer drinkers
Consumption, litres per person, 2017

1	Czech Republic	183.1
2	Austria	106.6
3	Germany	100.1
4	Poland	99.4
5	Romania	95.2
6	Ireland	94.9
7	Spain	87.3
8	Namibia	83.2
9	Slovakia	81.1
10	Estonia	80.5
11	Lithuania	79.9
12	Croatia	79.5
13	Slovenia	79.1
14	Panama	78.7
15	Latvia	76.7
16	Netherlands	76.5
17	Finland	76.3
18	Bulgaria	74.0
19	United States	73.8
20	Gabon	73.5
21	Hungary	71.7
22	Australia	71.2

Wine consumption
Litres per person, 2015

1	Croatia	47.6
2	Portugal	46.5
3	Slovenia	42.8
4	France	41.9
5	Macedonia	41.3
6	Switzerland	36.7
7	Italy	34.5
8	Uruguay	28.1
9	Denmark	27.9
10	Austria	27.5
11	Sweden	26.2
12	Germany	25.0
13	Argentina	23.3
	Greece	23.3
15	Australia	22.1
	Malta	22.1
17	Hungary	21.6
	Spain	21.6
19	Belgium	21.2
20	Bulgaria	20.6
21	Georgia	19.9
22	Romania	19.8

Gambling losses
Total, $bn, 2018

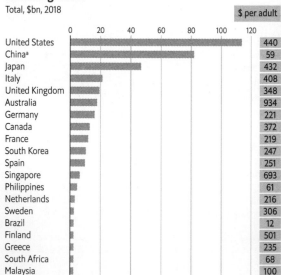

	$ per adult
United States	440
Chinaa	59
Japan	432
Italy	408
United Kingdom	348
Australia	934
Germany	221
Canada	372
France	219
South Korea	247
Spain	251
Singapore	693
Philippines	61
Netherlands	216
Sweden	306
Brazil	12
Finland	501
Greece	235
South Africa	68
Malaysia	100

a Includes Macau and Hong Kong.

Tourism

Most tourist arrivals
Number of arrivals, '000, 2017

1	France	86,861	21	Saudi Arabia	16,109
2	Spain	81,786	22	Croatia	15,593
3	United States	76,941	23	India	15,543
4	China	60,740	24	Portugal	15,432
5	Italy	58,253	25	Ukraine	14,230
6	Mexico	39,291	26	Indonesia	14,040
7	United Kingdom	37,651	27	Singapore	13,903
8	Turkey	37,601	28	South Korea	13,336
9	Germany	37,452	29	Vietnam	12,922
10	Thailand	35,592	30	Denmark	11,743
11	Austria	29,460	31	Bahrain	11,370
12	Japan	28,691	32	Morocco	11,349
13	Hong Kong	27,884	33	Belarus	11,060
14	Greece	27,194	34	Romania	10,926
15	Malaysia	25,948	35	Ireland	10,338
16	Russia	24,390	36	South Africa	10,285
17	Canada	20,798	37	Czech Republic	10,160
18	Poland	18,258	38	Switzerland	9,889
19	Netherlands	17,924	39	Bulgaria	8,883
20	Macau	17,255	40	Australia	8,815

Biggest tourist spenders
$bn, 2017

1	China	257.7	13	Belgium	23.0
2	United States	173.9		Brazil	23.0
3	Germany	97.6	15	Spain	22.3
4	United Kingdom	71.7	16	Netherlands	22.0
5	France	50.3	17	India	21.9
6	Australia	39.5	18	Switzerland	19.5
7	Russia	35.6	19	Saudi Arabia	18.7
8	South Korea	33.4	20	Japan	18.2
9	Canada	31.8	21	Norway	17.8
10	Italy	27.9	22	United Arab Emirates	17.6
11	Hong Kong	25.4	23	Sweden	17.1
12	Singapore	24.5	24	Kuwait	13.7

Largest tourist receipts
$bn, 2017

1	United States	251.4	13	Turkey	31.9
2	France	69.9	14	India	27.9
3	Spain	68.4	15	Mexico	22.5
4	Thailand	62.2	16	Austria	22.4
5	Germany	56.2	17	Portugal	21.1
6	United Kingdom	51.5	18	United Arab Emirates	21.0
7	Italy	44.5	19	Canada	20.4
8	Australia	44.0		Netherlands	20.4
9	Hong Kong	38.0	21	Switzerland	20.1
10	Japan	37.0	22	Singapore	19.7
11	Macau	35.7	23	Greece	18.8
12	China	32.6	24	Malaysia	18.4

Country profiles

ALGERIA

Area, sq km	2,381,741	Capital	Algiers
Arable as % of total land	3.2	Currency	Algerian dinar (AD)

People

Population, m	41.3	Life expectancy: men	76.2 yrs
Pop. per sq km	17.3	women	78.7 yrs
Total change in population		Adult literacy	79.6
2010–20, %	20.0	Fertility rate (per woman)	2.7
Pop. aged 0–19, %	36.4	Urban population, %	71.5
Pop. aged 65 and over, %	6.9		per 1,000 pop.
No. of men per 100 women	102.0	Crude birth rate	21.6
Human Development Index	75.4	Crude death rate	4.8

The economy

GDP	$168bn	GDP per head	$4,238
GDP	AD18,594bn	GDP per head in purchasing	
Av. ann. growth in real		power parity (USA=100)	24.7
GDP 2012–17	3.0%	Economic freedom index	46.2

Origins of GDP

Components of GDP

	% of total		% of total
Agriculture	12	Private consumption	43
Industry, of which:	37	Public consumption	19
manufacturing	35	Investment	48
Services	51	Exports	23
		Imports	-34

Structure of employment

	% of total		% of labour force
Agriculture	9.3	Unemployed 2018	12.1
Industry	30.7	Av. ann. rate 2010–18	10.7
Services	60.0		

Energy

	m TOE		
Total output	174.3	Net energy imports as %	
Total consumption	59.4	of energy use	-177
Consumption per head			
kg oil equivalent	1,321		

Inflation and finance

Consumer price			% change 2017–18
inflation 2018	4.3%	Narrow money (M1)	7.8
Av. ann. inflation 2013–18	4.8%	Broad money	11.1
Deposit rate, Dec. 2018	1.75%		

Exchange rates

	end 2018		December 2018
AD per $	118.29	Effective rates	2010 = 100
AD per SDR	164.52	– nominal	77.1
AD per €	135.97	– real	95.0

Trade

Principal exports		Principal imports	
	$bn fob		*$bn cif*
Hydrocarbons	33.2	Capital goods	14.0
Semi-finished goods	1.4	Intermediate goods	11.0
Capital goods	0.1	Consumer goods	8.5
		Food	8.4
Total incl. others	**35.0**	Total	**45.6**

Main export destinations		Main origins of imports	
	% of total		*% of total*
Italy	17.1	China	18.2
Spain	12.8	France	9.1
France	11.7	Italy	8.0
United States	9.3	Germany	7.0

Balance of payments, reserves and debt, $bn

Visible exports fob	34.6	Change in reserves	-16.0
Visible imports fob	-48.8	Level of reserves	
Trade balance	-14.2	end Dec.	104.8
Invisibles inflows	5.3	No. months of import cover	19.4
Invisibles outflows	-16.2	Official gold holdings, m oz	5.6
Net transfers	3.1	Foreign debt	5.7
Current account balance	-22.1	– as % of GDP	3.3
– as % of GDP	-13.2	– as % of total exports	13.6
Capital balance	0.3	Debt service ratio	0.6
Overall balance	-21.8		

Health and education

Health spending, % of GDP	6.6	Education spending, % of GDP	...
Doctors per 1,000 pop.	1.2	Enrolment, %: primary	111.7
Hospital beds per 1,000 pop.	6.6	secondary	...
At least basic drinking water,		tertiary	47.7
% of pop.	93.5		

Society

No. of households, m	7.8	Cost of living, Dec. 2018	
Av. no. per household	5.3	New York = 100	43
Marriages per 1,000 pop.	...	Cars per 1,000 pop.	91
Divorces per 1,000 pop.	...	Telephone lines per 100 pop.	9.9
Religion, % of pop.		Mobile telephone subscribers	
Muslim	97.9	per 100 pop.	111.0
Non-religious	1.8	Internet access, %	47.7
Christian	0.2	Broadband subs per 100 pop.	7.8
Hindu	<0.1	Broadband speed, Mbps	47.7
Jewish	<0.1		
Other	<0.1		

ARGENTINA

Area, sq km	2,780,400	Capital	Buenos Aires
Arable as % of total land	13.9	Currency	Peso (P)

People

Population, m	44.3	Life expectancy: men	74.0 yrs
Pop. per sq km	15.9	women	81.2 yrs
Total change in population		Adult literacy	99.1
2010–20, %	10.4	Fertility rate (per woman)	2.3
Pop. aged 0–19, %	32.2	Urban population, %	91.6
Pop. aged 65 and over, %	12.1		per 1,000 pop.
No. of men per 100 women	95.9	Crude birth rate	16.9
Human Development Index	82.5	Crude death rate	7.6

The economy

GDP	$637bn	GDP per head	$11,627
GDP	P10,644	GDP per head in purchasing	
Av. ann. growth in real		power parity (USA=100)	32.8
GDP 2012–17	0.7%	Economic freedom index	52.2

Origins of GDP

	% of total
Agriculture	6
Industry, of which:	22
manufacturing	13
Services	72

Components of GDP

	% of total
Private consumption	66
Public consumption	18
Investment	19
Exports	11
Imports	-14

Structure of employment

	% of total		% of labour force
Agriculture	0.1	Unemployed 2018	9.5
Industry	22.4	Av. ann. rate 2010–18	7.8
Services	77.5		

Energy

	m TOE		
Total output	81.3	Net energy imports as %	
Total consumption	93.2	of energy use	13
Consumption per head			
kg oil equivalent	2,015		

Inflation and finance

			% change 2017–18
Consumer price			
inflation 2018	34.3%	Narrow money (M1)	9.5
Av. ann. inflation 2013–18	26.7%	Broad money	12.2
Deposit rate, Aug. 2018	32.6%		

Exchange rates

	end 2018		December 2018
P per $	37.6	Effective rates	2010 = 100
P per SDR	52.3	– nominal	...
P per €	43.2	– real	...

Trade

Principal exports

	$bn fob
Processed agricultural products	22.6
Manufactures	18.8
Primary products	14.8
Fuels & energy	2.5
Total	**58.6**

Principal imports

	$bn cif
Intermediate goods	17.8
Capital goods	14.9
Consumer goods	8.9
Fuels	5.7
Total incl. others	**66.9**

Main export destinations

	% of total
Brazil	15.9
United States	7.6
China	7.4
Chile	4.5

Main origins of imports

	% of total
Brazil	26.9
China	18.4
United States	11.3
Germany	4.8

Balance of payments, reserves and debt, $bn

Visible exports fob	58.6	Change in reserves	16.9
Visible imports fob	-64.1	Level of reserves	
Trade balance	-5.5	end Dec.	55.3
Invisibles inflows	18.8	No. months of import cover	6.1
Invisibles outflows	-45.3	Official gold holdings, m oz	1.8
Net transfers	0.4	Foreign debt	229.0
Current account balance	-31.6	– as % of GDP	35.9
– as % of GDP	-5.0	– as % of total exports	293.8
Capital balance	46.0	Debt service ratio	18.0
Overall balance	14.5		

Health and education

Health spending, % of GDP	7.5	Education spending, % of GDP	5.6
Doctors per 1,000 pop.	3.9	Enrolment, %: primary	110
Hospital beds per 1,000 pop.	5.0	secondary	108
At least basic drinking water,		tertiary	89
% of pop.	99.6		

Society

No. of households, m	13.8	Cost of living, Dec. 2018	
Av. no. per household	3.2	New York = 100	41
Marriages per 1,000 pop.	2.7	Cars per 1,000 pop.	238
Divorces per 1,000 pop.	...	Telephone lines per 100 pop.	22.0
Religion, % of pop.		Mobile telephone subscribers	
Christian	85.2	per 100 pop.	139.8
Non-religious	12.2	Internet access, %	75.8
Other	1.1	Broadband subs per 100 pop.	17.7
Muslim	1.0	Broadband speed, Mbps	1.2
Jewish	0.5		
Hindu	<0.1		

AUSTRALIA

Area, sq km	7,692,024	Capital	Canberra
Arable as % of total land	6.2	Currency	Australian dollar (A$)

People

Population, m	24.5	Life expectancy: men	82.3 yrs
Pop. per sq km	3.2	women	85.7 yrs
Total change in population		Adult literacy	...
2010–20, %	14.8	Fertility rate (per woman)	1.8
Pop. aged 0–19, %	25.2	Urban population, %	85.8
Pop. aged 65 and over, %	16.3		per 1,000 pop.
No. of men per 100 women	99.3	Crude birth rate	12.8
Human Development Index	93.9	Crude death rate	6.7

The economy

GDP	$1,323bn	GDP per head	$56,352
GDP	A$1,808bn	GDP per head in purchasing	
Av. ann. growth in real		power parity (USA=100)	83.7
GDP 2012–17	2.5%	Economic freedom index	80.9

Origins of GDP

	% of total
Agriculture	3
Industry, of which:	23
manufacturing	6
Services	74

Components of GDP

	% of total
Private consumption	57
Public consumption	19
Investment	24
Exports	21
Imports	-21

Structure of employment

	% of total		% of labour force
Agriculture	2.6	Unemployed 2018	5.4
Industry	19.4	Av. ann. rate 2010–18	5.6
Services	78.1		

Energy

	m TOE		
Total output	401.4	Net energy imports as %	
Total consumption	151.0	of energy use	-190
Consumption per head			
kg oil equivalent	5,484		

Inflation and finance

			% change 2017–18
Consumer price			
inflation 2018	2.0%	Narrow money (M1)	3.8
Av. ann. inflation 2013–18	1.8%	Broad money	2.4
Policy rate, Dec. 2018	1.50%		

Exchange rates

	end 2018		December 2018
A$ per $	1.42	Effective rates	2010 = 100
A$ per SDR	1.97	– nominal	89.0
A$ per €	1.63	– real	89.0

Trade

Principal exports		Principal imports	
	$bn fob		*$bn cif*
Crude materials	76.4	Machinery & transport equip.	90.5
Fuels	69.4	Mineral fuels	31.2
Food	28.1	Manufactured goods	22.0
Machinery & transport equip.	13.5		
Total incl. others	**231.1**	Total incl. others	**221.4**

Main export destinations		Main origins of imports	
	% of total		*% of total*
China	33.2	China	23.5
Japan	14.5	United States	11.1
South Korea	6.5	Japan	7.7
India	4.9	Thailand	5.3

Balance of payments, reserves and aid, $bn

Visible exports fob	231.6	Overall balance	8.7
Visible imports fob	-221.1	Change in reserves	13.0
Trade balance	10.5	Level of reserves	
Invisibles inflows	107.9	end Dec.	66.6
Invisibles outflows	-152.8	No. months of import cover	2.1
Net transfers	-1.3	Official gold holdings, m oz	2.3
Current account balance	-35.8	Aid given	3.0
– as % of GDP	-2.7	– as % of GNI	0.2
Capital balance	44.0		

Health and education

Health spending, % of GDP	9.3	Education spending, % of GDP	5.3
Doctors per 1,000 pop.	3.5	Enrolment, %: primary	101
Hospital beds per 1,000 pop.	3.8	secondary	154
At least basic drinking water,		tertiary	122
% of pop.	100		

Society

No. of households, m	9.9	Cost of living, Dec. 2018	
Av. no. per household	2.5	New York = 100	89
Marriages per 1,000 pop.	4.9	Cars per 1,000 pop.	562
Divorces per 1,000 pop.	1.9	Telephone lines per 100 pop.	34.6
Religion, % of pop.		Mobile telephone subscribers	
Christian	67.3	per 100 pop.	112.7
Non-religious	24.2	Internet access, %	86.5
Other	4.2	Broadband subs per 100 pop.	32.4
Muslim	2.4	Broadband speed, Mbps	7.7
Hindu	1.4		
Jewish	0.5		

AUSTRIA

Area, sq km	83,871	Capital	Vienna
Arable as % of total land	16.5	Currency	Euro (€)

People

Population, m	8.7	Life expectancy: men	80.6 yrs
Pop. per sq km	103.7	women	84.9 yrs
Total change in population		Adult literacy	...
2010–20, %	4.4	Fertility rate (per woman)	1.5
Pop. aged 0–19, %	19.0	Urban population, %	57.9
Pop. aged 65 and over, %	19.9		per 1,000 pop.
No. of men per 100 women	96.6	Crude birth rate	9.7
Human Development Index	90.8	Crude death rate	9.8

The economy

GDP	$417bn	GDP per head	$51,509
GDP	€370bn	GDP per head in purchasing	
Av. ann. growth in real		power parity (USA=100)	75.1
GDP 2012–17	1.3%	Economic freedom index	72.0

Origins of GDP		Components of GDP	
	% of total		% of total
Agriculture	1	Private consumption	52
Industry, of which:	25	Public consumption	20
manufacturing	17	Investment	25
Services	74	Exports	54
		Imports	-51

Structure of employment

	% of total		% of labour force
Agriculture	3.9	Unemployed 2018	4.8
Industry	24.7	Av. ann. rate 2010–18	5.2
Services	71.4		

Energy

	m TOE		
Total output	13.8	Net energy imports as %	
Total consumption	37.3	of energy use	64
Consumption per head			
kg oil equivalent	3,800		

Inflation and finance

Consumer price			% change 2017–18
inflation 2018	2.1%	Narrow money (M1)	0.7
Av. ann. inflation 2013–18	1.5%	Broad money	4.2
Deposit rate, Dec. 2018	0.20%		

Exchange rates

	end 2018		December 2018
€ per $	0.87	Effective rates	2010 = 100
€ per SDR	1.21	– nominal	101.4
		– real	102.8

Trade

Principal exports

	$bn fob
Machinery & transport equip.	68.8
Chemicals & related products	22.8
Food, drink & tobacco	12.4
Raw materials	5.5
Total incl. others	**168.0**

Principal imports

	$bn cif
Machinery & transport equip.	65.3
Chemicals & related products	23.3
Mineral fuels & lubricants	12.7
Food, drink & tobacco	12.1
Total incl. others	**175.7**

Main export destinations

	% of total
Germany	29.5
United States	6.3
Italy	6.2
Switzerland	5.1
EU28	71.2

Main origins of imports

	% of total
Germany	41.9
Italy	5.8
Switzerland	5.5
Czech Republic	4.4
EU28	77.3

Balance of payments, reserves and aid, $bn

Visible exports fob	157.3	Overall balance	-3.5
Visible imports fob	-156.3	Change in reserves	-1.7
Trade balance	1.0	Level of reserves	
Invisibles inflows	98.3	end Dec.	21.5
Invisibles outflows	-88.1	No. months of import cover	1.1
Net transfers	-3.2	Official gold holdings, m oz	9.0
Current account balance	8.0	Aid given	1.3
– as % of GDP	1.9	– as % of GNI	0.3
Capital balance	-14.0		

Health and education

Health spending, % of GDP	10.4	Education spending, % of GDP	5.5
Doctors per 1,000 pop.	5.2	Enrolment, %: primary	102
Hospital beds per 1,000 pop.	7.6	secondary	101
At least basic drinking water,		tertiary	84
% of pop.	100		

Society

No. of households, m	3.9	Cost of living, Dec. 2018	
Av. no. per household	2.2	New York = 100	91
Marriages per 1,000 pop.	5.1	Cars per 1,000 pop.	546
Divorces per 1,000 pop.	1.8	Telephone lines per 100 pop.	43.1
Religion, % of pop.		Mobile telephone subscribers	
Christian	80.4	per 100 pop.	170.9
Non-religious	13.5	Internet access, %	87.9
Muslim	5.4	Broadband subs per 100 pop.	28.8
Other	0.5	Broadband speed, Mbps	15.3
Jewish	0.2		
Hindu	<0.1		

BANGLADESH

| Area, sq km | 147,570 | Capital | Dhaka |
| Arable as % of total land | 58.6 | Currency | Taka (Tk) |

People

Population, m	164.7	Life expectancy: men	72.7 yrs
Pop. per sq km	1,116.1	women	76.3 yrs
Total change in population		Adult literacy	72.9
2010–20, %	11.6	Fertility rate (per woman)	2.1
Pop. aged 0–19, %	36.4	Urban population, %	35.1
Pop. aged 65 and over, %	5.2		per 1,000 pop.
No. of men per 100 women	101.5	Crude birth rate	18.5
Human Development Index	60.8	Crude death rate	5.3

The economy

GDP	$250bn	GDP per head	$1,745
GDP	Tk21,131bn	GDP per head in purchasing	
Av. ann. growth in real		power parity (USA=100)	7.4
GDP 2012–17	6.6%	Economic freedom index	55.6

Origins of GDP		**Components of GDP**	
	% of total		% of total
Agriculture	13	Private consumption	69
Industry, of which:	28	Public consumption	6
manufacturing	17	Investment	31
Services	59	Exports	15
		Imports	-20

Structure of employment

	% of total		% of labour force
Agriculture	40.2	Unemployed 2018	4.3
Industry	20.5	Av. ann. rate 2010–18	4.2
Services	39.4		

Energy

	m TOE		
Total output	25.7	Net energy imports as %	
Total consumption	31.7	of energy use	17
Consumption per head			
kg oil equivalent	222		

Inflation and finance

Consumer price			% change 2017–18
inflation 2018	5.6%	Narrow money (M1)	8.2
Av. ann. inflation 2013–18	6.0%	Broad money	11.5
Deposit rate, Dec. 2018	6.20%		

Exchange rates

	end 2018		December 2018
Tk per $	83.90	Effective rates	2010 = 100
Tk per SDR	116.69	– nominal	...
Tk per €	96.44	– real	...

Trade

Principal exports

	$bn fob
Clothing	21.6
Jute goods	0.8
Fish & fish products	0.5
Leather	0.2
Total incl. others	**31.4**

Principal imports

	$bn cif
Iron & steel	4.2
Capital machinery	3.8
Textiles & yarns	3.7
Fuels	3.5
Total incl. others	**47.6**

Main export destinations

	% of total
Germany	12.9
United States	12.2
United Kingdom	8.7
Spain	5.3

Main origins of imports

	% of total
China	21.9
India	15.2
Singapore	5.7
Japan	3.5

Balance of payments, reserves and debt, $bn

Visible exports fob	35.3	Change in reserves	1.1
Visible imports fob	-47.6	Level of reserves	
Trade balance	-12.3	end Dec.	33.4
Invisibles inflows	4.0	No. months of import cover	6.7
Invisibles outflows	-12.1	Official gold holdings, m oz	0.4
Net transfers	14.0	Foreign debt	47.2
Current account balance	-6.4	– as % of GDP	18.9
– as % of GDP	-2.5	– as % of total exports	89.3
Capital balance	8.4	Debt service ratio	4.1
Overall balance	0.6		

Health and education

Health spending, % of GDP	2.4	Education spending, % of GDP	1.5
Doctors per 1,000 pop.	0.5	Enrolment, %: primary	111
Hospital beds per 1,000 pop.	0.8	secondary	67
At least basic drinking water,		tertiary	18
% of pop.	97.3		

Society

No. of households, m	33.3	Cost of living, Dec. 2018	
Av. no. per household	4.9	New York = 100	68
Marriages per 1,000 pop.	...	Cars per 1,000 pop.	2
Divorces per 1,000 pop.	...	Telephone lines per 100 pop.	0.4
Religion, % of pop. of pop.		Mobile telephone subscribers	
Muslim	89.8	per 100 pop.	91.7
Hindu	9.1	Internet access, %	18.0
Other	0.9	Broadband subs per 100 pop.	4.4
Christian	0.2	Broadband speed, Mbps	1.3
Jewish	<0.1		
Non-religious	<0.1		

BELGIUM

Area, sq km	30,528	Capital	Brussels
Arable as % of total land	27.3	Currency	Euro (€)

People

Population, m	11.4	Life expectancy: men	80.1 yrs
Pop. per sq km	373.4	women	84.3 yrs
Total change in population		Adult literacy	...
2010–20, %	6.2	Fertility rate (per woman)	1.8
Pop. aged 0–19, %	22.8	Urban population, %	97.9
Pop. aged 65 and over, %	19.2		per 1,000 pop.
No. of men per 100 women	98.3	Crude birth rate	11.4
Human Development Index	91.6	Crude death rate	9.7

The economy

GDP	$495bn	GDP per head	$46,724
GDP	€439bn	GDP per head in purchasing	
Av. ann. growth in real		power parity (USA=100)	77.1
GDP 2012–17	1.2%	Economic freedom index	67.3

Origins of GDP		**Components of GDP**	
	% of total		% of total
Agriculture	1	Private consumption	51
Industry, of which:	20	Public consumption	23
manufacturing	13	Investment	25
Services	79	Exports	86
		Imports	-85

Structure of employment

	% of total		% of labour force
Agriculture	1.2	Unemployed 2018	6.3
Industry	20.6	Av. ann. rate 2010–18	7.7
Services	78.2		

Energy

	m TOE		
Total output	14.8	Net energy imports as %	
Total consumption	67.7	of energy use	80
Consumption per head			
kg oil equivalent	4,688		

Inflation and finance

Consumer price			% change 2017–18
inflation 2018	2.3%	Narrow money (M1)	0.7
Av. ann. inflation 2013–18	1.5%	Broad money	4.2
Deposit rate, Dec. 2018	0.39%		

Exchange rates

	end 2018		December 2018
€ per $	0.87	Effective rates	2010 = 100
€ per SDR	1.21	– nominal	102.8
		– real	101.8

Trade

Principal exports		Principal imports	
	$bn fob		*$bn cif*
Chemicals & related products	121.4	Machinery & transport equip.	106.4
Machinery & transport equip.	96.5	Chemicals & related products	98.6
Mineral fuels & lubricants	41.7	Mineral fuels & lubricants	48.2
Food, drink & tobacco	35.9	Food, drink & tobacco	35.4
Total incl. others	**430.7**	Total incl. others	**409.1**

Main export destinations		Main origins of imports	
	% of total		*% of total*
Germany	16.7	Netherlands	17.2
France	14.9	Germany	14.0
Netherlands	12.0	France	9.5
United Kingdom	8.4	United States	7.0
EU28	72.1	EU28	64.5

Balance of payments, reserves and debt, $bn

Visible exports fob	304.3	Overall balance	1.2
Visible imports fob	-303.8	Change in reserves	2.6
Trade balance	0.5	Level of reserves	
Invisibles inflows	178.0	end Dec.	26.1
Invisibles outflows	-167.6	No. months of import cover	0.7
Net transfers	-7.3	Official gold holdings, m oz	7.3
Current account balance	3.6	Aid given	2.2
– as % of GDP	0.7	– as % of GNI	0.4
Capital balance	6.2		

Health and education

Health spending, % of GDP	10.0	Education spending, % of GDP	6.6
Doctors per 1,000 pop.	3.0	Enrolment, %: primary	103
Hospital beds per 1,000 pop.	6.2	secondary	161
At least basic drinking water,		tertiary	76
% of pop.	100		

Society

No. of households, m	4.8	Cost of living, Dec. 2018	
Av. no. per household	2.4	New York = 100	80
Marriages per 1,000 pop.	3.9	Cars per 1,000 pop.	490
Divorces per 1,000 pop.	2.0	Telephone lines per 100 pop.	37.2
Religion, % of pop.		Mobile telephone subscribers	
Christian	64.2	per 100 pop.	104.7
Non-religious	29.0	Internet access, %	87.7
Muslim	5.9	Broadband subs per 100 pop.	38.3
Other	0.6	Broadband speed, Mbps	27.4
Jewish	0.3		
Hindu	<0.1		

BRAZIL

Area, sq km	8,513,887	Capital	Brasília
Arable as % of total land	8.5	Currency	Real (R)

People

Population, m	209.3	Life expectancy: men	73.4 yrs
Pop. per sq km	24.6	women	80.4 yrs
Total change in population		Adult literacy	92.0
2010–20, %	8.7	Fertility rate (per woman)	1.7
Pop. aged 0–19, %	28.3	Urban population, %	86.0
Pop. aged 65 and over, %	9.5		per 1,000 pop.
No. of men per 100 women	96.5	Crude birth rate	13.8
Human Development Index	75.9	Crude death rate	6.7

The economy

GDP	$2,054bn	GDP per head	$8,968
GDP	R6,553bn	GDP per head in purchasing	
Av. ann. growth in real		power parity (USA=100)	25.8
GDP 2012–17	-0.5%	Economic freedom index	51.9

Origins of GDP		Components of GDP	
	% of total		% of total
Agriculture	5	Private consumption	64
Industry, of which:	18	Public consumption	20
manufacturing	11	Investment	15
Services	77	Exports	13
		Imports	-12

Structure of employment

	% of total		% of labour force
Agriculture	9.4	Unemployed 2018	12.5
Industry	20.4	Av. ann. rate 2010–18	9.0
Services	70.2		

Energy

	m TOE		
Total output	293.2	Net energy imports as %	
Total consumption	314.7	of energy use	12
Consumption per head			
kg oil equivalent	1,485		

Inflation and finance

Consumer price		% change 2017–18	
inflation 2018	3.7%	Narrow money (M1)	1.6
Av. ann. inflation 2013–18	6.2%	Broad money	8.1
Deposit rate, Dec. 2018	5.66%		

Exchange rates

	end 2018		December 2018
R per $	3.87	Effective rates	2010 = 100
R per SDR	5.39	– nominal	63.5
R per €	4.45	– real	69.7

Trade

Principal exports		**Principal imports**	
	$bn fob		*$bn cif*
Primary products	101.1	Intermediate products & raw	
Manufactured goods	80.3	materials	93.6
Semi-manufactured goods	31.4	Consumer goods	23.3
		Fuels & lubricants	17.6
		Capital goods	16.1
Total incl. others	**217.7**	Total incl. others	**150.8**

Main export destinations		**Main origins of imports**	
	% of total		*% of total*
China	21.8	China	19.2
United States	12.5	United States	17.7
Argentina	8.1	Argentina	6.6
Netherlands	4.2	Germany	6.5

Balance of payments, reserves and debt, $bn

Visible exports fob	217.2	Change in reserves	9.0
Visible imports fob	-153.2	Level of reserves	
Trade balance	64.0	end Dec.	373.9
Invisibles inflows	57.7	No. months of import cover	15.8
Invisibles outflows	-131.6	Official gold holdings, m oz	2.2
Net transfers	2.6	Foreign debt	543.0
Current account balance	-7.2	– as % of GDP	26.4
– as % of GDP	-0.4	– as % of total exports	195.6
Capital balance	5.9	Debt service ratio	34.4
Overall balance	5.1		

Health and education

Health spending, % of GDP	11.8	Education spending, % of GDP	6.2
Doctors per 1,000 pop.	1.9	Enrolment, %: primary	114
Hospital beds per 1,000 pop.	2.2	secondary	102
At least basic drinking water,		tertiary	51
% of pop.	97.5		

Society

No. of households, m	62.1	Cost of living, Dec. 2018	
Av. no. per household	3.3	New York = 100	52
Marriages per 1,000 pop.	...	Cars per 1,000 pop.	171
Divorces per 1,000 pop.	...	Telephone lines per 100 pop.	19.5
Religion, % of pop.		Mobile telephone subscribers	
Christian	88.9	per 100 pop.	113
Non-religious	7.9	Internet access, %	67.5
Other	3.1	Broadband subs per 100 pop.	13.8
Hindu	<0.1	Broadband speed, Mbps	1.5
Jewish	<0.1		
Muslim	<0.1		

BULGARIA

Area, sq km	111,002	Capital	Sofia
Arable as % of total land	29.9	Currency	Lev (BGL)

People

Population, m	7.1	Life expectancy: men	72.3 yrs
Pop. per sq km	64.0	women	79.0 yrs
Total change in population		Adult literacy	...
2010–20, %	-6.3	Fertility rate (per woman)	1.6
Pop. aged 0–19, %	19.0	Urban population, %	74.3
Pop. aged 65 and over, %	21.5		per 1,000 pop.
No. of men per 100 women	94.6	Crude birth rate	9.3
Human Development Index	81.3	Crude death rate	15.5

The economy

GDP	$58bn	GDP per head	$9,267
GDP	BGL101bn	GDP per head in purchasing	
Av. ann. growth in real		power parity (USA=100)	37.0
GDP 2012–17	2.7%	Economic freedom index	69.0

Origins of GDP		Components of GDP	
	% of total		% of total
Agriculture	4	Private consumption	61
Industry, of which:	25	Public consumption	16
manufacturing	15	Investment	20
Services	71	Exports	67
		Imports	-64

Structure of employment

	% of total		% of labour force
Agriculture	6.9	Unemployed 2018	5.3
Industry	29.8	Av. ann. rate 2010–18	9.6
Services	63.3		

Energy

	m TOE		
Total output	11.4	Net energy imports as %	
Total consumption	19.1	of energy use	37
Consumption per head			
kg oil equivalent	2,478		

Inflation and finance

			% change 2017–18
Consumer price			
inflation 2018	2.6%	Narrow money (M1)	11.0
Av. ann. inflation 2013–18	0.0%	Broad money	8.8
Deposit rate, Dec. 2018	0.03%		

Exchange rates

	end 2018		December 2018
			2010 = 100
BGL per $	1.71	Effective rates	
BGL per SDR	2.38	– nominal	110.2
BGL per €	1.97	– real	101.8

Trade

Principal exports		**Principal imports**	
	$bn fob		*$bn cif*
Raw materials	12.3	Raw materials	12.6
Capital goods	7.9	Capital goods	8.8
Consumer goods	7.7	Consumer goods	7.4
Mineral fuels & lubricants	2.6	Mineral fuels & lubricants	4.0
Total incl. others	**31.6**	Total incl. others	**34.2**

Main export destinations		**Main origins of imports**	
	% of total		*% of total*
Germany	12.8	Germany	12.3
Turkey	8.8	Russia	10.3
Italy	7.9	Italy	7.2
Romania	7.8	Romania	7.1
EU28	63.6	EU28	64.0

Balance of payments, reserves and debt, $bn

Visible exports fob	30.5	Change in reserves	3.2
Visible imports fob	-31.4	Level of reserves	
Trade balance	-0.9	end Dec.	28.4
Invisibles inflows	10.4	No. months of import cover	8.3
Invisibles outflows	-9.8	Official gold holdings, m oz	1.3
Net transfers	2.1	Foreign debt	40.4
Current account balance	1.8	– as % of GDP	69.5
– as % of GDP	3.2	– as % of total exports	94.2
Capital balance	-0.8	Debt service ratio	20.5
Overall balance	-0.1		

Health and education

Health spending, % of GDP	8.2	Education spending, % of GDP	...
Doctors per 1,000 pop.	4.0	Enrolment, %: primary	95
Hospital beds per 1,000 pop.	6.8	secondary	100
At least basic drinking water,		tertiary	71
% of pop.	99.3		

Society

No. of households, m	3.0	Cost of living, Dec. 2018	
Av. no. per household	2.4	New York = 100	58
Marriages per 1,000 pop.	4.0	Cars per 1,000 pop.	445
Divorces per 1,000 pop.	1.5	Telephone lines per 100 pop.	18.2
Religion, % of pop.		Mobile telephone subscribers	
Christian	82.1	per 100 pop.	120.4
Muslim	13.7	Internet access, %	63.4
Non-religious	4.2	Broadband subs per 100 pop.	25.4
Hindu	<0.1	Broadband speed, Mbps	17.5
Jewish	<0.1		
Other	<0.1		

CAMEROON

Area, sq km	475,650	Capital	Yaoundé
Arable as % of total land	13.1	Currency	CFA franc (CFAfr)

People

Population, m	24.1	Life expectancy: men	60.0 yrs
Pop. per sq km	50.7	women	62.5 yrs
Total change in population		Adult literacy	74.9
2010–20, %	30.0	Fertility rate (per woman)	4.6
Pop. aged 0–19, %	52.6	Urban population, %	55.2
Pop. aged 65 and over, %	3.2		per 1,000 pop.
No. of men per 100 women	100.3	Crude birth rate	35.5
Human Development Index	55.6	Crude death rate	8.5

The economy

GDP	$35bn	GDP per head	$1,548
GDP	CFEfr20,328bn	GDP per head in purchasing	
Av. ann. growth in real		power parity (USA=100)	6.1
GDP 2012–17	5.0%	Economic freedom index	52.4

Origins of GDP

	% of total
Agriculture	14
Industry, of which:	25
manufacturing	15
Services	61

Components of GDP

	% of total
Private consumption	70
Public consumption	11
Investment	23
Exports	19
Imports	-23

Structure of employment

	% of total		% of labour force
Agriculture	46.3	Unemployed 2018	3.4
Industry	14.1	Av. ann. rate 2010–18	3.7
Services	39.6		

Energy

	m TOE		
Total output	6.8	Net energy imports as %	
Total consumption	3.8	of energy use	-28
Consumption per head			
kg oil equivalent	342		

Inflation and finance

		% change 2017–18	
Consumer price			
inflation 2018	0.9%	Narrow money (M1)	15.1
Av. ann. inflation 2013–18	1.4%	Broad money	13.9
Deposit rate, Oct. 2018	2.45%		

Exchange rates

	end 2018		December 2018
CFAfr per $	572.89	Effective rates	2010 = 100
CFAfr per SDR	796.77	– nominal	103.0
CFAfr per €	658.49	– real	98.0

Trade

Principal exports		Principal imports	
	$bn fob		*$bn cif*
Fuels	1.4	Machinery & transport equip.	1.2
Timber	0.5	Food, drink & tobacco	1.2
Cocoa beans & products	0.4	Fuels	0.9
Cotton	0.2	Chemicals	0.6
Total incl. others	**3.2**	Total incl. others	**5.2**

Main export destinations		Main origins of imports	
	% of total		*% of total*
Italy	13.9	China	17.3
China	12.1	France	9.8
France	10.5	Thailand	5.8
Netherlands	9.6	Togo	5.1

Balance of payments, reserves and debt, $bn

Visible exports fob	4.6	Change in reserves	1.0
Visible imports fob	-4.8	Level of reserves	
Trade balance	-0.2	end Dec.	3.2
Invisibles inflows	2.1	No. months of import cover	4.7
Invisibles outflows	-3.3	Official gold holdings, m oz	0.0
Net transfers	0.4	Foreign debt	9.6
Current account balance	-0.9	– as % of GDP	27.7
– as % of GDP	-2.7	– as % of total exports	136.5
Capital balance	1.6	Debt service ratio	10.6
Overall balance	0.4		

Health and education

Health spending, % of GDP	4.7	Education spending, % of GDP	3.1
Doctors per 1,000 pop.	...	Enrolment, %: primary	113
Hospital beds per 1,000 pop.	...	secondary	62
At least basic drinking water,		tertiary	19
% of pop.	65.3		

Society

No. of households, m	5.0	Cost of living, Dec. 2018	
Av. no. per household	4.8	New York = 100	...
Marriages per 1,000 pop.	...	Cars per 1,000 pop.	11
Divorces per 1,000 pop.	...	Telephone lines per 100 pop.	3.7
Religion, % of pop.		Mobile telephone subscribers	
Christian	70.3	per 100 pop.	83.7
Muslim	18.3	Internet access, %	23.2
Other	6.0	Broadband subs per 100 pop.	0.2
Non-religious	5.3	Broadband speed, Mbps	1.0
Hindu	<0.1		
Jewish	<0.1		

CANADA

Area, sq km[a]	9,984,670	Capital	Ottawa
Arable as % of total land	4.7	Currency	Canadian dollar (C$)

People

Population, m	36.6	Life expectancy: men	81.8 yrs
Pop. per sq km	3.7	women	85.1 yrs
Total change in population		Adult literacy	...
2010–20, %	10.1	Fertility rate (per woman)	1.6
Pop. aged 0–19, %	21.4	Urban population, %	81.3
Pop. aged 65 and over, %	18.3		per 1,000 pop.
No. of men per 100 women	98.6	Crude birth rate	10.5
Human Development Index	92.6	Crude death rate	7.8

The economy

GDP	$1,647bn	GDP per head	$46,260
GDP	C$2,142bn	GDP per head in purchasing	
Av. ann. growth in real		power parity (USA=100)	79.3
GDP 2012–17	2.2%	Economic freedom index	77.7

Origins of GDP		**Components of GDP**	
	% of total		% of total
Agriculture	2	Private consumption	58
Industry, of which:	25	Public consumption	21
manufacturing	10	Investment	24
Services	73	Exports	31
		Imports	-33

Structure of employment

	% of total		% of labour force
Agriculture	1.5	Unemployed 2018	5.9
Industry	19.5	Av. ann. rate 2010–18	7.0
Services	79.0		

Energy

	m TOE		
Total output	534.1	Net energy imports as %	
Total consumption	370.1	of energy use	-73
Consumption per head			
kg oil equivalent	7,604		

Inflation and finance

		% change 2017–18	
Consumer price			
inflation 2018	2.2%	Narrow money (M1)	4.7
Av. ann. inflation 2013–18	1.7%	Broad money	4.5
Treasury bill rate, Apr. 2017	0.55%		

Exchange rates

	end 2018		December 2018
C$ per $	1.36	Effective rates	2010 = 100
C$ per SDR	1.90	– nominal	82.7
C$ per €	1.56	– real	80.9

Trade

Principal exports

	$bn fob
Energy products	74.6
Motor vehicles & parts	71.8
Consumer goods	48.5
Metal & mineral products	47.5
Total incl. others	**424.2**

Principal imports

	$bn cif
Consumer goods	89.1
Motor vehicles & parts	87.5
Electronic & electrical equip.	52.1
Industrial machinery & equip.	48.3
Total incl. others	**442.6**

Main export destinations

	% of total
United States	76.4
China	4.3
United Kingdom	3.2
Japan	2.2
EU28	7.3

Main origins of imports

	% of total
United States	51.5
China	12.6
Mexico	6.3
Germany	3.2
EU28	11.7

Balance of payments, reserves and aid, $bn

Visible exports fob	423.4	Overall balance	0.9
Visible imports fob	-442.6	Change in reserves	4.0
Trade balance	-19.2	Level of reserves	
Invisibles inflows	178.9	end Dec.	86.7
Invisibles outflows	-203.9	No. months of import cover	1.6
Net transfers	-2.2	Official gold holdings, m oz	0.0
Current account balance	-46.4	Aid given	4.3
– as % of GDP	-2.8	– as % of GNI	0.3
Capital balance	41.4		

Health and education

Health spending, % of GDP	10.5	Education spending, % of GDP	...
Doctors per 1,000 pop.	2.5	Enrolment, %: primary	101
Hospital beds per 1,000 pop.	2.6	secondary	113
At least basic drinking water,		tertiary	67
% of pop.	98.9		

Society

No. of households, m	14.1	Cost of living, Dec. 2018	
Av. no. per household	2.6	New York = 100	77
Marriages per 1,000 pop.	...	Cars per 1,000 pop.	608
Divorces per 1,000 pop.	...	Telephone lines per 100 pop.	39.5
Religion, % of pop.		Mobile telephone subscribers	
Christian	69.0	per 100 pop.	86.5
Non-religious	23.7	Internet access, %	92.7
Other	2.8	Broadband subs per 100 pop.	38.0
Muslim	2.1	Broadband speed, Mbps	18.4
Hindu	1.4		
Jewish	1.0		

a Including freshwater.

CHILE

Area, sq km	756,102	Capital	Santiago
Arable as % of total land	1.8	Currency	Chilean peso (Ps)

People

Population, m	18.1	Life expectancy: men	78.5 yrs
Pop. per sq km	23.9	women	83.0 yrs
Total change in population		Adult literacy	96.9
2010–20, %	8.7	Fertility rate (per woman)	1.8
Pop. aged 0–19, %	26.5	Urban population, %	87.4
Pop. aged 65 and over, %	12.2		per 1,000 pop.
No. of men per 100 women	98.3	Crude birth rate	13.1
Human Development Index	84.3	Crude death rate	6.5

The economy

GDP	$277bn	GDP per head	$16,079
GDP	180trn peso	GDP per head in purchasing	
Av. ann. growth in real		power parity (USA=100)	41.5
GDP 2012–17	2.2%	Economic freedom index	75.4

Origins of GDP

	% of total
Agriculture	4
Industry, of which:	30
manufacturing	10
Services	66

Components of GDP

	% of total
Private consumption	62
Public consumption	14
Investment	22
Exports	29
Imports	-27

Structure of employment

	% of total		% of labour force
Agriculture	9.2	Unemployed 2018	7.2
Industry	22.7	Av. ann. rate 2010–18	7.0
Services	68.1		

Energy

	m TOE		
Total output	10.4	Net energy imports as %	
Total consumption	37.3	of energy use	65
Consumption per head			
kg oil equivalent	2,029		

Inflation and finance

			% change 2017–18
Consumer price			
inflation 2018	2.3%	Narrow money (M1)	1.7
Av. ann. inflation 2013–18	3.5%	Broad money	4.2
Deposit rate, Dec. 2018	2.92%		

Exchange rates

	end 2018		December 2018
Ps per $	695.69	Effective rates	2010 = 100
Ps per SDR	967.56	– nominal	94.2
Ps per €	799.64	– real	94.8

Trade

Principal exports

	$bn fob
Copper	28.3
Fresh fruit	5.0
Salmon & trout	4.2
Cellulose & paper products	3.2
Total incl. others	**68.9**

Principal imports

	$bn cif
Intermediate goods	31.0
Consumer goods	20.6
Capital goods	13.6
Total incl. others	**66.1**

Main export destinations

	% of total
United States	14.5
China	13.6
Japan	9.3
South Korea	6.2

Main origins of imports

	% of total
China	23.4
United States	17.8
Brazil	8.5
Argentina	4.4

Balance of payments, reserves and debt, $bn

Visible exports fob	68.9	Change in reserves	-1.5
Visible imports fob	-61.5	Level of reserves	
Trade balance	7.4	end Dec.	39.0
Invisibles inflows	18.7	No. months of import cover	4.9
Invisibles outflows	-33.5	Official gold holdings, m oz	0.0
Net transfers	1.4	Foreign debt	183.4
Current account balance	-6.0	– as % of GDP	66.2
– as % of GDP	-2.2	– as % of total exports	211.9
Capital balance	2.0	Debt service ratio	38.5
Overall balance	-2.8		

Health and education

Health spending, % of GDP	8.5	Education spending, % of GDP	5.4
Doctors per 1,000 pop.	...	Enrolment, %: primary	100
Hospital beds per 1,000 pop.	2.2	secondary	100
At least basic drinking water,		tertiary	90
% of pop.	100		

Society

No. of households, m	6.4	Cost of living, Dec. 2018	
Av. no. per household	2.8	New York = 100	66
Marriages per 1,000 pop.	3.4	Cars per 1,000 pop.	175
Divorces per 1,000 pop.	...	Telephone lines per 100 pop.	17.7
Religion, % of pop.		Mobile telephone subscribers	
Christian	89.4	per 100 pop.	127.5
Non-religious	8.6	Internet access, %	82.3
Other	1.9	Broadband subs per 100 pop.	16.9
Jewish	0.1	Broadband speed, Mbps	1.7
Hindu	<0.1		
Muslim	<0.1		

CHINA

Area, sq km	9,596,961	Capital	Beijing
Arable as % of total land	12.0	Currency	Yuan

People

Population, m	1,409.5	Life expectancy: men	75.8 yrs
Pop. per sq km	146.9	women	78.9 yrs
Total change in population		Adult literacy	96.4
2010–20, %	4.8	Fertility rate (per woman)	1.6
Pop. aged 0–19, %	23.0	Urban population, %	56.7
Pop. aged 65 and over, %	12.2		per 1,000 pop.
No. of men per 100 women	106.3	Crude birth rate	11.6
Human Development Index	75.2	Crude death rate	8.1

The economy

GDP	$12,238bn	GDP per head	$9,608
GDP	Yuan 81,526bn	GDP per head in purchasing	
Av. ann. growth in real		power parity (USA=100)	28.9
GDP 2012–17	7.1%	Economic freedom index	58.4

Origins of GDP		**Components of GDP**	
	% of total		% of total
Agriculture	8	Private consumption	38
Industry, of which:	40	Public consumption	14
manufacturing	29	Investment	44
Services	52	Exports	20
		Imports	-18

Structure of employment

	% of total		% of labour force
Agriculture	26.8	Unemployed 2018	4.4
Industry	28.6	Av. ann. rate 2010–18	4.5
Services	44.6		

Energy

	m TOE		
Total output	2,701.4	Net energy imports as %	
Total consumption	3,510.4	of energy use	15
Consumption per head			
kg oil equivalent	2,237		

Inflation and finance

			% change 2017–18
Consumer price			
inflation 2018	2.1%	Narrow money (M1)	1.5
Av. ann. inflation 2013–18	1.8%	Broad money	8.1
Deposit rate, Dec. 2018	1.50%		

Exchange rates

	end 2018		December 2018
Yuan per $	6.85	Effective rates	2010 = 100
Yuan per SDR	9.53	– nominal	116.8
Yuan per €	7.87	– real	120.2

Trade

Principal exports		Principal imports	
	$bn fob		$bn cif
Telecoms equipment	303.2	Electrical machinery	378.3
Electrical goods	289.4	Petroleum products	190.0
Office machinery	195.5	Metal ores & scrap	140.7
Clothing & apparel	158.4	Professional instruments	76.6
Total incl. others	**2,263.3**	Total incl. others	**1,843.8**

Main export destinations		Main origins of imports	
	% of total		% of total
United States	19.2	South Korea	9.6
Hong Kong	12.5	Japan	9.0
Japan	6.1	Taiwan	8.4
South Korea	4.6	United States	8.4
EU28	16.4	EU28	13.4

Balance of payments, reserves and debt, $bn

Visible exports fob	2,216.2	Change in reserves	137.7
Visible imports fob	-1,740.3	Level of reserves	
Trade balance	475.9	end Dec.	3,235.4
Invisibles inflows	500.6	No. months of import cover	15.5
Invisibles outflows	-769.6	Official gold holdings, m oz	59.2
Net transfers	-11.9	Foreign debt	1,710.2
Current account balance	195.1	– as % of GDP	14.2
– as % of GDP	1.6	– as % of total exports	63.1
Capital balance	109.4	Debt service ratio	7.5
Overall balance	91.5		

Health and education

Health spending, % of GDP	5.0	Education spending, % of GDP	...
Doctors per 1,000 pop.	1.8	Enrolment, %: primary	102
Hospital beds per 1,000 pop.	3.9	secondary	...
At least basic drinking water,		tertiary	51
% of pop.	95.8		

Society

No. of households, m	466.8	Cost of living, Dec. 2018	
Av. no. per household	3.0	New York = 100	76
Marriages per 1,000 pop.	...	Cars per 1,000 pop.	97
Divorces per 1,000 pop.	...	Telephone lines per 100 pop.	13.8
Religion, % of pop.		Mobile telephone subscribers	
Non-religious	52.2	per 100 pop.	104.3
Other	22.7	Internet access, %	54.3
Buddhist	18.2	Broadband subs per 100 pop.	28.0
Christian	5.1	Broadband speed, Mbps	1.6
Muslim	1.8		
Jewish	<0.1		

Note: Data exclude Special Administrative Regions, ie, Hong Kong and Macau.

COLOMBIA

Area, sq km	1,141,748	Capital	Bogotá
Arable as % of total land	1.9	Currency	Colombian peso (peso)

People

Population, m	49.1	Life expectancy: men	72.1 yrs
Pop. per sq km	43.0	women	79.1 yrs
Total change in population		Adult literacy	94.7
2010–20, %	9.4	Fertility rate (per woman)	1.8
Pop. aged 0–19, %	30.3	Urban population, %	80.1
Pop. aged 65 and over, %	8.7		per 1,000 pop.
No. of men per 100 women	96.7	Crude birth rate	14.8
Human Development Index	74.7	Crude death rate	6.6

The economy

GDP	$314bn	GDP per head	$6,684
GDP	920trn peso	GDP per head in purchasing	
Av. ann. growth in real		power parity (USA=100)	23.9
GDP 2012–17	3.2%	Economic freedom index	67.3

Origins of GDP

	% of total
Agriculture	6
Industry, of which:	27
manufacturing	12
Services	67

Components of GDP

	% of total
Private consumption	68
Public consumption	15
Investment	22
Exports	15
Imports	-20

Structure of employment

	% of total		% of labour force
Agriculture	16.4	Unemployed 2018	9.1
Industry	19.4	Av. ann. rate 2010–18	9.3
Services	64.3		

Energy

	m TOE		
Total output	130.6	Net energy imports as %	
Total consumption	44.6	of energy use	-274
Consumption per head			
kg oil equivalent	712		

Inflation and finance

			% change 2017–18
Consumer price			
inflation 2018	3.2%	Narrow money (M1)	10.4
Av. ann. inflation 2013–18	4.6%	Broad money	5.1
Deposit rate, Dec. 2018	4.54%		

Exchange rates

	end 2018		December 2018
Peso per $	3,275.01	Effective rates	2010 = 100
Peso per SDR	4,554.86	– nominal	74.6
Peso per €	3,764.38	– real	73.8

Trade

Principal exports

	$bn fob
Petroleum & products	13.2
Coal	7.4
Coffee	2.5
Animal & vegatable products	1.5
Total incl. others	**37.9**

Principal imports

	$bn cif
Intermediate goods & raw materials	20.9
Capital goods	14.2
Consumer goods	11.0
Total	**46.1**

Main export destinations

	% of total
United States	28.0
Panama	8.2
China	4.5
Mexico	4.1

Main origins of imports

	% of total
United States	26.3
China	19.0
Mexico	7.5
Brazil	5.0

Balance of payments, reserves and debt, $bn

Visible exports fob	39.7	Change in reserves	1.0
Visible imports fob	-44.2	Level of reserves	
Trade balance	-4.6	end Dec.	47.1
Invisibles Inflows	13.9	No. months of import cover	8.0
Invisibles outflows	-26.3	Official gold holdings, m oz	0.3
Net transfers	6.6	Foreign debt	124.4
Current account balance	-10.3	– as % of GDP	39.5
– as % of GDP	-3.3	– as % of total exports	210.6
Capital balance	10.1	Debt service ratio	37.7
Overall balance	0.5		

Health and education

Health spending, % of GDP	5.9	Education spending, % of GDP	4.4
Doctors per 1,000 pop.	1.8	Enrolment, %: primary	113
Hospital beds per 1,000 pop.	1.5	secondary	99
At least basic drinking water, % of pop.	96.5	tertiary	60

Society

No. of households, m	14.4	Cost of living, Dec. 2018	
Av. no. per household	3.4	New York = 100	59
Marriages per 1,000 pop.	...	Cars per 1,000 pop.	64
Divorces per 1,000 pop.	...	Telephone lines per 100 pop.	14.2
Religion, % of pop.		Mobile telephone subscribers	
Christian	92.5	per 100 pop.	126.8
Non-religious	6.6	Internet access, %	62.3
Other	0.8	Broadband subs per 100 pop.	12.9
Hindu	<0.1	Broadband speed, Mbps	2.1
Jewish	<0.1		
Muslim	<0.1		

CZECH REPUBLIC

Area, sq km	78,867	Capital	Prague
Arable as % of total land	41.0	Currency	Koruna (Kc)

People

Population, m	10.6	Life expectancy: men	77.0 yrs
Pop. per sq km	134.4	women	82.4 yrs
Total change in population		Adult literacy	...
2010–20, %	0.9	Fertility rate (per woman)	1.6
Pop. aged 0–19, %	20.2	Urban population, %	73.6
Pop. aged 65 and over, %	20.2		per 1,000 pop.
No. of men per 100 women	96.8	Crude birth rate	10.1
Human Development Index	88.8	Crude death rate	11.0

The economy

GDP	$216bn	GDP per head	$22,820
GDP	Kc5,047bn	GDP per head in purchasing	
Av. ann. growth in real		power parity (USA=100)	59.7
GDP 2012–17	2.9%	Economic freedom index	73.7

Origins of GDP		**Components of GDP**	
	% of total		% of total
Agriculture	2	Private consumption	47
Industry, of which:	33	Public consumption	19
manufacturing	24	Investment	26
Services	65	Exports	80
		Imports	-72

Structure of employment

	% of total		% of labour force
Agriculture	2.8	Unemployed 2018	2.4
Industry	37.9	Av. ann. rate 2010–18	5.4
Services	59.4		

Energy

	m TOE		
Total output	26.1	Net energy imports as %	
Total consumption	41.8	of energy use	32
Consumption per head			
kg oil equivalent	3,860		

Inflation and finance

			% change 2017–18
Consumer price			
inflation 2018	2.2%	Narrow money (M1)	1.1
Av. ann. inflation 2013–18	1.2%	Broad money	6.3
Deposit rate, Dec. 2018	0.30%		

Exchange rates

	end 2018		December 2018
Kc per $	22.47	Effective rates	2010 = 100
Kc per SDR	31.25	– nominal	100.8
Kc per €	25.83	– real	98.4

Trade

Principal exports

	$bn fob
Machinery & transport equip.	103.9
Semi-manufactures	27.2
Miscellaneous manufactured goods	24.3
Chemicals	11.1
Total incl. others	**182.2**

Principal imports

	$bn cif
Machinery & transport equip.	75.5
Semi-manufactures	27.5
Miscellaneous manufactured goods	20.5
Chemicals	17.9
Total incl. others	**163.4**

Main export destinations

	% of total
Germany	32.6
Slovakia	7.6
Poland	6.0
France	5.0
EU28	83.9

Main origins of imports

	% of total
Germany	29.8
Poland	9.1
China	7.3
Slovakia	5.8
EU28	78.0

Balance of payments, reserves and debt, $bn

Visible exports fob	145.8	Change in reserves	62.2
Visible imports fob	-135.0	Level of reserves	
Trade balance	10.9	end Dec.	148.0
Invisibles inflows	39.0	No. months of import cover	9.9
Invisibles outflows	-44.7	Official gold holdings, m oz	0.3
Net transfers	-2.0	Foreign debt	205.1
Current account balance	3.1	– as % of GDP	94.9
– as % of GDP	1.5	– as % of total exports	111.2
Capital balance	46.4	Debt service ratio	9.5
Overall balance	49.4		

Health and education

Health spending, % of GDP	7.1	Education spending, % of GDP	5.8
Doctors per 1,000 pop.	3.7	Enrolment, %: primary	100
Hospital beds per 1,000 pop.	6.5	secondary	105
At least basic drinking water, % of pop.	99.9	tertiary	64

Society

No. of households, m	4.4	Cost of living, Dec. 2018	
Av. no. per household	2.4	New York = 100	63
Marriages per 1,000 pop.	5.0	Cars per 1,000 pop.	487
Divorces per 1,000 pop.	2.4	Telephone lines per 100 pop.	15.5
Religion, % of pop.		Mobile telephone subscribers	
Non-religious	76.4	per 100 pop.	119.0
Christian	23.3	Internet access, %	78.7
Other	0.2	Broadband subs per 100 pop.	29.6
Hindu	<0.1	Broadband speed, Mbps	17.3
Jewish	<0.1		
Muslim	<0.1		

DENMARK

Area, sq km	42,921	Capital	Copenhagen
Arable as % of total land	58.9	Currency	Danish krone (DKr)

People

Population, m	5.7	Life expectancy: men	79.9 yrs
Pop. per sq km	132.8	women	83.4 yrs
Total change in population		Adult literacy	...
2010–20, %	4.4	Fertility rate (per woman)	1.8
Pop. aged 0–19, %	22.1	Urban population, %	87.6
Pop. aged 65 and over, %	20.2		per 1,000 pop.
No. of men per 100 women	98.9	Crude birth rate	10.7
Human Development Index	92.9	Crude death rate	9.8

The economy

GDP	$330bn	GDP per head	$60,692
GDP	DKr2,178bn	GDP per head in purchasing	
Av. ann. growth in real		power parity (USA=100)	83.3
GDP 2012–17	1.7%	Economic freedom index	76.7

Origins of GDP

Components of GDP

	% of total		% of total
Agriculture	1	Private consumption	47
Industry, of which:	20	Public consumption	25
manufacturing	13	Investment	22
Services	79	Exports	55
		Imports	-47

Structure of employment

	% of total		% of labour force
Agriculture	2.2	Unemployed 2018	5.0
Industry	18.6	Av. ann. rate 2010–18	6.6
Services	79.2		

Energy

	m TOE		
Total output	16.5	Net energy imports as %	
Total consumption	18.6	of energy use	2
Consumption per head			
kg oil equivalent	2,817		

Inflation and finance

		% change 2017–18
Consumer price		
inflation 2018	0.7%	Narrow money (M1)	-10.4
Av. ann. inflation 2013–18	0.5%	Broad money	1.5
Money market rate, Dec. 2018	-0.42%		

Exchange rates

	end 2018		December 2018
DKr per $	6.52	Effective rates	2010 = 100
DKr per SDR	9.07	– nominal	102.4
DKr per €	7.49	– real	96.5

Trade

Principal exports

	$bn fob
Machinery & transport equip.	27.1
Chemicals & related products	20.9
Food, drink & tobacco	19.3
Mineral fuels & lubricants	5.1
Total incl. others	**101.7**

Principal imports

	$bn cif
Machinery & transport equip.	31.2
Food, drink & tobacco	12.6
Chemicals & related products	11.6
Mineral fuels & lubricants	5.4
Total incl. others	**92.4**

Main export destinations

	% of total
Germany	15.6
Sweden	11.8
United Kingdom	8.2
United States	7.6
EU28	61.8

Main origins of imports

	% of total
Germany	21.5
Sweden	11.9
Netherlands	7.9
China	7.2
EU28	69.8

Balance of payments, reserves and aid, $bn

Visible exports fob	113.3	Overall balance	2.6
Visible imports fob	-94.7	Change in reserves	11.0
Trade balance	18.6	Level of reserves	
Invisibles inflows	94.7	end Dec.	75.2
Invisibles outflows	-82.6	No. months of import cover	5.1
Net transfers	-4.5	Official gold holdings, m oz	2.1
Current account balance	26.3	Aid given	2.4
– as % of GDP	8.0	– as % of GNI	0.7
Capital balance	-21.0		

Health and education

Health spending, % of GDP	10.4	Education spending, % of GDP	7.6
Doctors per 1,000 pop.	3.7	Enrolment, %: primary	102
Hospital beds per 1,000 pop.	2.5	secondary	129
At least basic drinking water,		tertiary	81
% of pop.	100		

Society

No. of households, m	2.7	Cost of living, Dec. 2018	
Av. no. per household	2.1	New York = 100	100
Marriages per 1,000 pop.	5.5	Cars per 1,000 pop.	420
Divorces per 1,000 pop.	2.6	Telephone lines per 100 pop.	25.1
Religion, % of pop.		Mobile telephone subscribers	
Christian	83.5	per 100 pop.	121.7
Non-religious	11.8	Internet access, %	97.1
Muslim	4.1	Broadband subs per 100 pop.	43.7
Hindu	0.4	Broadband speed, Mbps	33.5
Other	0.2		
Jewish	<0.1		

EGYPT

Area, sq km	1,002,000	Capital	Cairo
Arable as % of total land	2.9	Currency	Egyptian pound (£E)

People

Population, m	97.6	Life expectancy: men	70.3 yrs
Pop. per sq km	97.4	women	75.0 yrs
Total change in population		Adult literacy	80.8
2010–20, %	22.4	Fertility rate (per woman)	3.2
Pop. aged 0–19, %	41.8	Urban population, %	42.7
Pop. aged 65 and over, %	5.3		per 1,000 pop.
No. of men per 100 women	102.3	Crude birth rate	25.0
Human Development Index	69.6	Crude death rate	5.7

The economy

GDP	$235bn	GDP per head	$2,573
GDP	£E3,470bn	GDP per head in purchasing	
Av. ann. growth in real		power parity (USA=100)	21.4
GDP 2012–17	3.6%	Economic freedom index	52.5

Origins of GDP		**Components of GDP**	
	% of total		% of total
Agriculture	11	Private consumption	88
Industry, of which:	34	Public consumption	10
manufacturing	16	Investment	15
Services	55	Exports	16
		Imports	-29

Structure of employment

	% of total		% of labour force
Agriculture	24.9	Unemployed 2018	11.4
Industry	26.6	Av. ann. rate 2010–18	12.0
Services	48.6		

Energy

	m TOE		
Total output	80.3	Net energy imports as %	
Total consumption	96.2	of energy use	-7
Consumption per head			
kg oil equivalent	815		

Inflation and finance

			% change 2017–18
Consumer price			
inflation 2018	20.9%	Narrow money (M1)	12.6
Av. ann. inflation 2013–18	15.0%	Broad money	13.3
Deposit rate, Dec. 2018	12.20%		

Exchange rates

	end 2018		December 2018
£E per $	17.87	Effective rates	2010 = 100
£E per SDR	24.85	– nominal	...
£E per €	20.54	– real	...

Trade

Principal exports

	$bn fob
Petroleum & products	6.6
Food	3.0
Chemicals	2.2
Finished goods incl. textiles	2.0
Total incl. others	**23.3**

Principal imports

	$bn cif
Petroleum & products	12.0
Machinery & equip.	8.9
Chemicals	5.7
Vehicles	2.9
Total incl. others	**59.9**

Main export destinations

	% of total
United Arab Emirates	11.2
Italy	10.2
United States	8.4
United Kingdom	6.0

Main origins of imports

	% of total
China	7.7
Saudi Arabia	5.5
United Arab Emirates	5.4
Russia	4.9

Balance of payments, reserves and debt, $bn

Visible exports fob	23.3	Change in reserves	12.7
Visible imports fob	-52.4	Level of reserves	
Trade balance	-29.1	end Dec.	36.4
Invisibles inflows	20.3	No. months of import cover	5.7
Invisibles outflows	-23.9	Official gold holdings, m oz	2.5
Net transfers	24.8	Foreign debt	82.9
Current account balance	-7.9	– as % of GDP	37.4
– as % of GDP	-3.4	– as % of total exports	123.2
Capital balance	23.7	Debt service ratio	9.8
Overall balance	8.8		

Health and education

Health spending, % of GDP	4.6	Education spending, % of GDP	...
Doctors per 1,000 pop.	0.8	Enrolment, %: primary	105
Hospital beds per 1,000 pop.	1.6	secondary	87
At least basic drinking water,		tertiary	34
% of pop.	98.4		

Society

No. of households, m	23.5	Cost of living, Dec. 2018	
Av. no. per household	4.2	New York = 100	49
Marriages per 1,000 pop.	9.6	Cars per 1,000 pop.	46
Divorces per 1,000 pop.	2.1	Telephone lines per 100 pop.	6.8
Religion, % of pop.		Mobile telephone subscribers	
Muslim	94.9	per 100 pop.	105.5
Christian	5.1	Internet access, %	45.0
Hindu	<0.1	Broadband subs per 100 pop.	5.4
Jewish	<0.1	Broadband speed, Mbps	1.2
Non-religious	<0.1		
Other	<0.1		

FINLAND

Area, sq km	336,855	Capital	Helsinki
Arable as % of total land	7.4	Currency	Euro (€)

People

Population, m	5.5	Life expectancy: men	79.9 yrs
Pop. per sq km	16.3	women	85.0 yrs
Total change in population		Adult literacy	...
2010–20, %	4.0	Fertility rate (per woman)	1.8
Pop. aged 0–19, %	21.8	Urban population, %	85.3
Pop. aged 65 and over, %	22.3		per 1,000 pop.
No. of men per 100 women	97.5	Crude birth rate	10.8
Human Development Index	92.0	Crude death rate	10.0

The economy

GDP	$252bn	GDP per head	$49,845
GDP	€224bn	GDP per head in purchasing	
Av. ann. growth in real		power parity (USA=100)	74.2
GDP 2012–17	0.7%	Economic freedom index	74.9

Origins of GDP

Components of GDP

	% of total		% of total
Agriculture	2	Private consumption	54
Industry, of which:	24	Public consumption	23
manufacturing	15	Investment	23
Services	74	Exports	39
		Imports	-38

Structure of employment

	% of total		% of labour force
Agriculture	3.7	Unemployed 2018	7.8
Industry	22.0	Av. ann. rate 2010–18	8.4
Services	74.3		

Energy

	m TOE		
Total output	13.0	Net energy imports as %	
Total consumption	31.0	of energy use	45
Consumption per head			
kg oil equivalent	5,925		

Inflation and finance

			% change 2017–18
Consumer price			
inflation 2018	1.2%	Narrow money (M1)	0.7
Av. ann. inflation 2013–18	0.7%	Broad money	4.2
Deposit rate, Dec. 2018	0.31%		

Exchange rates

	end 2018		December 2018
€ per $	0.87	Effective rates	2010 = 100
€ per SDR	1.21	– nominal	105.1
		– real	98.4

Trade

Principal exports

	$bn fob
Machinery & transport equip.	22.2
Raw materials	6.6
Chemicals & related products	6.4
Mineral fuels & lubricants	5.7
Total incl. others	**67.5**

Principal imports

	$bn cif
Machinery & transport equip.	25.1
Mineral fuels & lubricants	9.8
Chemicals & related products	8.1
Food, drink & tobacco	4.8
Total incl. others	**65.5**

Main export destinations

	% of total
Germany	14.3
Sweden	10.2
United States	7.0
Netherlands	6.9
EU28	59.5

Main origins of imports

	% of total
Germany	19.1
Sweden	17.0
Russia	14.1
Netherlands	9.4
EU28	71.7

Balance of payments, reserves and aid, $bn

Visible exports fob	67.5	Overall balance	-0.4
Visible imports fob	-65.5	Change in reserves	0.0
Trade balance	1.9	Level of reserves	
Invisibles inflows	48.6	end Dec.	10.5
Invisibles outflows	-48.9	No. months of import cover	1.1
Net transfers	-2.3	Official gold holdings, m oz	1.6
Current account balance	-0.7	Aid given	1.1
– as % of GDP	-0.3	– as % of GNI	0.4
Capital balance	6.1		

Health and education

Health spending, % of GDP	9.5	Education spending, % of GDP	7.1
Doctors per 1,000 pop.	3.2	Enrolment, %: primary	100
Hospital beds per 1,000 pop.	4.4	secondary	152
At least basic drinking water,		tertiary	87
% of pop.	100		

Society

No. of households, m	2.7	Cost of living, Dec. 2018	
Av. no. per household	2.0	New York = 100	89
Marriages per 1,000 pop.	4.5	Cars per 1,000 pop.	475
Divorces per 1,000 pop.	2.5	Telephone lines per 100 pop.	6.9
Religion, % of pop.		Mobile telephone subscribers	
Christian	81.6	per 100 pop.	132.3
Non-religious	17.6	Internet access, %	87.5
Muslim	0.8	Broadband subs per 100 pop.	31.0
Hindu	<0.1	Broadband speed, Mbps	20.9
Jewish	<0.1		
Other	<0.1		

FRANCE

Area, sq km	551,500	Capital	Paris
Arable as % of total land	33.5	Currency	Euro (€)

People

Population, m	65.0	Life expectancy: men	80.7 yrs
Pop. per sq km	117.9	women	86.4 yrs
Total change in population		Adult literacy	...
2010–20, %	4.3	Fertility rate (per woman)	2.0
Pop. aged 0–19, %	23.8	Urban population, %	79.9
Pop. aged 65 and over, %	20.7		per 1,000 pop.
No. of men per 100 women	96.9	Crude birth rate	11.7
Human Development Index	90.1	Crude death rate	9.2

The economy

GDP	$2,583bn	GDP per head	$42,878
GDP	€2,292bn	GDP per head in purchasing	
Av. ann. growth in real		power parity (USA=100)	73.1
GDP 2012–17	1.1%	Economic freedom index	63.8

Origins of GDP		**Components of GDP**	
	% of total		% of total
Agriculture	2	Private consumption	54
Industry, of which:	17	Public consumption	24
manufacturing	10	Investment	23
Services	81	Exports	31
		Imports	-32

Structure of employment

	% of total		% of labour force
Agriculture	2.6	Unemployed 2018	9.2
Industry	20.3	Av. ann. rate 2010–18	9.6
Services	77.1		

Energy

	m TOE		
Total output	128.1	Net energy imports as %	
Total consumption	256.0	of energy use	44
Consumption per head			
kg oil equivalent	3,690		

Inflation and finance

			% change 2017–18
Consumer price			
inflation 2018	2.1%	Narrow money (M1)	0.7
Av. ann. inflation 2013–18	0.9%	Broad money	4.2
Deposit rate, Dec. 2018	0.77%		

Exchange rates

	end 2018		December 2018
€ per $	0.87	Effective rates	2010 = 100
€ per SDR	1.21	– nominal	101.9
		– real	94.9

Trade

Principal exports

	$bn fob
Machinery & transport equip.	208.8
Chemicals & related products	100.8
Food, drink and tobacco	63.7
Mineral fuels & lubricants	16.0
Total incl. others	**536.2**

Principal imports

	$bn cif
Machinery & transport equip.	222.9
Chemicals & related products	84.5
Mineral fuels & lubricants	60.1
Food, drink and tobacco	56.8
Total incl. others	**601.0**

Main export destinations

	% of total
Germany	14.6
Spain	7.7
Italy	7.5
United States	7.2
EU28	58.8

Main origins of imports

	% of total
Germany	19.3
Belgium	10.6
Netherlands	8.6
Italy	8.2
EU28	69.6

Balance of payments, reserves and aid, $bn

Visible exports fob	554.3	Overall balance	-3.4
Visible imports fob	-608.4	Change in reserves	10.0
Trade balance	-54.1	Level of reserves	
Invisibles inflows	462.7	end Dec.	155.9
Invisibles outflows	-372.7	No. months of import cover	1.9
Net transfers	-49.3	Official gold holdings, m oz	78.3
Current account balance	-13.3	Aid given	11.3
– as % of GDP	-0.5	– as % of GNI	0.4
Capital balance	32.0		

Health and education

Health spending, % of GDP	11.5	Education spending, % of GDP	5.5
Doctors per 1,000 pop.	3.2	Enrolment, %: primary	102
Hospital beds per 1,000 pop.	6.5	secondary	103
At least basic drinking water,		tertiary	64
% of pop.	100		

Society

No. of households, m	29.3	Cost of living, Dec. 2018	
Av. no. per household	2.2	New York = 100	107
Marriages per 1,000 pop.	3.5	Cars per 1,000 pop.	495
Divorces per 1,000 pop.	1.9	Telephone lines per 100 pop.	59.5
Religion, % of pop.		Mobile telephone subscribers	
Christian	63.0	per 100 pop.	106.2
Non-religious	28.0	Internet access, %	80.5
Muslim	7.5	Broadband subs per 100 pop.	43.7
Other	1.0	Broadband speed, Mbps	13.4
Jewish	0.5		
Hindu	<0.1		

GERMANY

Area, sq km	357,340	Capital	Berlin
Arable as % of total land	34.1	Currency	Euro (€)

People

Population, m	82.1	Life expectancy: men	80.0 yrs
Pop. per sq km	229.6	women	84.2 yrs
Total change in population		Adult literacy	...
2010–20, %	2.0	Fertility rate (per woman)	1.5
Pop. aged 0–19, %	17.7	Urban population, %	77.2
Pop. aged 65 and over, %	22.2		per 1,000 pop.
No. of men per 100 women	97.3	Crude birth rate	8.9
Human Development Index	93.6	Crude death rate	11.7

The economy

GDP	$3,693bn	GDP per head	$48,264
GDP	€3,277bn	GDP per head in purchasing	
Av. ann. growth in real		power parity (USA=100)	84.0
GDP 2012–17	1.7%	Economic freedom index	73.5

Origins of GDP

Components of GDP

	% of total		% of total
Agriculture	1	Private consumption	53
Industry, of which:	28	Public consumption	19
manufacturing	21	Investment	20
Services	71	Exports	47
		Imports	-39

Structure of employment

	% of total		% of labour force
Agriculture	1.3	Unemployed 2018	3.4
Industry	27.1	Av. ann. rate 2010–18	4.9
Services	71.6		

Energy

	m TOE		
Total output	120.6	Net energy imports as %	
Total consumption	349.6	of energy use	61
Consumption per head			
kg oil equivalent	3,818		

Inflation and finance

		% change 2017–18	
Consumer price			
inflation 2018	1.9%	Narrow money (M1)	0.7
Av. ann. inflation 2013–18	1.1%	Broad money	4.2
Deposit rate, Dec. 2018	0.23%		

Exchange rates

	end 2018		December 2018
€ per $	0.87	Effective rates	2010 = 100
€ per SDR	1.21	– nominal	102.3
		– real	96.6

Trade

Principal exports		**Principal imports**	
	$bn fob		*$bn cif*
Machinery & transport equip.	722.8	Machinery & transport equip.	440.4
Chemicals & related products	233.4	Chemicals & related products	165.4
Food, drink and tobacco	76.9	Mineral fuels & lubricants	91.9
Mineral fuels & lubricants	29.3	Food, drink and tobacco	88.6
Total incl. others	**1,448.1**	Total incl. others	**1,166.6**

Main export destinations		**Main origins of imports**	
	% of total		*% of total*
United States	8.8	Netherlands	13.7
France	8.2	China	7.0
China	6.8	France	6.7
United Kingdom	6.7	Belgium	5.9
EU28	58.5	EU28	66.3

Balance of payments, reserves and aid, $bn

Visible exports fob	1,418.3	Overall balance	-1.5
Visible imports fob	-1,132.7	Change in reserves	15.4
Trade balance	285.6	Level of reserves	
Invisibles inflows	558.8	end Dec.	199.4
Invisibles outflows	-492.4	No. months of import cover	1.5
Net transfers	-55.8	Official gold holdings, m oz	108.5
Current account balance	296.2	Aid given	25.0
– as % of GDP	8.0	– as % of GNI	0.7
Capital balance	-323.5		

Health and education

Health spending, % of GDP	11.1	Education spending, % of GDP	4.8
Doctors per 1,000 pop.	4.2	Enrolment, %: primary	103
Hospital beds per 1,000 pop.	8.3	secondary	102
At least basic drinking water,		tertiary	68
% of pop.	100		

Society

No. of households, m	40.7	Cost of living, Dec. 2018	
Av. no. per household	2.0	New York = 100	77
Marriages per 1,000 pop.	4.9	Cars per 1,000 pop.	550
Divorces per 1,000 pop.	1.9	Telephone lines per 100 pop.	54.1
Religion, % of pop.		Mobile telephone subscribers	
Christian	68.7	per 100 pop.	133.6
Non-religious	24.7	Internet access, %	84.4
Muslim	5.8	Broadband subs per 100 pop.	40.5
Other	0.5	Broadband speed, Mbps	18.8
Jewish	0.3		
Hindu	<0.1		

GREECE

Area, sq km	131,957	Capital	Athens
Arable as % of total land	19.4	Currency	Euro (€)

People

Population, m	11.2	Life expectancy: men	80.1 yrs
Pop. per sq km	84.9	women	84.7 yrs
Total change in population		Adult literacy	...
2010–20, %	-3.0	Fertility rate (per woman)	1.3
Pop. aged 0–19, %	18.7	Urban population, %	78.4
Pop. aged 65 and over, %	21.1		per 1,000 pop.
No. of men per 100 women	96.9	Crude birth rate	7.9
Human Development Index	87.0	Crude death rate	11.1

The economy

GDP	$203bn	GDP per head	$20,408
GDP	€180bn	GDP per head in purchasing	
Av. ann. growth in real		power parity (USA=100)	46.5
GDP 2012–17	-0.3%	Economic freedom index	57.7

Origins of GDP		Components of GDP	
	% of total		% of total
Agriculture	4	Private consumption	69
Industry, of which:	15	Public consumption	20
manufacturing	9	Investment	13
Services	81	Exports	33
		Imports	-34

Structure of employment

	% of total		% of labour force
Agriculture	12.0	Unemployed 2018	19.2
Industry	15.3	Av. ann. rate 2010–18	22.0
Services	75.7		

Energy

	m TOE		
Total output	8.0	Net energy imports as %	
Total consumption	28.2	of energy use	64
Consumption per head			
kg oil equivalent	2,182		

Inflation and finance

Consumer price			% change 2017–18
inflation 2018	0.8%	Narrow money (M1)	0.7
Av. ann. inflation 2013–18	-0.1%	Broad money	4.2
Deposit rate, Dec. 2018	0.59%		

Exchange rates

	end 2018		December 2018
€ per $	0.87	Effective rates	2010 = 100
€ per SDR	1.21	– nominal	105.2
		– real	90.1

Trade

Principal exports
	$bn fob
Mineral fuels & lubricants	10.1
Food, drink and tobacco	5.7
Chemicals & related products	3.5
Machinery & transport equip.	2.9
Total incl. others	**32.7**

Principal imports
	$bn cif
Mineral fuels & lubricants	13.8
Machinery & transport equip.	12.7
Chemicals & related products	8.4
Food, drink and tobacco	7.1
Total incl. others	**56.8**

Main export destinations
	% of total
Italy	10.6
Germany	7.1
Turkey	6.8
Cyprus	6.4
EU28	53.7

Main origins of imports
	% of total
Germany	10.5
Italy	8.5
Russia	6.8
Iraq	6.3
EU28	52.0

Balance of payments, reserves and debt, $bn

Visible exports fob	31.7	Overall balance	1.0
Visible imports fob	-54.1	Change in reserves	0.9
Trade balance	-22.4	Level of reserves	
Invisibles inflows	45.7	end Dec.	7.8
Invisibles outflows	-26.0	No. months of import cover	1.2
Net transfers	-0.7	Official gold holdings, m oz	3.6
Current account balance	-3.3	Aid given	0.3
– as % of GDP	-1.6	– as % of GNI	0.2
Capital balance	3.7		

Health and education

Health spending, % of GDP	8.5	Education spending, % of GDP	...
Doctors per 1,000 pop.	6.3	Enrolment, %: primary	94
Hospital beds per 1,000 pop.	4.3	secondary	100
At least basic drinking water,		tertiary	126
% of pop.	100		

Society

No. of households, m	4.2	Cost of living, Dec. 2018	
Av. no. per household	2.7	New York = 100	64
Marriages per 1,000 pop.	4.7	Cars per 1,000 pop.	456
Divorces per 1,000 pop.	1.0	Telephone lines per 100 pop.	46.4
Religion, % of pop.		Mobile telephone subscribers	
Christian	88.1	per 100 pop.	115.9
Non-religious	6.1	Internet access, %	69.9
Muslim	5.3	Broadband subs per 100 pop.	33.9
Other	0.3	Broadband speed, Mbps	7.6
Hindu	0.1		
Jewish	<0.1		

HONG KONG

Area, sq km	1,075	Capital	Victoria
Arable as % of total land	...	Currency	Hong Kong dollar (HK$)

People

Population, m	7.4	Life expectancy: men	81.9 yrs
Pop. per sq km	6,883.7	women	87.9 yrs
Total change in population		Adult literacy	...
2010–20, %	7.4	Fertility rate (per woman)	1.3
Pop. aged 0–19, %	16.3	Urban population, %	100.0
Pop. aged 65 and over, %	18.1		per 1,000 pop.
No. of men per 100 women	84.1	Crude birth rate	11.1
Human Development Index	93.3	Crude death rate	7.4

The economy

GDP	$341bn	GDP per head	$48,517
GDP	HK$2,663bn	GDP per head in purchasing	
Av. ann. growth in real		power parity (USA=100)	102.6
GDP 2012–17	2.8%	Economic freedom index	90.2

Origins of GDP

Components of GDP

	% of total		% of total
Agriculture	0	Private consumption	67
Industry, of which:	7	Public consumption	10
manufacturing	1	Investment	22
Services	93	Exports	188
		Imports	-187

Structure of employment

	% of total		% of labour force
Agriculture	0.2	Unemployed 2018	2.8
Industry	11.8	Av. ann. rate 2010–18	3.4
Services	88.0		

Energy

	m TOE		
Total output	0.0	Net energy imports as %	
Total consumption	33.4	of energy use	99
Consumption per head			
kg oil equivalent	1,970		

Inflation and finance

		% change 2017–18	
Consumer price			
inflation 2018	2.4%	Narrow money (M1)	-0.4
Av. ann. inflation 2013–18	2.7%	Broad money	4.3
Treasury bill rate, Dec. 2018	1.75%		

Exchange rates

	end 2018		December 2018
HK$ per $	7.83	Effective rates	2010 = 100
HK$ per SDR	10.90	– nominal	105.2
HK$ per €	9.00	– real	...

Trade

Principal exports[a]

	$bn fob
Capital goods	199.5
Semi-finished goods	186.4
Consumer goods	97.1
Foodstuffs	8.7
Total incl. others	**497.7**

Principal imports[a]

	$bn cif
Capital goods & raw materials	217.6
Raw materials & semi-manufactures	193.9
Consumer goods	110.6
Foodstuffs	24.5
Total incl. others	**559.6**

Main export destinations

	% of total
China	54.3
United States	8.5
India	4.1
Japan	3.3

Main origins of imports

	% of total
China	46.6
Taiwan	7.6
Singapore	6.6
Japan	6.3

Balance of payments, reserves and debt, $bn

Visible exports fob	540.5	Change in reserves	45.1
Visible imports fob	-563.4	Level of reserves	
Trade balance	-22.9	end Dec.	431.4
Invisibles inflows	286.8	No. months of import cover	6.4
Invisibles outflows	-245.4	Official gold holdings, m oz	0.1
Net transfers	-2.6	Foreign debt	643.0
Current account balance	15.9	– as % of GDP	188.2
– as % of GDP	4.7	– as % of total exports	77.6
Capital balance	22.3	Debt service ratio	7.3
Overall balance	32.1		

Health and education

Health spending, % of GDP	...	Education spending, % of GDP	3.3
Doctors per 1,000 pop.	...	Enrolment, %: primary	107
Hospital beds per 1,000 pop.	...	secondary	104
At least basic drinking water,		tertiary	74
% of pop.	100		

Society

No. of households, m	2.5	Cost of living, Dec. 2018	
Av. no. per household	3.0	New York = 100	107
Marriages per 1,000 pop.	7.0	Cars per 1,000 pop.	74
Divorces per 1,000 pop.	...	Telephone lines per 100 pop.	57.7
Religion, % of pop.		Mobile telephone subscribers	
Non-religious	56.1	per 100 pop.	249.8
Christian	14.3	Internet access, %	89.4
Other	14.2	Broadband subs per 100 pop.	36.1
Buddhist	13.2	Broadband speed, Mbps	27.2
Muslim	1.8		
Hindu	0.4		

a Including re-exports.
Note: Hong Kong became a Special Administrative Region of China on July 1 1997.

HUNGARY

Area, sq km	93,024	Capital	Budapest
Arable as % of total land	48.5	Currency	Forint (Ft)

People

Population, m	9.7	Life expectancy: men	73.3 yrs
Pop. per sq km	104.3	women	80.1 yrs
Total change in population		Adult literacy	99.1
2010–20, %	-3.1	Fertility rate (per woman)	1.4
Pop. aged 0–19, %	19.3	Urban population, %	70.8
Pop. aged 65 and over, %	20.1		per 1,000 pop.
No. of men per 100 women	90.9	Crude birth rate	9.0
Human Development Index	83.8	Crude death rate	13.4

The economy

GDP	$140bn	GDP per head	$15,924
GDP	Ft38,355bn	GDP per head in purchasing	
Av. ann. growth in real		power parity (USA=100)	51.0
GDP 2012–17	3.2%	Economic freedom index	65.0

Origins of GDP		**Components of GDP**	
	% of total		% of total
Agriculture	4	Private consumption	50
Industry, of which:	26	Public consumption	20
manufacturing	20	Investment	23
Services	70	Exports	88
		Imports	-81

Structure of employment

	% of total		% of labour force
Agriculture	5.0	Unemployed 2018	3.7
Industry	31.3	Av. ann. rate 2010–18	7.9
Services	63.7		

Energy

	m TOE		
Total output	9.3	Net energy imports as %	
Total consumption	25.3	of energy use	58
Consumption per head			
kg oil equivalent	2,433		

Inflation and finance

		% change 2017–18	
Consumer price			
inflation 2018	2.8%	Narrow money (M1)	7.1
Av. ann. inflation 2013–18	1.1%	Broad money	11.8
Deposit rate, Dec. 2018	0.07%		

Exchange rates

	end 2018		December 2018
Ft per $	280.94	Effective rates	2010 = 100
Ft per SDR	390.73	– nominal	88.4
Ft per €	322.92	– real	89.2

Trade

Trade

Principal exports		**Principal imports**	
	$bn fob		*$bn cif*
Machinery & equipment	63.4	Machinery & equipment	50.5
Manufactured goods	36.5	Manufactured goods	38.0
Food, drink & tobacco	8.2	Fuels & energy	8.1
Raw materials	2.7	Food, drink & tobacco	5.6
Total incl. others	**113.4**	Total incl. others	**104.3**

Main export destinations		**Main origins of imports**	
	% of total		*% of total*
Germany	28.0	Germany	27.0
Romania	5.4	Austria	6.5
Italy	5.2	China	6.1
Austria	5.0	Poland	5.6
EU28	81.2	EU28	76.1

Balance of payments, reserves and debt, $bn

Visible exports fob	96.6	Change In reserves	2.2
Visible imports fob	-94.5	Level of reserves	
Trade balance	2.1	end Dec.	28.0
Invisibles inflows	41.9	No. months of import cover	2.5
Invisibles outflows	-39.3	Official gold holdings, m oz	0.1
Net transfers	-0.9	Foreign debt	153.2
Current account balance	3.8	– as % of GDP	109.8
– as % of GDP	2.8	– as % of total exports	110.3
Capital balance	-0.9	Debt service ratio	37.3
Overall balance	0.1		

Health and education

Health spending, % of GDP	7.4	Education spending, % of GDP	...
Doctors per 1,000 pop.	3.1	Enrolment, %: primary	102
Hospital beds per 1,000 pop.	7.0	secondary	103
At least basic drinking water,		tertiary	48
% of pop.	100		

Society

No. of households, m	4.1	Cost of living, Dec. 2018	
Av. no. per household	2.4	New York = 100	54
Marriages per 1,000 pop.	5.2	Cars per 1,000 pop.	326
Divorces per 1,000 pop.	1.9	Telephone lines per 100 pop.	32.2
Religion, % of pop.		Mobile telephone subscribers	
Christian	81.0	per 100 pop.	113.5
Non-religious	18.6	Internet access, %	76.8
Other	0.2	Broadband subs per 100 pop.	30.5
Jewish	0.1	Broadband speed, Mbps	23.2
Hindu	<0.1		
Muslim	<0.1		

INDIA

| Area, sq km | 3,287,263 | Capital | New Delhi |
| Arable as % of total land | 52.9 | Currency | Indian rupee (Rs) |

People

Population, m	1,339.2	Life expectancy: men	68.4 yrs
Pop. per sq km	407.4	women	71.8 yrs
Total change in population		Adult literacy	...
2010–20, %	12.4	Fertility rate (per woman)	2.3
Pop. aged 0–19, %	35.7	Urban population, %	33.2
Pop. aged 65 and over, %	6.6		per 1,000 pop.
No. of men per 100 women	107.4	Crude birth rate	18.7
Human Development Index	64.0	Crude death rate	7.5

The economy

GDP	$2,651bn	GDP per head	$2,306
GDP	Rs171trn	GDP per head in purchasing	
Av. ann. growth in real		power parity (USA=100)	12.6
GDP 2012–17	7.1%	Economic freedom index	55.2

Origins of GDP		Components of GDP	
	% of total		% of total
Agriculture	16	Private consumption	59
Industry, of which:	26	Public consumption	11
manufacturing	15	Investment	31
Services	58	Exports	19
		Imports	-22

Structure of employment

	% of total		% of labour force
Agriculture	43.9	Unemployed 2018	2.6
Industry	24.7	Av. ann. rate 2010–18	2.7
Services	31.5		

Energy

	m TOE		
Total output	410.7	Net energy imports as %	
Total consumption	732.3	of energy use	34
Consumption per head			
kg oil equivalent	637		

Inflation and finance

Consumer price			% change 2017–18
inflation 2018	3.5%	Narrow money (M1)	18.1
Av. ann. inflation 2013–18	4.5%	Broad money	10.5
Discount rate, Dec. 2018	6.75%		

Exchange rates

	end 2018		December 2018
Rs per $	69.79	Effective rates	2010 = 100
Rs per SDR	97.07	– nominal	...
Rs per €	80.22	– real	...

Trade

Principal exports		Principal imports	
	$bn fob		*$bn cif*
Engineering products	78.7	Petroleum & products	108.7
Gems & jewellery	41.5	Electronic goods	51.5
Petroleum & products	37.5	Gold & silver	36.9
Agricultural products	32.9	Machinery	34.3
Total incl. others	**303.4**	Total incl. others	**465.6**

Main export destinations		Main origins of imports	
	% of total		*% of total*
United States	15.2	China	15.5
United Arab Emirates	9.9	United States	5.2
Hong Kong	4.9	United Arab Emirates	5.0
United Kingdom	4.1	Saudi Arabia	4.5

Balance of payments, reserves and debt, $bn

Visible exports fob	304.1	Change in reserves	50.8
Visible imports fob	-452.2	Level of reserves	
Trade balance	-148.1	end Dec.	412.5
Invisibles inflows	203.8	No. months of import cover	8.2
Invisibles outflows	-154.3	Official gold holdings, m oz	17.9
Net transfers	60.5	Foreign debt	513.2
Current account balance	-38.2	– as % of GDP	19.7
– as % of GDP	-1.4	– as % of total exports	89.0
Capital balance	76.7	Debt service ratio	8.9
Overall balance	37.1		

Health and education

Health spending, % of GDP	3.7	Education spending, % of GDP	...
Doctors per 1,000 pop.	0.8	Enrolment, %: primary	115
Hospital beds per 1,000 pop.	...	secondary	75
At least basic drinking water,		tertiary	27
% of pop.	87.6		

Society

No. of households, m	278.2	Cost of living, Dec. 2018	
Av. no. per household	4.8	New York = 100	43
Marriages per 1,000 pop.	...	Cars per 1,000 pop.	17
Divorces per 1,000 pop.	...	Telephone lines per 100 pop.	1.7
Religion, % of pop.		Mobile telephone subscribers	
Hindu	79.5	per 100 pop.	87.3
Muslim	14.4	Internet access, %	34.5
Other	3.6	Broadband subs per 100 pop.	1.3
Christian	2.5	Broadband speed, Mbps	2.1
Jewish	<0.1		
Non-religious	<0.1		

INDONESIA

| Area, sq km | 1,910,931 | Capital | Jakarta |
| Arable as % of total land | 13.0 | Currency | Rupiah (Rp) |

People

Population, m	264.0	Life expectancy: men	68.0 yrs
Pop. per sq km	138.2	women	72.6 yrs
Total change in population		Adult literacy	95.4
2010–20, %	12.2	Fertility rate (per woman)	2.3
Pop. aged 0–19, %	35.0	Urban population, %	54.0
Pop. aged 65 and over, %	5.8		per 1,000 pop.
No. of men per 100 women	101.2	Crude birth rate	18.4
Human Development Index	69.4	Crude death rate	7.5

The economy

GDP	$1,015bn	GDP per head	$3,871
GDP	Rs13,587trn	GDP per head in purchasing	
Av. ann. growth in real		power parity (USA=100)	21.1
GDP 2012–17	5.1%	Economic freedom index	65.8

Origins of GDP

	% of total		
Agriculture	13
Industry, of which:	39
manufacturing	20
Services	48

Components of GDP

	% of total
Private consumption	57
Public consumption	9
Investment	34
Exports	20
Imports	-19

Structure of employment

	% of total		% of labour force
Agriculture	30.5	Unemployed 2018	4.3
Industry	22	Av. ann. rate 2010–18	4.5
Services	47.5		

Energy

	m TOE		
Total output	382.3	Net energy imports as %	
Total consumption	182.8	of energy use	-103
Consumption per head			
kg oil equivalent	884		

Inflation and finance

Consumer price			% change 2017–18
inflation 2018	3.2%	Narrow money (M1)	0.2
Av. ann. inflation 2013–18	4.6%	Broad money	6.3
Deposit rate, Dec. 2018	6.84%		

Exchange rates

	end 2018		December 2018
Rp per $	14,481.00	Effective rates	2010 = 100
Rp per SDR	20,140.05	– nominal	...
Rp per €	16,644.83	– real	...

Trade

Principal exports		Principal imports	
	$bn fob		*$bn cif*
Manufactured goods	122.1	Raw materials & auxiliary	
Mining & other sector products	37.6	materials	110.3
Agricultural goods	5.9	Capital goods	25.0
Unclassified exports	1.3	Consumer goods	20.8
Total incl. others	**168.8**	Total incl. others	**157.0**

Main export destinations		Main origins of imports	
	% of total		*% of total*
China	13.7	China	22.8
Japan	10.5	Singapore	10.8
United States	10.5	Japan	9.7
India	8.3	Thailand	5.9

Balance of payments, reserves and debt, $bn

Visible exports fob	168.9	Change in reserves	13.8
Visible imports fob	-150.1	Level of reserves	
Trade balance	18.8	end Dec.	130.2
Invisibles inflows	30.9	No. months of import cover	7.1
Invisibles outflows	-70.4	Official gold holdings, m oz	2.6
Net transfers	4.5	Foreign debt	354.4
Current account balance	-16.2	– as % of GDP	34.9
– as % of GDP	-1.6	– as % of total exports	169.7
Capital balance	28.7	Debt service ratio	32.6
Overall balance	11.6		

Health and education

Health spending, % of GDP	3.1	Education spending, % of GDP	3.6
Doctors per 1,000 pop.	0.2	Enrolment, %: primary	104
Hospital beds per 1,000 pop.	1.2	secondary	88
At least basic drinking water,		tertiary	36
% of pop.	89.5		

Society

No. of households, m	66.9	Cost of living, Dec. 2018	
Av. no. per household	3.9	New York = 100	57
Marriages per 1,000 pop.	...	Cars per 1,000 pop.	52
Divorces per 1,000 pop.	...	Telephone lines per 100 pop.	4.2
Religion, % of pop.		Mobile telephone subscribers	
Muslim	87.2	per 100 pop.	164.9
Christian	9.9	Internet access, %	32.3
Hindu	1.7	Broadband subs per 100 pop.	2.4
Other	1.1	Broadband speed, Mbps	5.2
Jewish	<0.1		
Non-religious	<0.1		

IRAN

Area, sq km	1,628,750	Capital	Tehran
Arable as % of total land	10.8	Currency	Rial (IR)

People

Population, m	81.2	Life expectancy: men	76.1 yrs
Pop. per sq km	49.9	women	78.5 yrs
Total change in population		Adult literacy	85.5
2010–20, %	12.1	Fertility rate (per woman)	1.6
Pop. aged 0–19, %	29.8	Urban population, %	73.9
Pop. aged 65 and over, %	6.3		per 1,000 pop.
No. of men per 100 women	101.0	Crude birth rate	15.6
Human Development Index	79.8	Crude death rate	4.6

The economy

GDP	$454bn	GDP per head	$5,491
GDP	IR14,807trn	GDP per head in purchasing	
Av. ann. growth in real		power parity (USA=100)	31.2
GDP 2012–17	3.9%	Economic freedom index	51.1

Origins of GDP

	% of total
Agriculture	9
Industry, of which:	35
manufacturing	12
Services	56

Components of GDP

	% of total
Private consumption	48
Public consumption	13
Investment	35
Exports	25
Imports	-24

Structure of employment

	% of total		% of labour force
Agriculture	17.4	Unemployed 2018	12.0
Industry	32.0	Av. ann. rate 2010–18	11.9
Services	50.6		

Energy

	m TOE		
Total output	429.2	Net energy imports as %	
Total consumption	284.0	of energy use	-33
Consumption per head			
kg oil equivalent	3,023		

Inflation and finance

			% change 2017–18
Consumer price			
inflation 2018	31.2%	Narrow money (M1)	41.0
Av. ann. inflation 2013–18	15.2%	Broad money	22.1
Deposit rate, Feb. 2017	12.70%		

Exchange rates

	end 2018		December 2018
IR per $	42,000.00	Effective rates	2010 = 100
IR per SDR	58,180.23	– nominal	29.0
IR per €	48,275.86	– real	117.2

Trade

Principal exports[a]		**Principal imports[a]**	
	$bn fob		*$bn fob*
Oil & gas	65.8	Machinery & transport equip.	21.9
Petrochemicals	9.0	Intermediate goods	7.8
Fresh & dry fruits	2.3	Foodstuffs	7.6
Carpets	0.4	Chemicals	7.2
Total incl. others	**98.1**	**Total incl. others**	**75.5**

Main export destinations		**Main origins of imports**	
	% of total		*% of total*
China	26.7	China	25.4
India	15.9	United Arab Emirates	15.9
Turkey	11.0	South Korea	7.1
South Korea	10.8	Turkey	6.2

Balance of payments[a], reserves and debt, $bn

Visible exports fob	98.1	Change in reserves	...
Visible imports fob	-75.5	Level of reserves	
Trade balance	22.6	end Dec.	...
Invisibles inflows	12.8	No. months of import cover	...
Invisibles outflows	-20.1	Official gold holdings, m oz	...
Net transfers	0.5	Foreign debt	6.3
Current account balance	15.8	– as % of GDP	1.4
– as % of GDP	3.5	– as % of total exports	5.6
Capital balance	9.0	Debt service ratio	0.4
Overall balance	20.2		

Health and education

Health spending, % of GDP	8.1	Education spending, % of GDP	3.8
Doctors per 1,000 pop.	1.5	Enrolment, %: primary	109
Hospital beds per 1,000 pop.	1.5	secondary	89
At least basic drinking water,		tertiary	69
% of pop.	94.9		

Society

No. of households, m	24.7	Cost of living, Dec. 2018	
Av. no. per household	3.3	New York = 100	46
Marriages per 1,000 pop.	8.8	Cars per 1,000 pop.	158
Divorces per 1,000 pop.	2.3	Telephone lines per 100 pop.	38.4
Religion, % of pop.		Mobile telephone subscribers	
Muslim	99.5	per 100 pop.	107.0
Christian	0.2	Internet access, %	60.4
Other	0.2	Broadband subs per 100 pop.	12.4
Non-religious	0.1	Broadband speed, Mbps	1.6
Hindu	<0.1		
Jewish	<0.1		

a Iranian year ending March 20 2019.

IRELAND

Area, sq km	69,797	Capital	Dublin
Arable as % of total land	15.4	Currency	Euro (€)

People

Population, m	4.8	Life expectancy: men	80.8 yrs
Pop. per sq km	68.8	women	84.3 yrs
Total change in population		Adult literacy	...
2010–20, %	5.6	Fertility rate (per woman)	2.0
Pop. aged 0–19, %	27.6	Urban population, %	62.7
Pop. aged 65 and over, %	15.0		per 1,000 pop.
No. of men per 100 women	98.6	Crude birth rate	13.5
Human Development Index	93.8	Crude death rate	6.8

The economy

GDP	$331bn	GDP per head	$76,099
GDP	€294bn	GDP per head in purchasing	
Av. ann. growth in real		power parity (USA=100)	125.8
GDP 2012–17	9.4%	Economic freedom index	80.5

Origins of GDP

	% of total
Agriculture	1
Industry, of which:	36
manufacturing	32
Services	63

Components of GDP

	% of total
Private consumption	32
Public consumption	12
Investment	25
Exports	120
Imports	-90

Structure of employment

	% of total		% of labour force
Agriculture	5.0	Unemployed 2018	5.7
Industry	18.5	Av. ann. rate 2010–18	11.3
Services	76.5		

Energy

	m TOE		
Total output	4.6	Net energy imports as %	
Total consumption	15.9	of energy use	86
Consumption per head			
kg oil equivalent	2,820		

Inflation and finance

			% change 2017–18
Consumer price			
inflation 2018	0.7%	Narrow money (M1)	0.7
Av. ann. inflation 2013–18	0.2%	Broad money	4.2
Deposit rate, Dec. 2018	0.29%		

Exchange rates

	end 2018		December 2018
€ per $	0.87	Effective rates	2010 = 100
€ per SDR	1.21	– nominal	98.3
		– real	89.8

Trade

Principal exports		Principal imports	
	$bn fob		*$bn cif*
Chemicals & related products	76.5	Machinery & transport equip.	35.7
Machinery & transport equip.	23.4	Chemicals & related products	20.0
Food, drink and tobacco	14.4	Food, drink and tobacco	9.1
Raw materials	2.2	Mineral fuels & lubricants	5.4
Total incl. others	**138.6**	Total incl. others	**93.6**

Main export destinations		Main origins of imports	
	% of total		*% of total*
United States	26.9	United Kingdom	27.1
United Kingdom	13.3	United States	18.6
Belgium	10.8	France	11.9
Germany	8.2	Germany	8.9
EU28	51.1	EU28	65.6

Balance of payments, reserves and aid, $bn

Visible exports fob	218.2	Overall balance	5.9
Visible imports fob	-96.2	Change in reserves	0.8
Trade balance	122.0	Level of reserves	
Invisibles inflows	269.3	end Dec.	4.4
Invisibles outflows	-357.0	No. months of import cover	0.1
Net transfers	-5.2	Official gold holdings, m oz	0.2
Current account balance	29.1	Aid given	0.8
– as % of GDP	8.8	– as % of GNI	0.3
Capital balance	-38.5		

Health and education

Health spending, % of GDP	7.4	Education spending, % of GDP	3.8
Doctors per 1,000 pop.	3.0	Enrolment, %: primary	101
Hospital beds per 1,000 pop.	2.8	secondary	117
At least basic drinking water,		tertiary	78
% of pop.	98.9		

Society

No. of households, m	1.8	Cost of living, Dec. 2018	
Av. no. per household	2.7	New York = 100	88
Marriages per 1,000 pop.	4.6	Cars per 1,000 pop.	422
Divorces per 1,000 pop.	0.6	Telephone lines per 100 pop.	38.7
Religion, % of pop.		Mobile telephone subscribers	
Christian	92.0	per 100 pop.	102.9
Non-religious	6.2	Internet access, %	84.5
Muslim	1.1	Broadband subs per 100 pop.	29.4
Other	0.4	Broadband speed, Mbps	13.9
Hindu	0.2		
Jewish	<0.1		

ISRAEL

Area, sq km	22,072	Capital	Jerusalem[a]
Arable as % of total land	14.0	Currency	New Shekel (NIS)

People

Population, m	8.3	Life expectancy: men	82.1 yrs
Pop. per sq km	376.0	women	85.0 yrs
Total change in population		Adult literacy	...
2010–20, %	17.3	Fertility rate (per woman)	2.9
Pop. aged 0–19, %	35.3	Urban population, %	92.3
Pop. aged 65 and over, %	12.5		per 1,000 pop.
No. of men per 100 women	99.1	Crude birth rate	19.6
Human Development Index	90.3	Crude death rate	5.3

The economy

GDP	$353bn	GDP per head	$41,644
GDP	NIS1,272bn	GDP per head in purchasing	
Av. ann. growth in real		power parity (USA=100)	60.7
GDP 2012–17	3.6%	Economic freedom index	72.8

Origins of GDP

	% of total
Agriculture	1
Industry, of which:	20
manufacturing	12
Services	79

Components of GDP

	% of total
Private consumption	55
Public consumption	23
Investment	21
Exports	29
Imports	-28

Structure of employment

	% of total		% of labour force
Agriculture	1.0	Unemployed 2018	4.0
Industry	17.3	Av. ann. rate 2010–18	5.9
Services	81.7		

Energy

	m TOE		
Total output	9.2	Net energy imports as %	
Total consumption	26.2	of energy use	65
Consumption per head			
kg oil equivalent	2,778		

Inflation and finance

Consumer price			% change 2017–18
inflation 2018	0.8%	Narrow money (M1)	12.8
Av. ann. inflation 2013–18	0.1%	Broad money	4.6
Deposit rate, Dec. 2018	0.65%		

Exchange rates

	end 2018		December 2018
NIS per $	3.75	Effective rates	2010 = 100
NIS per SDR	5.21	– nominal	116.4
NIS per €	4.31	– real	103.7

Trade

Principal exports		Principal imports	
	$bn fob		*$bn cif*
Chemicals & chemical products	14.2	Machinery & equipment	8.4
Communications, medical &		Fuel	7.6
scientific equipment	8.7	Diamonds	5.8
Polished diamonds	6.7	Chemicals	4.9
Electronic components &			
computers	4.3		
Total incl. others	**53.1**	Total incl. others	**68.0**

Main export destinations		Main origins of imports	
	% of total		*% of total*
United States	32.6	United States	11.9
United Kingdom	9.2	China	9.6
Hong Kong	7.9	Switzerland	8.1
China	6.1	Germany	6.9

Balance of payments, reserves and debt, $bn

Visible exports fob	58.7	Change in reserves	17.6
Visible imports fob	-68.6	Level of reserves	
Trade balance	-9.9	end Dec.	113.0
Invisibles inflows	56.4	No. months of import cover	12.0
Invisibles outflows	-44.3	Official gold holdings, m oz	0.0
Net transfers	7.8	Foreign debt	88.8
Current account balance	10.0	– as % of GDP	25.1
– as % of GDP	2.8	– as % of total exports	76.3
Capital balance	-1.4	Debt service ratio	12.7
Overall balance	8.3		

Health and education

Health spending, % of GDP	7.3	Education spending, % of GDP	5.9
Doctors per 1,000 pop.	3.6	Enrolment, %: primary	104
Hospital beds per 1,000 pop.	3.1	secondary	104
At least basic drinking water,		tertiary	64
% of pop.	100		

Society

No. of households, m	2.5	Cost of living, Dec. 2018	
Av. no. per household	3.3	New York = 100	99
Marriages per 1,000 pop.	6.2	Cars per 1,000 pop.	318
Divorces per 1,000 pop.	1.7	Telephone lines per 100 pop.	38.9
Religion, % of pop.		Mobile telephone subscribers	
Jewish	75.6	per 100 pop.	126.7
Muslim	18.6	Internet access, %	81.6
Non-religious	3.1	Broadband subs per 100 pop.	28.1
Christian	2.0	Broadband speed, Mbps	7.2
Other	0.6		
Hindu	<0.1		

a Sovereignty over the city is disputed.

ITALY

Area, sq km	302,073	Capital	Rome
Arable as % of total land	23.1	Currency	Euro (€)

People

Population, m	59.4	Life expectancy: men	82.0 yrs
Pop. per sq km	196.6	women	86.1 yrs
Total change in population		Adult literacy	...
2010–20, %	-1.0	Fertility rate (per woman)	1.5
Pop. aged 0–19, %	18.0	Urban population, %	69.9
Pop. aged 65 and over, %	23.9		per 1,000 pop.
No. of men per 100 women	95.4	Crude birth rate	8.2
Human Development Index	88.0	Crude death rate	11.1

The economy

GDP	$1,944bn	GDP per head	$34,260
GDP	€1,724bn	GDP per head in purchasing	
Av. ann. growth in real		power parity (USA=100)	63.3
GDP 2012–17	0.3%	Economic freedom index	62.2

Origins of GDP

Components of GDP

	% of total		% of total
Agriculture	2	Private consumption	61
Industry, of which:	22	Public consumption	19
manufacturing	15	Investment	18
Services	76	Exports	31
		Imports	-28

Structure of employment

	% of total		% of labour force
Agriculture	3.8	Unemployed 2018	10.2
Industry	25.8	Av. ann. rate 2010–18	10.8
Services	70.4		

Energy

	m TOE		
Total output	35.4	Net energy imports as %	
Total consumption	169.6	of energy use	76
Consumption per head			
kg oil equivalent	2,482		

Inflation and finance

			% change 2017–18
Consumer price			
inflation 2018	1.2%	Narrow money (M1)	0.7
Av. ann. inflation 2013–18	0.6%	Broad money	4.2
Treasury bill rate, Dec. 2018	0.37%		

Exchange rates

	end 2018		December 2018
€ per $	0.87	Effective rates	2010 = 100
€ per SDR	1.21	– nominal	103.6
		– real	96.1

Trade

Principal exports		Principal imports	
	$bn fob		*$bn cif*
Machinery & transport equip.	183.8	Machinery & transport equip.	131.4
Chemicals & related products	66.3	Chemicals & related products	71.6
Food, drink and tobacco	42.4	Mineral fuels & lubricants	54.1
Mineral fuels & lubricants	17.2	Food, drink and tobacco	42.1
Total incl. others	**510.5**	**Total incl. others**	**456.7**

Main export destinations		Main origins of imports	
	% of total		*% of total*
Germany	12.4	Germany	16.3
France	10.2	France	8.7
United States	9.0	China	7.0
Spain	5.2	Netherlands	5.6
EU28	55.7	EU28	60.2

Balance of payments, reserves and aid, $bn

Visible exports fob	497.3	Overall balance	2.9
Visible imports fob	-434.8	Change in reserves	15.6
Trade balance	62.5	Level of reserves	
Invisibles inflows	193.2	end Dec.	150.7
Invisibles outflows	-187.2	No. months of import cover	2.9
Net transfers	-16.9	Official gold holdings, m oz	78.8
Current account balance	51.6	Aid given	5.9
– as % of GDP	2.7	– as % of GNI	0.3
Capital balance	-55.3		

Health and education

Health spending, % of GDP	8.9	Education spending, % of GDP	4.1
Doctors per 1,000 pop.	4.0	Enrolment, %: primary	100
Hospital beds per 1,000 pop.	3.2	secondary	103
At least basic drinking water,		tertiary	63
% of pop.	100		

Society

No. of households, m	25.9	Cost of living, Dec. 2018	
Av. no. per household	2.3	New York = 100	81
Marriages per 1,000 pop.	3.4	Cars per 1,000 pop.	629
Divorces per 1,000 pop.	1.6	Telephone lines per 100 pop.	34.9
Religion, % of pop.		Mobile telephone subscribers	
Christian	83.3	per 100 pop.	141.3
Non-religious	12.4	Internet access, %	61.3
Muslim	3.7	Broadband subs per 100 pop.	27.9
Other	0.4	Broadband speed, Mbps	10.7
Hindu	0.1		
Jewish	<0.1		

IVORY COAST

Area, sq km	322,463	Capital	Yamoussoukro
Arable as % of total land	9.1	Currency	CFA franc (CFAfr)

People

Population, m	24.3	Life expectancy: men	55.2 yrs
Pop. per sq km	75.4	women	58.3 yrs
Total change in population		Adult literacy	43.9
2010–20, %	28.3	Fertility rate (per woman)	4.8
Pop. aged 0–19, %	52.7	Urban population, %	49.9
Pop. aged 65 and over, %	3.0		per 1,000 pop.
No. of men per 100 women	102.1	Crude birth rate	36.4
Human Development Index	49.2	Crude death rate	10.6

The economy

GDP	$37bn	GDP per head	$1,680
GDP	CFAfr22,151	GDP per head in purchasing	
Av. ann. growth in real		power parity (USA=100)	6.7
GDP 2012–17	8.4%	Economic freedom index	62.4

Origins of GDP

	% of total
Agriculture	22
Industry, of which:	25
manufacturing	12
Services	53

Components of GDP

	% of total
Private consumption	66
Public consumption	14
Investment	18
Exports	34
Imports	-32

Structure of employment

	% of total		% of labour force
Agriculture	48.0	Unemployed 2018	2.5
Industry	6.2	Av. ann. rate 2010–18	4.4
Services	45.8		

Energy

	m TOE		
Total output	5.1	Net energy imports as %	
Total consumption	4.9	of energy use	7
Consumption per head			
kg oil equivalent	616		

Inflation and finance

			% change 2017–18
Consumer price			
inflation 2018	0.3%	Narrow money (M1)	8.8
Av. ann. inflation 2013–18	0.7%	Broad money	13.4
Deposit rate, Feb. 2017	6.60%		

Exchange rates

	end 2018		December 2018
CFAfr per $	572.89	Effective rates	2010 = 100
CFAfr per SDR	796.77	– nominal	111.9
CFAfr per €	658.49	– real	97.0

Trade

Principal exports		Principal imports	
	$bn fob		*$bn cif*
Cocoa beans & butter	5.0	Fuels & lubricants	2.2
Petroleum products	1.5	Foodstuffs	2.1
Cashew nuts	1.0	Capital equip.	2.0
Gold	1.0	Raw materials & intermediate goods	2.0
Total incl. others	**11.7**	Total incl. others	**11.3**

Main export destinations		Main origins of imports	
	% of total		*% of total*
Netherlands	12.0	China	13.5
United States	9.5	France	11.1
Vietnam	6.2	Nigeria	9.3
France	5.1	Spain	9.1

Balance of payments, reserves and debt, $bn

Visible exports fob	11.9	Change in reserves	1.2
Visible imports fob	-8.5	Level of reserves	
Trade balance	3.4	end Dec.	5.6
Invisibles inflows	1.3	No. months of import cover	4.9
Invisibles outflows	-5.2	Official gold holdings, m oz	0.0
Net transfers	-0.5	Foreign debt	13.4
Current account balance	-1.0	– as % of GDP	35.3
– as % of GDP	-2.8	– as % of total exports	99.5
Capital balance	1.5	Debt service ratio	16.7
Overall balance	0.5		

Health and education

Health spending, % of GDP	˙4.4	Education spending, % of GDP	4.4
Doctors per 1,000 pop.	...	Enrolment, %: primary	99
Hospital beds per 1,000 pop.	...	secondary	50
At least basic drinking water, % of pop.	...	tertiary	9

Society

No. of households, m	3.7	Cost of living, Dec. 2018	
Av. no. per household	6.6	New York = 100	56
Marriages per 1,000 pop.	...	Cars per 1,000 pop.	18
Divorces per 1,000 pop.	...	Telephone lines per 100 pop.	1.3
Religion, % of pop.	...	Mobile telephone subscribers	
		per 100 pop.	130.7
		Internet access, %	43.8
		Broadband subs per 100 pop.	0.6
		Broadband speed, Mbps	1.2

JAPAN

Area, sq km	377,930	Capital	Tokyo
Arable as % of total land	11.7	Currency	Yen (¥)

People

Population, m	127.5	Life expectancy: men	81.4 yrs
Pop. per sq km	337.4	women	87.9 yrs
Total change in population		Adult literacy	...
2010–20, %	-1.6	Fertility rate (per woman)	1.5
Pop. aged 0–19, %	17.2	Urban population, %	91.5
Pop. aged 65 and over, %	28.2		per 1,000 pop.
No. of men per 100 women	95.3	Crude birth rate	8.1
Human Development Index	90.9	Crude death rate	11.7

The economy

GDP	$4,872bn	GDP per head	$39,305
GDP	Yen 545trn	GDP per head in purchasing	
Av. ann. growth in real		power parity (USA=100)	70.6
GDP 2012–17	1.3%	Economic freedom index	72.1

Origins of GDP		**Components of GDP**	
	% of total		% of total
Agriculture	1	Private consumption	55
Industry, of which:	29	Public consumption	20
manufacturing	21	Investment	24
Services	70	Exports	18
		Imports	-17

Structure of employment

	% of total		% of labour force
Agriculture	3.4	Unemployed 2018	2.4
Industry	24.5	Av. ann. rate 2010–18	3.7
Services	72.1		

Energy

	m TOE		
Total output	51.5	Net energy imports as %	
Total consumption	495.5	of energy use	93
Consumption per head			
kg oil equivalent	3,429		

Inflation and finance

			% change 2017–18
Consumer price			
inflation 2018	1.0%	Narrow money (M1)	5.0
Av. ann. inflation 2013–18	1.0%	Broad money	2.9
Policy rate, Dec. 2018	-0.10%		

Exchange rates

	end 2018		December 2018
¥ per $	110.83	Effective rates	2010 = 100
¥ per SDR	154.14	– nominal	85.4
¥ per €	127.39	– real	74.8

Trade

Principal exports

	$bn fob
Capital equipment	354.7
Industrial supplies	161.9
Consumer durable goods	114.0
Consumer non-durable goods	6.7
Total incl. others	**698.3**

Principal imports

	$bn cif
Industrial supplies	294.8
Capital equipment	191.9
Food & direct consumer goods	62.0
Consumer durable goods	56.1
Total incl. others	**672.1**

Main export destinations

	% of total
United States	19.3
China	19.0
South Korea	7.6
Taiwan	5.8

Main origins of imports

	% of total
China	24.5
United States	11.0
Australia	5.8
South Korea	4.2

Balance of payments, reserves and aid, $bn

Visible exports fob	688.7	Overall balance	23.6
Visible imports fob	-644.8	Change in reserves	47.5
Trade balance	43.8	Level of reserves	
Invisibles inflows	465.7	end Dec.	1,264.0
Invisibles outflows	-289.0	No. months of import cover	16.2
Net transfers	-18.9	Official gold holdings, m oz	24.6
Current account balance	201.6	Aid given	11.5
– as % of GDP	4.1	– as % of GNI	0.2
Capital balance	-145.1		

Health and education

Health spending, % of GDP	10.9	Education spending, % of GDP	3.5
Doctors per 1,000 pop.	2.4	Enrolment, %: primary	98
Hospital beds per 1,000 pop.	13.2	secondary	102
At least basic drinking water,		tertiary	64
% of pop.	100		

Society

No. of households, m	53.4	Cost of living, Dec. 2018	
Av. no. per household	2.4	New York = 100	96
Marriages per 1,000 pop.	4.0	Cars per 1,000 pop.	478
Divorces per 1,000 pop.	1.7	Telephone lines per 100 pop.	50.2
Religion, % of pop.		Mobile telephone subscribers	
Non-religious	57.0	per 100 pop.	135.5
Buddhist	36.2	Internet access, %	90.9
Other	5.0	Broadband subs per 100 pop.	31.8
Christian	1.6	Broadband speed, Mbps	24.5
Muslim	0.2		
Jewish	<0.1		

KENYA

Area, sq km	591,958	Capital	Nairobi
Arable as % of total land	9.7	Currency	Kenyan shilling (KSh)

People

Population, m	49.7	Life expectancy: men	66.2 yrs
Pop. per sq km	84.0	women	70.7 yrs
Total change in population		Adult literacy	78.7
2010–20, %	29.4	Fertility rate (per woman)	3.8
Pop. aged 0–19, %	50.1	Urban population, %	26.1
Pop. aged 65 and over, %	2.9		per 1,000 pop.
No. of men per 100 women	98.8	Crude birth rate	30.7
Human Development Index	59.0	Crude death rate	5.4

The economy

GDP	$79bn	GDP per head	$1,857
GDP	KSh8,199bn	GDP per head in purchasing	
Av. ann. growth in real		power parity (USA=100)	5.9
GDP 2012–17	5.5%	Economic freedom index	55.1

Origins of GDP		**Components of GDP**	
	% of total		% of total
Agriculture	35	Private consumption	81
Industry, of which:	17	Public consumption	14
manufacturing	8	Investment	18
Services	48	Exports	13
		Imports	-24

Structure of employment

	% of total		% of labour force
Agriculture	57.5	Unemployed 2018	9.3
Industry	7.6	Av. ann. rate 2010–18	9.6
Services	35.0		

Energy

	m TOE		
Total output	1.8	Net energy imports as %	
Total consumption	8.0	of energy use	17
Consumption per head			
kg oil equivalent	513		

Inflation and finance

Consumer price		% change 2017–18	
inflation 2018	4.7%	Narrow money (M1)	19.0
Av. ann. inflation 2013–18	6.5%	Broad money	10.9
Deposit rate, Aug. 2018	8.28%		

Exchange rates

	end 2018		December 2018
KSh per $	101.85	Effective rates	2010 = 100
KSh per SDR	141.65	– nominal	...
KSh per €	117.07	– real	...

Trade

Principal exports

	$bn fob
Tea	1.4
Horticultural products	0.8
Coffee	0.2
Total incl. others	**5.8**

Principal imports

	$bn cif
Industrial supplies	5.3
Machinery & other capital equip.	3.2
Transport equipment	1.5
Food & beverages	1.2
Total incl. others	**16.2**

Main export destinations

	% of total
Pakistan	10.8
Uganda	10.4
United States	8.0
Netherlands	7.4

Main origins of imports

	% of total
China	22.6
India	9.9
United Arab Emirates	8.0
Saudi Arabia	6.6

Balance of payments, reserves and debt, $bn

Visible exports fob	5.8	Change in reserves	-0.2
Visible imports fob	-16.0	Level of reserves	
Trade balance	-10.2	end Dec.	7.4
Invisibles Inflows	5.0	No. months of import cover	4.3
Invisibles outflows	-4.3	Official gold holdings, m oz	0.0
Net transfers	4.4	Foreign debt	26.4
Current account balance	-5.0	– as % of GDP	33.3
– as % of GDP	-6.3	– as % of total exports	206.5
Capital balance	4.8	Debt service ratio	12.1
Overall balance	-0.1		

Health and education

Health spending, % of GDP	4.5	Education spending, % of GDP	5.2
Doctors per 1,000 pop.	0.2	Enrolment, %: primary	105
Hospital beds per 1,000 pop.	1.4	secondary	...
At least basic drinking water,		tertiary	12
% of pop.	58.5		

Society

No. of households, m	11.0	Cost of living, Dec. 2018	
Av. no. per household	4.5	New York = 100	69
Marriages per 1,000 pop.	...	Cars per 1,000 pop.	17
Divorces per 1,000 pop.	...	Telephone lines per 100 pop.	0.1
Religion, % of pop.		Mobile telephone subscribers	
Christian	84.8	per 100 pop.	86.2
Muslim	9.7	Internet access, %	17.8
Other	3.0	Broadband subs per 100 pop.	0.6
Non-religious	2.5	Broadband speed, Mbps	8.8
Hindu	0.1		
Jewish	<0.1		

MALAYSIA

Area, sq km	330,396	Capital	Kuala Lumpur
Arable as % of total land	5.5	Currency	Malaysian dollar/ringgit (M$)

People

Population, m	31.6	Life expectancy: men	74.2 yrs
Pop. per sq km	95.6	women	78.7 yrs
Total change in population		Adult literacy	94.6
2010–20, %	16.9	Fertility rate (per woman)	2.0
Pop. aged 0–19, %	31.6	Urban population, %	74.8
Pop. aged 65 and over, %	7.0		per 1,000 pop.
No. of men per 100 women	106.1	Crude birth rate	17.0
Human Development Index	80.2	Crude death rate	5.4

The economy

GDP	$315bn	GDP per head	$10,942
GDP	M$1,354bn	GDP per head in purchasing	
Av. ann. growth in real		power parity (USA=100)	49.3
GDP 2012–17	5.2%	Economic freedom index	74.0

Origins of GDP		**Components of GDP**	
	% of total		% of total
Agriculture	9	Private consumption	55
Industry, of which:	39	Public consumption	12
manufacturing	22	Investment	26
Services	52	Exports	71
		Imports	-64

Structure of employment

	% of total		% of labour force
Agriculture	11.1	Unemployed 2018	3.4
Industry	27.3	Av. ann. rate 2010–18	3.2
Services	61.6		

Energy

	m TOE		
Total output	102.3	Net energy imports as %	
Total consumption	83.4	of energy use	-6
Consumption per head			
kg oil equivalent	2,968		

Inflation and finance

Consumer price			% change 2017–18
inflation 2018	1.0%	Narrow money (M1)	5.5
Av. ann. inflation 2013–18	2.4%	Broad money	6.3
Deposit rate, Dec. 2018	3.15%		

Exchange rates

	end 2018		December 2018
M$ per $	4.14	Effective rates	2010 = 100
M$ per SDR	5.76	– nominal	86.5
M$ per €	4.76	– real	87.8

Trade

Principal exports

	$bn fob
Machinery & transport equip.	93.1
Mineral fuels	33.2
Manufactured goods	19.3
Chemicals	17.5
Total incl. others	**217.8**

Principal imports

	$bn cif
Machinery & transport equip.	87.1
Mineral fuels	24.9
Manufactured goods	22.8
Chemicals	20.0
Total incl. others	**195.1**

Main export destinations

	% of total
Singapore	14.4
China	13.5
United States	9.5
Japan	8.0

Main origins of imports

	% of total
China	19.6
Singapore	11.1
United States	8.3
Japan	7.6

Balance of payments, reserves and debt, $bn

Visible exports fob	187.9	Change in reserves	8.0
Visible imports fob	-160.7	Level of reserves	
Trade balance	27.2	end Dec.	102.4
Invisibles inflows	49.5	No. months of import cover	5.5
Invisibles outflows	-63.3	Official gold holdings, m oz	1.2
Net transfers	-4.0	Foreign debt	215.9
Current account balance	9.4	– as % of GDP	68.6
– as % of GDP	3.0	– as % of total exports	90.3
Capital balance	1.0	Debt service ratio	4.8
Overall balance	3.9		

Health and education

Health spending, % of GDP	3.8	Education spending, % of GDP	4.7
Doctors per 1,000 pop.	1.5	Enrolment, %: primary	103
Hospital beds per 1,000 pop.	1.9	secondary	86
At least basic drinking water,		tertiary	42
% of pop.	96.4		

Society

No. of households, m	7.7	Cost of living, Dec. 2018	
Av. no. per household	4.1	New York = 100	59
Marriages per 1,000 pop.	...	Cars per 1,000 pop.	386
Divorces per 1,000 pop.	...	Telephone lines per 100 pop.	20.8
Religion, % of pop.		Mobile telephone subscribers	
Muslim	63.7	per 100 pop.	133.9
Buddhist	17.7	Internet access, %	80.1
Christian	9.4	Broadband subs per 100 pop.	8.5
Hindu	6.0	Broadband speed, Mbps	6.7
Other	2.5		
Non-religious	0.7		

MEXICO

Area, sq km	1,964,375	Capital	Mexico City
Arable as % of total land	13.1	Currency	Mexican peso (PS)

People

Population, m	129.2	Life expectancy: men	76.0 yrs
Pop. per sq km	65.8	women	80.6 yrs
Total change in population		Adult literacy	94.9
2010–20, %	14.1	Fertility rate (per woman)	2.1
Pop. aged 0–19, %	34.1	Urban population, %	79.6
Pop. aged 65 and over, %	7.5		per 1,000 pop.
No. of men per 100 women	99.2	Crude birth rate	17.6
Human Development Index	77.4	Crude death rate	5.1

The economy

GDP	$1,151bn	GDP per head	$9,807
GDP	PS21,921bn	GDP per head in purchasing	
Av. ann. growth in real		power parity (USA=100)	32.9
GDP 2012–17	2.5%	Economic freedom index	64.7

Origins of GDP

Components of GDP

	% of total		% of total
Agriculture	3	Private consumption	66
Industry, of which:	30	Public consumption	12
manufacturing	17	Investment	23
Services	67	Exports	38
		Imports	-40

Structure of employment

	% of total		% of labour force
Agriculture	13.0	Unemployed 2018	3.3
Industry	26.0	Av. ann. rate 2010–18	4.4
Services	61.1		

Energy

	m TOE		
Total output	185.1	Net energy imports as %	
Total consumption	200.3	of energy use	-5
Consumption per head			
kg oil equivalent	1,488		

Inflation and finance

		% change 2017–18	
Consumer price			
inflation 2018	4.9%	Narrow money (M1)	8.3
Av. ann. inflation 2013–18	4.1%	Broad money	5.4
Deposit rate, Dec. 2018	3.60%		

Exchange rates

	end 2018		December 2018
PS per $	19.68	Effective rates	2010 = 100
PS per SDR	27.37	– nominal	67.5
PS per €	22.62	– real	79.8

Trade

Principal exports		Principal imports	
	$bn fob		*$bn cif*
Manufactured goods	364.4	Intermediate goods	322.0
Crude oil & products	23.3	Consumer goods	57.3
Agricultural products	15.8	Capital goods	41.0
Mining products	5.4		
Total	**409.4**	Total	**420.4**

Main export destinations		Main origins of imports	
	% of total		*% of total*
United States	79.8	United States	49.1
Canada	2.8	China	18.7
Germany	1.7	Japan	4.6
China	1.6	Germany	4.1

Balance of payments, reserves and debt, $bn

Visible exports fob	409.8	Change in reserves	-2.5
Visible imports fob	-420.8	Level of reserves	
Trade balance	-11.0	end Dec.	175.4
Invisibles inflows	38.3	No. months of import cover	4.2
Invisibles outflows	-76.4	Official gold holdings, m oz	3.9
Net transfers	29.7	Foreign debt	455.1
Current account balance	-19.4	– as % of GDP	39.3
– as % of GDP	-1.7	– as % of total exports	95.4
Capital balance	24.4	Debt service ratio	13.2
Overall balance	-4.8		

Health and education

Health spending, % of GDP	5.5	Education spending, % of GDP	5.2
Doctors per 1,000 pop.	2.2	Enrolment, %: primary	104
Hospital beds per 1,000 pop.	1.5	secondary	97
At least basic drinking water,		tertiary	37
% of pop.	93.5		

Society

No. of households, m	33.8	Cost of living, Dec. 2018	
Av. no. per household	3.8	New York = 100	72
Marriages per 1,000 pop.	4.4	Cars per 1,000 pop.	211
Divorces per 1,000 pop.	1.1	Telephone lines per 100 pop.	16.1
Religion, % of pop.		Mobile telephone subscribers	
Christian	95.1	per 100 pop.	88.5
Non-religious	4.7	Internet access, %	63.9
Hindu	<0.1	Broadband subs per 100 pop.	13.3
Jewish	<0.1	Broadband speed, Mbps	7.6
Muslim	<0.1		
Other	<0.1		

MOROCCO

Area, sq km	447,400	Capital	Rabat
Arable as % of total land	17.8	Currency	Dirham (Dh)

People

Population, m	35.7	Life expectancy: men	76.1 yrs
Pop. per sq km	79.8	women	78.5 yrs
Total change in population		Adult literacy	69.4
2010–20, %	14.4	Fertility rate (per woman)	2.4
Pop. aged 0–19, %	34.8	Urban population, %	61.4
Pop. aged 65 and over, %	7.6		per 1,000 pop.
No. of men per 100 women	98.3	Crude birth rate	19.2
Human Development Index	66.7	Crude death rate	5.2

The economy

GDP	$110bn	GDP per head	$3,359
GDP	Dh1,063bn	GDP per head in purchasing	
Av. ann. growth in real		power parity (USA=100)	14.3
GDP 2012–17	3.4%	Economic freedom index	62.9

Origins of GDP		Components of GDP	
	% of total		% of total
Agriculture	12	Private consumption	58
Industry, of which:	26	Public consumption	19
manufacturing	16	Investment	33
Services	62	Exports	37
		Imports	-47

Structure of employment

	% of total		% of labour force
Agriculture	38.1	Unemployed 2018	9.0
Industry	21.6	Av. ann. rate 2010–18	9.2
Services	40.3		

Energy

	m TOE		
Total output	1.2	Net energy imports as %	
Total consumption	19.7	of energy use	91
Consumption per head			
kg oil equivalent	553		

Inflation and finance

Consumer price			% change 2017–18
inflation 2018	1.9%	Narrow money (M1)	7.2
Av. ann. inflation 2013–18	1.3%	Broad money	3.7
Deposit rate, Dec. 2018	3.04%		

Exchange rates

	end 2018		December 2018
Dh per $	9.57	Effective rates	2010 = 100
Dh per SDR	13.30	– nominal	109.0
Dh per €	11.00	– real	100.4

Trade

Principal exports		**Principal imports**	
	$bn fob		*$bn cif*
Electric cables & wires	2.7	Capital goods	11.2
Fertilisers & chemicals	2.6	Consumer goods	10.3
Phosphoric acid	2.4	Semi-finished goods	9.9
Finished clothes	1.1	Fuel & lubricants	7.2
Total incl. others	**25.6**	Total incl. others	**45.1**

Main export destinations		**Main origins of imports**	
	% of total		*% of total*
Spain	23.2	Spain	16.6
France	22.6	France	12.2
Italy	4.5	China	9.2
United States	4.1	United States	6.9

Balance of payments, reserves and debt, $bn

Visible exports fob	21.5	Change in reserves	1.1
Visible imports fob	-39.6	Level of reserves	
Trade balance	-18.1	end Dec.	26.2
Invisibles inflows	18.2	No. months of import cover	6.0
Invisibles outflows	-12.6	Official gold holdings, m oz	0.7
Net transfers	8.8	Foreign debt	49.8
Current account balance	-3.7	– as % of GDP	45.3
– as % of GDP	-3.4	– as % of total exports	107.0
Capital balance	2.1	Debt service ratio	8.4
Overall balance	-0.8		

Health and education

Health spending, % of GDP	5.8	Education spending, % of GDP	...
Doctors per 1,000 pop.	0.6	Enrolment, %: primary	112
Hospital beds per 1,000 pop.	1.1	secondary	79.7
At least basic drinking water,		tertiary	33.8
% of pop.	99.7		

Society

No. of households, m	7.9	Cost of living, Dec. 2018	
Av. no. per household	4.5	New York = 100	57
Marriages per 1,000 pop.	...	Cars per 1,000 pop.	72
Divorces per 1,000 pop.	...	Telephone lines per 100 pop.	5.7
Religion, % of pop.		Mobile telephone subscribers	
Muslim	99.9	per 100 pop.	122.9
Christian	<0.1	Internet access, %	61.8
Hindu	<0.1	Broadband subs per 100 pop.	3.9
Jewish	<0.1	Broadband speed, Mbps	4.4
Non-religious	<0.1		
Other	<0.1		

NETHERLANDS

Area, sq km[a]	37,354	Capital	Amsterdam
Arable as % of total land	30.9	Currency	Euro (€)

People

Population, m	17.0	Life expectancy: men	81.3 yrs
Pop. per sq km	455.1	women	84.4 yrs
Total change in population		Adult literacy	...
2010–20, %	3.0	Fertility rate (per woman)	1.8
Pop. aged 0–19, %	21.8	Urban population, %	90.6
Pop. aged 65 and over, %	20.0		per 1,000 pop.
No. of men per 100 women	99.3	Crude birth rate	10.6
Human Development Index	93.1	Crude death rate	9.1

The economy

GDP	$831bn	GDP per head	$53,106
GDP	€737bn	GDP per head in purchasing	
Av. ann. growth in real		power parity (USA=100)	90.1
GDP 2012–17	1.8%	Economic freedom index	76.8

Origins of GDP		**Components of GDP**	
	% of total		% of total
Agriculture	2	Private consumption	44
Industry, of which:	17	Public consumption	24
manufacturing	11	Investment	21
Services	81	Exports	83
		Imports	-72

Structure of employment

	% of total		% of labour force
Agriculture	2.2	Unemployed 2018	3.9
Industry	16.6	Av. ann. rate 2010–18	5.7
Services	81.4		

Energy

	m TOE		
Total output	49.2	Net energy imports as %	
Total consumption	100.2	of energy use	34
Consumption per head			
kg oil equivalent	4,233		

Inflation and finance

Consumer price			% change 2017–18
inflation 2018	1.6%	Narrow money (M1)	0.7
Av. ann. inflation 2013–18	0.7%	Broad money	4.2
Deposit rate, Dec. 2018	1.13%		

Exchange rates

	end 2018		December 2018
€ per $	0.87	Effective rates	2010 = 100
€ per SDR	1.21	– nominal	102.1
		– real	99.5

Trade

Principal exports		**Principal imports**	
	$bn fob		*$bn cif*
Machinery & transport equip.	213.3	Machinery & transport equip.	196.8
Chemicals & related products	105.9	Mineral fuels & lubricants	88.1
Mineral fuels & lubricants	82.7	Chemicals & related products	73.7
Food, drink & tobacco	82.0	Food, drink & tobacco	55.2
Total incl. others	**528.1**	Total incl. others	**462.1**

Main export destinations		**Main origins of imports**	
	% of total		*% of total*
Germany	24.1	China	16.5
Belgium	10.9	Germany	15.2
United Kingdom	8.9	Belgium	8.4
France	8.8	United States	6.9
EU28	75.3	EU28	46.0

Balance of payments, reserves and aid, $bn

Visible exports fob	521.9	Overall balance	-1.9
Visible imports fob	-441.8	Change in reserves	2.4
Trade balance	80.0	Level of reserves	
Invisibles inflows	444.7	end Dec.	38.3
Invisibles outflows	-431.8	No. months of import cover	0.5
Net transfers	-5.5	Official gold holdings, m oz	19.7
Current account balance	87.4	Aid given	5.0
– as % of GDP	10.5	– as % of GNI	0.6
Capital balance	-87.5		

Health and education

Health spending, % of GDP	10.4	Education spending, % of GDP	5.4
Doctors per 1,000 pop.	3.5	Enrolment, %: primary	103
Hospital beds per 1,000 pop.	...	secondary	133
At least basic drinking water,		tertiary	80
% of pop.	100		

Society

No. of households, m	7.8	Cost of living, Dec. 2018	
Av. no. per household	2.2	New York = 100	78
Marriages per 1,000 pop.	3.8	Cars per 1,000 pop.	490
Divorces per 1,000 pop.	1.9	Telephone lines per 100 pop.	38.5
Religion, % of pop.		Mobile telephone subscribers	
Christian	50.6	per 100 pop.	120.5
Non-religious	42.1	Internet access, %	93.2
Muslim	6.0	Broadband subs per 100 pop.	42.3
Other	0.6	Broadband speed, Mbps	33.5
Hindu	0.5		
Jewish	0.2		

a Includes water.

NEW ZEALAND

Area, sq km	268,107	Capital	Wellington
Arable as % of total land	1.8	Currency	New Zealand dollar (NZ$)

People

Population, m	4.7	Life expectancy: men	81.4 yrs
Pop. per sq km	17.5	women	84.4 yrs
Total change in population		Adult literacy	...
2010–20, %	10.6	Fertility rate (per woman)	2.0
Pop. aged 0–19, %	25.9	Urban population, %	86.4
Pop. aged 65 and over, %	16.3		per 1,000 pop.
No. of men per 100 women	96.7	Crude birth rate	13.1
Human Development Index	91.7	Crude death rate	7.2

The economy

GDP	$204bn	GDP per head	$41,267
GDP	NZ$282bn	GDP per head in purchasing	
Av. ann. growth in real		power parity (USA=100)	64.1
GDP 2012–17	3.3%	Economic freedom index	84.4

Origins of GDP		**Components of GDP**	
	% of total		% of total
Agriculture	5	Private consumption	57
Industry, of which:	20	Public consumption	18
manufacturing	11	Investment	24
Services	75	Exports	27
		Imports	-26

Structure of employment

	% of total		% of labour force
Agriculture	6.2	Unemployed 2018	4.5
Industry	20.4	Av. ann. rate 2010–18	5.7
Services	73.4		

Energy

	m TOE		
Total output	16.7	Net energy imports as %	
Total consumption	22.6	of energy use	19
Consumption per head			
kg oil equivalent	4,445		

Inflation and finance

Consumer price			% change 2017–18
inflation 2018	1.6%	Narrow money (M1)	-2.8
Av. ann. inflation 2013–18	1.1%	Broad money	6.4
Deposit rate, Dec. 2018	3.26%		

Exchange rates

	end 2018		December 2018
NZ$ per $	1.49	Effective rates	2010 = 100
NZ$ per SDR	2.07	– nominal	108.5
NZ$ per €	1.71	– real	104.8

Trade

Principal exports		Principal imports	
	$bn fob		*$bn cif*
Dairy produce	9.9	Machinery & electrical equip.	9.1
Meat	4.7	Transport equipment	7.2
Forestry products	3.3	Mineral fuels	3.8
Fruit	1.9	Textiles	1.8
Total incl. others	**38.1**	**Total incl. others**	**40.2**

Main export destinations		Main origins of imports	
	% of total		*% of total*
China	22.4	China	19.3
Australia	16.5	Australia	12.3
United States	10.0	United States	10.7
Japan	6.1	Japan	7.4

Balance of payments, reserves and aid, $bn

Visible exports fob	38.2	Overall balance	1.9
Visible imports fob	-39.7	Change in reserves	2.9
Trade balance	-1.6	Level of reserves	
Invisibles inflows	22.7	end Dec.	20.7
Invisibles outflows	-26.6	No. months of import cover	3.7
Net transfers	-0.3	Official gold holdings, m oz	0.0
Current account balance	-5.9	Aid given	0.4
– as % of GDP	-2.9	– as % of GNI	0.2
Capital balance	5.8		

Health and education

Health spending, % of GDP	9.2	Education spending, % of GDP	6.3
Doctors per 1,000 pop.	3.1	Enrolment, %: primary	99
Hospital beds per 1,000 pop.	2.8	secondary	114
At least basic drinking water,		tertiary	82
% of pop.	100		

Society

No. of households, m	1.7	Cost of living, Dec. 2018	
Av. no. per household	2.8	New York = 100	78
Marriages per 1,000 pop.	4.3	Cars per 1,000 pop.	655
Divorces per 1,000 pop.	1.7	Telephone lines per 100 pop.	38.0
Religion, % of pop.		Mobile telephone subscribers	
Christian	57.0	per 100 pop.	136.0
Non-religious	36.6	Internet access, %	90.8
Other	2.8	Broadband subs per 100 pop.	33.6
Hindu	2.1	Broadband speed, Mbps	16.9
Muslim	1.2		
Jewish	0.2		

NIGERIA

Area, sq km	923,768	Capital	Abuja
Arable as % of total land	39.5	Currency	Naira (N)

People

Population, m	190.9	Life expectancy: men	55.4 yrs
Pop. per sq km	206.7	women	57.3 yrs
Total change in population		Adult literacy	59.6
2010–20, %	30.0	Fertility rate (per woman)	5.4
Pop. aged 0–19, %	54.1	Urban population, %	48.7
Pop. aged 65 and over, %	2.7		per 1,000 pop.
No. of men per 100 women	102.9	Crude birth rate	38.1
Human Development Index	53.2	Crude death rate	10.7

The economy

GDP	$376bn	GDP per head	$2,049
GDP	N114,899bn	GDP per head in purchasing	
Av. ann. growth in real		power parity (USA=100)	9.6
GDP 2012–17	2.9%	Economic freedom index	57.3

Origins of GDP		**Components of GDP**	
	% of total		% of total
Agriculture	21	Private consumption	80
Industry, of which:	22	Public consumption	5
manufacturing	9	Investment	15
Services	57	Exports	13
		Imports	-13

Structure of employment

	% of total		% of labour force
Agriculture	36.6	Unemployed 2018	6.0
Industry	11.6	Av. ann. rate 2010–18	4.8
Services	51.8		

Energy

	m TOE		
Total output	143.8	Net energy imports as %	
Total consumption	40.1	of energy use	-93
Consumption per head			
kg oil equivalent	763		

Inflation and finance

			% change 2017–18
Consumer price			
inflation 2018	12.1%	Narrow money (M1)	5.2
Av. ann. inflation 2013–18	12.2%	Broad money	12.2
Deposit rate, Dec. 2018	9.50%		

Exchange rates

	end 2018		December 2018
N per $	307.00	Effective rates	2010 = 100
N per SDR	426.97	– nominal	57.5
N per €	352.87	– real	117.8

Trade

Principal exports

	$bn fob
Crude oil	36.1
Gas	6.3
Food, drink & tobacco	0.5
Vegetable products	0.3
Total incl. others	**44.5**

Principal imports

	$bn cif
Mineral fuels	8.7
Machinery & transport equip.	8.0
Food & live animals	4.6
Chemicals	4.5
Total incl. others	**31.3**

Main export destinations

	% of total
India	32.5
United States	13.1
Spain	7.1
China	6.1

Main origins of imports

	% of total
China	21.5
Belgium	8.9
United States	8.5
South Korea	7.7

Balance of payments, reserves and debt, $bn

Visible exports fob	45.7	Change in reserves	12.5
Visible imports fob	-32.6	Level of reserves	
Trade balance	13.1	end Dec.	40.5
Invisibles inflows	6.6	No. months of import cover	7.6
Invisibles outflows	-31.3	Official gold holdings, m oz	0.7
Net transfers	22.0	Foreign debt	40.2
Current account balance	10.4	– as % of GDP	10.7
– as % of GDP	2.8	– as % of total exports	54.1
Capital balance	7.9	Debt service ratio	4.8
Overall balance	12.2		

Health and education

Health spending, % of GDP	3.6	Education spending, % of GDP	...
Doctors per 1,000 pop.	0.4	Enrolment, %: primary	85
Hospital beds per 1,000 pop.	...	secondary	42
At least basic drinking water,		tertiary	...
% of pop.	68.5		

Society

No. of households, m	40.6	Cost of living, Dec. 2018	
Av. no. per household	4.7	New York = 100	40
Marriages per 1,000 pop.	...	Cars per 1,000 pop.	16
Divorces per 1,000 pop.	...	Telephone lines per 100 pop.	0.1
Religion, % of pop.		Mobile telephone subscribers	
Christian	49.3	per 100 pop.	75.9
Muslim	48.8	Internet access, %	27.7
Other	1.4	Broadband subs per 100 pop.	0.1
Non-religious	0.4	Broadband speed, Mbps	3.2
Hindu	<0.1		
Jewish	<0.1		

NORWAY

Area, sq km	323,787	Capital	Oslo
Arable as % of total land	2.7	Currency	Norwegian krone (Nkr)

People

Population, m	5.3	Life expectancy: men	81.6 yrs
Pop. per sq km	16.4	women	84.9 yrs
Total change in population		Adult literacy	...
2010–20, %	11.5	Fertility rate (per woman)	1.8
Pop. aged 0–19, %	23.5	Urban population, %	81.5
Pop. aged 65 and over, %	17.5		per 1,000 pop.
No. of men per 100 women	102.4	Crude birth rate	12.0
Human Development Index	95.3	Crude death rate	7.7

The economy

GDP	$399bn	GDP per head	$81,695
GDP	Nkr3,304bn	GDP per head in purchasing	
Av. ann. growth in real		power parity (USA=100)	118.8
GDP 2012–17	1.6%	Economic freedom index	73.0

Origins of GDP		**Components of GDP**	
	% of total		% of total
Agriculture	2	Private consumption	45
Industry, of which:	29	Public consumption	24
manufacturing	6	Investment	28
Services	69	Exports	36
		Imports	-33

Structure of employment

	% of total		% of labour force
Agriculture	2.0	Unemployed 2018	3.9
Industry	19.2	Av. ann. rate 2010–18	3.8
Services	78.7		

Energy

	m TOE		
Total output	243.2	Net energy imports as %	
Total consumption	49.1	of energy use	-581
Consumption per head			
kg oil equivalent	5,818		

Inflation and finance

			% change 2017–18
Consumer price			
inflation 2018	1.8%	Narrow money (M1)	7.8
Av. ann. inflation 2013–18	2.5%	Broad money	5.3
Central bank policy rate, Dec. 2018	0.75%		

Exchange rates

	end 2018		December 2018
Nkr per $	8.69	Effective rates	2010 = 100
Nkr per SDR	12.09	– nominal	82.5
Nkr per €	9.99	– real	85.0

Trade

Principal exports		Principal imports	
	$bn fob		*$bn cif*
Mineral fuels & lubricants	60.5	Machinery & transport equip.	32.2
Food & beverages	11.9	Manufactured goods	14.3
Machinery & transport equip.	9.9	Miscellaneous manufactured	
Manufactured goods	9.8	goods	12.1
		Chemicals & mineral products	8.4
Total incl. others	**104.1**	Total incl. others	**82.9**

Main export destinations		Main origins of imports	
	% of total		*% of total*
United Kingdom	21.0	Sweden	11.4
Germany	14.7	Germany	11.2
Netherlands	9.6	China	9.6
Sweden	6.6	United States	6.7
EU28	80.9	EU28	61.4

Balance of payments, reserves and aid, $bn

Visible exports fob	103.4	Overall balance	-0.1
Visible imports fob	-81.7	Change in reserves	5.5
Trade balance	21.7	Level of reserves	
Invisibles inflows	83.6	end Dec.	65.9
Invisibles outflows	-76.3	No. months of import cover	5.0
Net transfers	-6.7	Official gold holdings, m oz	0.0
Current account balance	22.4	Aid given	4.1
– as % of GDP	5.6	– as % of GNI	1.0
Capital balance	-10.7		

Health and education

Health spending, % of GDP	10.5	Education spending, % of GDP	7.6
Doctors per 1,000 pop.	4.4	Enrolment, %: primary	100
Hospital beds per 1,000 pop.	3.9	secondary	116
At least basic drinking water,		tertiary	81
% of pop.	100		

Society

No. of households, m	2.4	Cost of living, Dec. 2018	
Av. no. per household	2.2	New York = 100	98
Marriages per 1,000 pop.	4.3	Cars per 1,000 pop.	489
Divorces per 1,000 pop.	1.9	Telephone lines per 100 pop.	12.8
Religion, % of pop.		Mobile telephone subscribers	
Christian	84.7	per 100 pop.	107.9
Non-religious	10.1	Internet access, %	96.5
Muslim	3.7	Broadband subs per 100 pop.	40.6
Other	0.9	Broadband speed, Mbps	29.1
Hindu	0.5		
Jewish	<0.1		

PAKISTAN

Area, sq km	796,095	Capital	Islamabad
Arable as % of total land	26.9	Currency	Pakistan rupee (PRs)

People

Population, m	197.0	Life expectancy: men	66.3 yrs
Pop. per sq km	247.5	women	68.7 yrs
Total change in population		Adult literacy	57.0
2010–20, %	22.2	Fertility rate (per woman)	3.4
Pop. aged 0–19, %	43.6	Urban population, %	36.2
Pop. aged 65 and over, %	4.5		per 1,000 pop.
No. of men per 100 women	105.6	Crude birth rate	27.4
Human Development Index	56.2	Crude death rate	7.0

The economy

GDP	$305bn	GDP per head	$1,555
GDP	PRs31,962bn	GDP per head in purchasing	
Av. ann. growth in real		power parity (USA=100)	9.1
GDP 2012–17	5.0%	Economic freedom index	55.0

Origins of GDP		Components of GDP	
	% of total		% of total
Agriculture	23	Private consumption	82
Industry, of which:	18	Public consumption	11
manufacturing	12	Investment	16
Services	59	Exports	8
		Imports	-18

Structure of employment

	% of total		% of labour force
Agriculture	41.7	Unemployed 2018	3.0
Industry	23.6	Av. ann. rate 2010–18	2.3
Services	34.7		

Energy

	m TOE		
Total output	46.9	Net energy imports as %	
Total consumption	78.6	of energy use	24
Consumption per head			
kg oil equivalent	484		

Inflation and finance

			% change 2017–18
Consumer price			
inflation 2018	3.9%	Narrow money (M1)	15.7
Av. ann. inflation 2013–18	4.8%	Broad money	9.0
Deposit rate, Dec. 2018	7.16%		

Exchange rates

	end 2018		December 2018
PRs per $	138.79	Effective rates	2010 = 100
PRs per SDR	193.03	– nominal	71.4
PRs per €	159.53	– real	99.1

Trade

Principal exports	$bn fob	Principal imports	$bn cif
Cotton fabrics	2.3	Petroleum products	7.7
Knitwear	2.0	Crude oil	3.8
Rice	1.6	Palm oil	2.1
Cotton yard & thread	1.1	Telecoms equipment	1.4
Total incl. others	**21.5**	**Total incl. others**	**57.3**

Main export destinations	% of total	Main origins of imports	% of total
United States	16.5	China	26.8
United Kingdom	7.6	United Arab Emirates	13.1
China	6.8	Saudi Arabia	4.8
Afghanistan	6.5	United States	4.8

Balance of payments, reserves and debt, $bn

Visible exports fob	23.2	Change in reserves	-3.6
Visible imports fob	-53.3	Level of reserves	
Trade balance	-30.1	end Dec.	18.4
Invisibles Inflows	6.4	No. months of import cover	3.2
Invisibles outflows	-16.4	Official gold holdings, m oz	2.1
Net transfers	23.8	Foreign debt	84.5
Current account balance	-16.3	– as % of GDP	27.7
– as % of GDP	-5.3	– as % of total exports	171.4
Capital balance	12.7	Debt service ratio	13.7
Overall balance	-4.0		

Health and education

Health spending, % of GDP	2.8	Education spending, % of GDP	2.8
Doctors per 1,000 pop.	1.0	Enrolment, %: primary	96
Hospital beds per 1,000 pop.	0.6	secondary	46
At least basic drinking water,		tertiary	10
% of pop.	93.4		

Society

No. of households, m	29.4	Cost of living, Dec. 2018	
Av. no. per household	6.7	New York = 100	40
Marriages per 1,000 pop.	...	Cars per 1,000 pop.	14
Divorces per 1,000 pop.	...	Telephone lines per 100 pop.	1.5
Religion, % of pop.		Mobile telephone subscribers	
Muslim	96.4	per 100 pop.	73.4
Hindu	1.9	Internet access, %	15.5
Christian	1.6	Broadband subs per 100 pop.	0.9
Jewish	<0.1	Broadband speed, Mbps	0.9
Non-religious	<0.1		
Other	<0.1		

PERU

Area, sq km	1,285,216	Capital	Lima
Arable as % of total land	2.9	Currency	Nuevo Sol (new Sol)

People

Population, m	32.2	Life expectancy: men	73.9 yrs
Pop. per sq km	25.1	women	79.1 yrs
Total change in population		Adult literacy	94.2
2010–20, %	13.4	Fertility rate (per woman)	2.4
Pop. aged 0–19, %	34.9	Urban population, %	77.5
Pop. aged 65 and over, %	7.7		per 1,000 pop.
No. of men per 100 women	99.7	Crude birth rate	18.7
Human Development Index	75.0	Crude death rate	5.8

The economy

GDP	$211bn	GDP per head	$7,002
GDP	New Soles 698bn	GDP per head in purchasing	
Av. ann. growth in real		power parity (USA=100)	22.7
GDP 2012–17	3.6%	Economic freedom index	67.8

Origins of GDP		**Components of GDP**	
	% of total		% of total
Agriculture	7	Private consumption	64
Industry, of which:	30	Public consumption	13
manufacturing	13	Investment	21
Services	63	Exports	24
		Imports	-23

Structure of employment

	% of total		% of labour force
Agriculture	27.5	Unemployed 2018	2.8
Industry	15.6	Av. ann. rate 2010–18	3.2
Services	56.9		

Energy

	m TOE		
Total output	27.7	Net energy imports as %	
Total consumption	27.8	of energy use	-15
Consumption per head			
kg oil equivalent	768		

Inflation and finance

			% change 2017–18
Consumer price			
inflation 2018	1.3%	Narrow money (M1)	7.3
Av. ann. inflation 2013–18	2.9%	Broad money	5.4
Policy rate, Dec. 2018	3.25%		

Exchange rates

	end 2018		December 2018
New Soles per $	3.37	Effective rates	2010 = 100
New Soles per SDR	4.69	– nominal	...
New Soles per €	3.87	– real	...

Trade

Principal exports

	$bn fob
Copper	13.8
Gold	8.2
Zinc	2.4
Fishmeal	1.8
Total incl. others	**45.3**

Principal imports

	$bn cif
Intermediate goods	17.9
Capital goods	11.3
Consumer goods	9.3
Total incl. others	**38.7**

Main export destinations

	% of total
China	25.7
United States	15.3
Switzerland	5.2
South Korea	4.7

Main origins of imports

	% of total
China	24.1
United States	21.7
Brazil	6.5
Mexico	4.8

Balance of payments, reserves and debt, $bn

Visible exports fob	44.9	Change in reserves	2.0
Visible imports fob	-38.3	Level of reserves	
Trade balance	6.7	end Dec.	63.8
Invisibles inflows	8.6	No. months of import cover	12.8
Invisibles outflows	-21.7	Official gold holdings, m oz	1.1
Net transfers	3.7	Foreign debt	68.1
Current account balance	-2.7	– as % of GDP	31.8
– as % of GDP	-1.3	– as % of total exports	120.4
Capital balance	4.3	Debt service ratio	15.1
Overall balance	1.9		

Health and education

Health spending, % of GDP	5.1	Education spending, % of GDP	3.9
Doctors per 1,000 pop.	1.1	Enrolment, %: primary	102
Hospital beds per 1,000 pop.	1.6	secondary	99
At least basic drinking water,		tertiary	70
% of pop.	86.7		

Society

No. of households, m	8.4	Cost of living, Dec. 2018	
Av. no. per household	3.8	New York = 100	66
Marriages per 1,000 pop.	2.5	Cars per 1,000 pop.	47
Divorces per 1,000 pop.	0.5	Telephone lines per 100 pop.	9.6
Religion, % of pop.		Mobile telephone subscribers	
Christian	95.5	per 100 pop.	121.0
Non-religious	3.0	Internet access, %	48.7
Other	1.5	Broadband subs per 100 pop.	7.2
Hindu	<0.1	Broadband speed, Mbps	1.4
Jewish	<0.1		
Muslim	<0.1		

PHILIPPINES

Area, sq km	300,000	Capital	Manila
Arable as % of total land	18.1	Currency	Philippine peso (P)

People

Population, m	104.9	Life expectancy: men	66.6 yrs
Pop. per sq km	349.7	women	73.7 yrs
Total change in population		Adult literacy	96.4
2010–20, %	17.0	Fertility rate (per woman)	2.9
Pop. aged 0–19, %	40.4	Urban population, %	46.5
Pop. aged 65 and over, %	5.2		per 1,000 pop.
No. of men per 100 women	101.0	Crude birth rate	22.9
Human Development Index	69.9	Crude death rate	6.7

The economy

GDP	$314bn	GDP per head	$3,104
GDP	P15,806bn	GDP per head in purchasing	
Av. ann. growth in real		power parity (USA=100)	14.3
GDP 2012–17	6.6%	Economic freedom index	63.8

Origins of GDP

	% of total
Agriculture	10
Industry, of which:	30
manufacturing	19
Services	60

Components of GDP

	% of total
Private consumption	74
Public consumption	11
Investment	25
Exports	31
Imports	-41

Structure of employment

	% of total		% of labour force
Agriculture	25.2	Unemployed 2018	2.5
Industry	18.3	Av. ann. rate 2010–18	3.2
Services	56.5		

Energy

	m TOE		
Total output	16.1	Net energy imports as %	
Total consumption	41.1	of energy use	46
Consumption per head			
kg oil equivalent	476		

Inflation and finance

			% change 2017–18
Consumer price			
inflation 2018	5.2%	Narrow money (M1)	6.4
Av. ann. inflation 2013–18	2.7%	Broad money	9.0
Deposit rate, Dec. 2018	3.23%		

Exchange rates

	end 2018		December 2018
P per $	52.72	Effective rates	2010 = 100
P per SDR	73.33	– nominal	94.6
P per €	60.60	– real	104.3

Trade

Principal exports

	$bn fob
Electrical & electronic equip.	35.8
Machinery & transport equip.	5.2
Mineral products	4.3
Agricultural products	4.0
Total incl. others	**68.7**

Principal imports

	$bn cif
Raw materials & intermediate goods	36.6
Capital goods	30.0
Consumer goods	16.1
Mineral fuels & lubricants	10.6
Total incl. others	**101.9**

Main export destinations

	% of total
Japan	14.9
United States	13.4
Hong Kong	12.6
China	10.2

Main origins of imports

	% of total
China	16.5
Japan	10.4
South Korea	7.9
United States	7.3

Balance of payments, reserves and debt, $bn

Visible exports fob	51.8	Change in reserves	0.7
Visible imports fob	-92.0	Level of reserves	
Trade balance	-40.2	end Dec.	81.4
Invisibles inflows	45.4	No. months of import cover	7.8
Invisibles outflows	-33.5	Official gold holdings, m oz	6.3
Net transfers	26.2	Foreign debt	73.1
Current account balance	-2.1	– as % of GDP	23.3
– as % of GDP	-0.7	– as % of total exports	55.8
Capital balance	2.9	Debt service ratio	8.5
Overall balance	-0.9		

Health and education

Health spending, % of GDP	4.4	Education spending, % of GDP	...
Doctors per 1,000 pop.	...	Enrolment, %: primary	111
Hospital beds per 1,000 pop.	...	secondary	89
At least basic drinking water,		tertiary	35
% of pop.	91.8		

Society

No. of households, m	23.9	Cost of living, Dec. 2018	
Av. no. per household	4.4	New York = 100	57
Marriages per 1,000 pop.	...	Cars per 1,000 pop.	33
Divorces per 1,000 pop.	...	Telephone lines per 100 pop.	3.97
Religion, % of pop.		Mobile telephone subscribers	
Christian	92.6	per 100 pop.	110.4
Muslim	5.5	Internet access, %	60.1
Other	1.7	Broadband subs per 100 pop.	3.2
Non-religious	0.1	Broadband speed, Mbps	3.7
Hindu	<0.1		
Jewish	<0.1		

POLAND

Area, sq km	312,888	Capital	Warsaw
Arable as % of total land	36.5	Currency	Zloty (Zl)

People

Population, m	38.2	Life expectancy: men	74.9 yrs
Pop. per sq km	122.1	women	82.3 yrs
Total change in population		Adult literacy	99.8
2010–20, %	-1.0	Fertility rate (per woman)	1.3
Pop. aged 0–19, %	19.5	Urban population, %	60.2
Pop. aged 65 and over, %	18.6		per 1,000 pop.
No. of men per 100 women	93.3	Crude birth rate	9.1
Human Development Index	86.5	Crude death rate	11.0

The economy

GDP	$526bn	GDP per head	$15,431
GDP	Zl1,989bn	GDP per head in purchasing	
Av. ann. growth in real		power parity (USA=100)	51.0
GDP 2012–17	3.3%	Economic freedom index	67.8

Origins of GDP		Components of GDP	
	% of total		% of total
Agriculture	3	Private consumption	59
Industry, of which:	29	Public consumption	18
manufacturing	18	Investment	20
Services	68	Exports	54
		Imports	-50

Structure of employment

	% of total		% of labour force
Agriculture	10.1	Unemployed 2018	3.7
Industry	31.5	Av. ann. rate 2010–18	7.9
Services	58.4		

Energy

	m TOE		
Total output	66.2	Net energy imports as %	
Total consumption	104.2	of energy use	29
Consumption per head			
kg oil equivalent	2,490		

Inflation and finance

Consumer price		% change 2017–18	
inflation 2018	1.6%	Narrow money (M1)	24.0
Av. ann. inflation 2013–18	0.4%	Broad money	9.2
Central bank policy rate, Dec. 2018 1.50%			

Exchange rates

	end 2018		December 2018
Zl per $	3.76	Effective rates	2010 = 100
Zl per SDR	5.23	– nominal	98.5
Zl per €	4.32	– real	92.4

Trade

Principal exports

	$bn fob
Machinery & transport equip.	84.8
Manufactured goods	42.9
Foodstuffs & live animals	25.0
Total incl. others	**228.2**

Principal imports

	$bn cif
Machinery & transport equip.	79.0
Manufactured goods	40.4
Chemicals & mineral products	33.3
Total incl. others	**227.8**

Main export destinations

	% of total
Germany	28.2
Czech Republic	6.6
United Kingdom	6.6
France	5.7
EU28	80.0

Main origins of imports

	% of total
Germany	28.8
China	8.1
Russia	6.4
Netherlands	6.1
EU28	71.7

Balance of payments, reserves and debt, $bn

Visible exports fob	228.0	Change in reserves	-1.1
Visible imports fob	-226.5	Level of reserves	
Trade balance	1.5	end Dec.	113.2
Invisibles inflows	71.8	No. months of import cover	4.5
Invisibles outflows	-72.6	Official gold holdings, m oz	3.3
Net transfers	-0.1	Foreign debt	242.6
Current account balance	0.6	– as % of GDP	46.1
– as % of GDP	0.1	– as % of total exports	79.5
Capital balance	0.4	Debt service ratio	7.8
Overall balance	-7.8		

Health and education

Health spending, % of GDP	6.5	Education spending, % of GDP	4.8
Doctors per 1,000 pop.	2.3	Enrolment, %: primary	110
Hospital beds per 1,000 pop.	6.5	secondary	107
At least basic drinking water,		tertiary	…
% of pop.	98.3		

Society

No. of households, m	14.5	Cost of living, Dec. 2018	
Av. no. per household	2.6	New York = 100	57
Marriages per 1,000 pop.	5.1	Cars per 1,000 pop.	542
Divorces per 1,000 pop.	1.7	Telephone lines per 100 pop.	19.4
Religion, % of pop.		Mobile telephone subscribers	
Christian	94.3	per 100 pop.	132.2
Non-religious	5.6	Internet access, %	76.0
Hindu	<0.1	Broadband subs per 100 pop.	20.0
Jewish	<0.1	Broadband speed, Mbps	14.9
Muslim	<0.1		
Other	<0.1		

PORTUGAL

Area, sq km	92,225	Capital	Lisbon
Arable as % of total land	12.0	Currency	Euro (€)

People

Population, m	10.3	Life expectancy: men	79.8 yrs
Pop. per sq km	111.7	women	85.0 yrs
Total change in population		Adult literacy	...
2010–20, %	-4.1	Fertility rate (per woman)	1.2
Pop. aged 0–19, %	18.1	Urban population, %	64.1
Pop. aged 65 and over, %	22.7		per 1,000 pop.
No. of men per 100 women	90.0	Crude birth rate	7.5
Human Development Index	84.7	Crude death rate	11.2

The economy

GDP	$219bn	GDP per head	$23,186
GDP	€195bn	GDP per head in purchasing	
Av. ann. growth in real		power parity (USA=100)	51.1
GDP 2012–17	1.2%	Economic freedom index	65.3

Origins of GDP

	% of total
Agriculture	2
Industry, of which:	19
manufacturing	12
Services	79

Components of GDP

	% of total
Private consumption	65
Public consumption	17
Investment	17
Exports	43
Imports	-42

Structure of employment

	% of total		% of labour force
Agriculture	6.3	Unemployed 2018	12.0
Industry	24.6	Av. ann. rate 2010–18	7.8
Services	69.1		

Energy

	m TOE		
Total output	26.7	Net energy imports as %	
Total consumption	34.6	of energy use	77
Consumption per head			
kg oil equivalent	1,592		

Inflation and finance

			% change 2017–18
Consumer price			
inflation 2018	1.2%	Narrow money (M1)	0.7
Av. ann. inflation 2013–18	0.7%	Broad money	4.2
Deposit rate, Dec. 2018	0.17%		

Exchange rates

	end 2018		December 2018
€ per $	0.87	Effective rates	2010 = 100
€ per SDR	1.21	– nominal	103.3
		– real	98.0

Trade

Principal exports		**Principal imports**	
	$bn fob		*$bn cif*
Machinery & transport equip.	16.9	Machinery & transport equip.	24.1
Food, drink & tobacco	6.7	Chemicals & related products	10.4
Chemicals & related products	5.5	Food, drink & tobacco	10.2
Mineral fuels & lubricants	4.6	Mineral fuels & lubricants	9.1
Total incl. others	**62.1**	Total incl. others	**78.5**

Main export destinations		**Main origins of imports**	
	% of total		*% of total*
Spain	25.2	Spain	32.4
France	12.5	Germany	13.7
Germany	11.4	France	7.3
United Kingdom	6.6	Italy	5.4
EU28	80.0	EU28	76.4

Balance of payments, reserves and debt, $bn

Visible exports fob	61.0	Overall balance	10.0
Visible imports fob	-74.7	Change in reserves	1.0
Trade balance	-13.7	Level of reserves	
Invisibles inflows	43.2	end Dec.	26.0
Invisibles outflows	-30.8	No. months of import cover	3.0
Net transfers	2.5	Official gold holdings, m oz	12.3
Current account balance	1.2	Aid given	0.4
– as % of GDP	0.5	– as % of GNI	0.2
Capital balance	8.3		

Health and education

Health spending, % of GDP	9.1	Education spending, % of GDP	4.9
Doctors per 1,000 pop.	4.4	Enrolment, %: primary	105
Hospital beds per 1,000 pop.	3.4	secondary	118
At least basic drinking water,		tertiary	63
% of pop.	100		

Society

No. of households, m	4.1	Cost of living, Dec. 2018	
Av. no. per household	2.5	New York = 100	63
Marriages per 1,000 pop.	3.3	Cars per 1,000 pop.	442
Divorces per 1,000 pop.	2.1	Telephone lines per 100 pop.	46.8
Religion, % of pop.		Mobile telephone subscribers	
Christian	93.8	per 100 pop.	113.9
Non-religious	4.4	Internet access, %	73.8
Other	1.0	Broadband subs per 100 pop.	34.6
Muslim	0.6	Broadband speed, Mbps	21.7
Hindu	0.1		
Jewish	<0.1		

ROMANIA

Area, sq km	238,391	Capital	Bucharest
Arable as % of total land	39.1	Currency	Leu (RON)

People

Population, m	19.7	Life expectancy: men	73.0 yrs
Pop. per sq km	82.5	women	79.7 yrs
Total change in population	-	Adult literacy	...
2010–20, %	-5.1	Fertility rate (per woman)	1.5
Pop. aged 0–19, %	20.5	Urban population, %	53.9
Pop. aged 65 and over, %	19.1		per 1,000 pop.
No. of men per 100 women	93.9	Crude birth rate	9.5
Human Development Index	81.1	Crude death rate	13.3

The economy

GDP	$212bn	GDP per head	$12,285
GDP	RON857bn	GDP per head in purchasing	
Av. ann. growth in real		power parity (USA=100)	42.2
GDP 2012–17	4.6%	Economic freedom index	68.6

Origins of GDP

Components of GDP

	% of total		% of total
Agriculture	4	Private consumption	63
Industry, of which:	30	Public consumption	15
manufacturing	21	Investment	24
Services	66	Exports	41
		Imports	-44

Structure of employment

	% of total		% of labour force
Agriculture	22.6	Unemployed 2018	4.3
Industry	30.1	Av. ann. rate 2010–18	6.3
Services	47.3		

Energy

	m TOE		
Total output	26.7	Net energy imports as %	
Total consumption	34.6	of energy use	17
Consumption per head			
kg oil equivalent	1,593		

Inflation and finance

		% change 2017–18	
Consumer price			
inflation 2018	4.6%	Narrow money (M1)	2.6
Av. ann. inflation 2013–18	1.0%	Broad money	8.9
Deposit rate, Dec. 2018	1.61%		

Exchange rates

	end 2018		December 2018
			2010 = 100
Lei per $	4.07	Effective rates	
Lei per SDR	5.67	– nominal	96.9
Lei per €	4.68	– real	98.1

Trade

Principal exports

	$bn fob
Machinery & transport equip.	32.7
Basic metals & products	6.0
Textiles & apparel	4.6
Minerals, fuels & lubricants	2.7
Total incl. others	**70.8**

Principal imports

	$bn cif
Machinery & transport equip.	31.9
Chemical products	8.4
Minerals, fuels & lubricants	6.1
Textiles & products	5.5
Total incl. others	**85.5**

Main export destinations

	% of total
Germany	22.9
Italy	11.2
France	6.8
Hungary	4.7
EU28	75.8

Main origins of imports

	% of total
Germany	20.0
Italy	10.0
Hungary	7.5
Poland	5.4
EU28	75.8

Balance of payments, reserves and debt, $bn

Visible exports fob	64.6	Change in reserves	4.5
Visible imports fob	-78.4	Level of reserves	
Trade balance	-13.8	end Dec.	44.4
Invisibles inflows	27.0	No. months of import cover	5.3
Invisibles outflows	-22.9	Official gold holdings, m oz	3.3
Net transfers	3.0	Foreign debt	109.4
Current account balance	-6.8	– as % of GDP	51.7
– as % of GDP	-3.2	– as % of total exports	114.0
Capital balance	6.5	Debt service ratio	21.4
Overall balance	0.3		

Health and education

Health spending, % of GDP	5.0	Education spending, % of GDP	3.1
Doctors per 1,000 pop.	2.7	Enrolment, %: primary	89
Hospital beds per 1,000 pop.	6.3	secondary	89
At least basic drinking water,		tertiary	48
% of pop.	96.9		

Society

No. of households, m	7.1	Cost of living, Dec. 2018	
Av. no. per household	2.8	New York = 100	47
Marriages per 1,000 pop.	7.3	Cars per 1,000 pop.	260
Divorces per 1,000 pop.	1.6	Telephone lines per 100 pop.	19.8
Religion, % of pop.		Mobile telephone subscribers	
Christian	99.5	per 100 pop.	113.8
Muslim	0.3	Internet access, %	63.7
Non-religious	0.1	Broadband subs per 100 pop.	24.3
Hindu	<0.1	Broadband speed, Mbps	21.3
Jewish	<0.1		
Other	<0.1		

RUSSIA

Area, sq km	17,098,246	Capital	Moscow
Arable as % of total land	7.4	Currency	Rouble (Rb)

People

Population, m	144.0	Life expectancy: men	66.5 yrs
Pop. per sq km	8.4	women	77.5 yrs
Total change in population		Adult literacy	99.7
2010–20, %	0.4	Fertility rate (per woman)	1.8
Pop. aged 0–19, %	23.1	Urban population, %	74.2
Pop. aged 65 and over, %	15.5		per 1,000 pop.
No. of men per 100 women	86.8	Crude birth rate	12.4
Human Development Index	81.6	Crude death rate	13.7

The economy

GDP	$1,578bn	GDP per head	$11,327
GDP	Rb92,089bn	GDP per head in purchasing	
Av. ann. growth in real		power parity (USA=100)	46.7
GDP 2012–17	0.2%	Economic freedom index	58.9

Origins of GDP

Components of GDP

	% of total		% of total
Agriculture	4	Private consumption	53
Industry, of which:	30	Public consumption	18
manufacturing	12	Investment	24
Services	66	Exports	26
		Imports	-21

Structure of employment

	% of total		% of labour force
Agriculture	5.8	Unemployed 2018	4.7
Industry	26.9	Av. ann. rate 2010–18	5.7
Services	67.2		

Energy

	m TOE		
Total output	1,491.8	Net energy imports as %	
Total consumption	794.0	of energy use	-84
Consumption per head			
kg oil equivalent	4,943		

Inflation and finance

		% change 2017–18	
Consumer price			
inflation 2018	2.9%	Narrow money (M1)	9.3
Av. ann. inflation 2013–18	7.3%	Broad money	10.5
Treasury bill rate, Dec. 2018	7.49%		

Exchange rates

	end 2018		December 2018
Rb per $	69.47	Effective rates	2010 = 100
Rb per SDR	96.62	– nominal	61.9
Rb per €	79.88	– real	82.4

Trade

Principal exports		Principal imports	
	$bn fob		*$bn cif*
Fuels	216.2	Machinery & equipment	110.5
Ores & metals	48.1	Chemicals	40.3
Machinery & equipment	28.3	Food & agricultural products	28.9
Chemicals	24.0	Metals	16.3
Total incl.others	**357.8**	Total incl.others	**226.8**

Main export destinations		Main origins of imports	
	% of total		*% of total*
China	10.9	China	21.2
Netherlands	10.0	Germany	10.6
Belarus	7.1	United States	5.6
Germany	5.1	Belarus	5.0
EU28	44.7	EU28	38.1

Balance of payments, reserves and debt, $bn

Visible exports fob	353.5	Change in reserves	55.4
Visible imports fob	-238.1	Level of reserves	
Trade balance	115.4	end Dec.	432.4
Invisibles inflows	104.2	No. months of import cover	12.5
Invisibles outflows	-177.5	Official gold holdings, m oz	59.1
Net transfers	-9.0	Foreign debt	492.8
Current account balance	33.2	– as % of GDP	31.3
– as % of GDP	2.1	– as % of total exports	105.7
Capital balance	-13.1	Debt service ratio	25.5
Overall balance	22.6		

Health and education

Health spending, % of GDP	5.3	Education spending, % of GDP	3.8
Doctors per 1,000 pop.	4.0	Enrolment, %: primary	102
Hospital beds per 1,000 pop.	8.2	secondary	105
At least basic drinking water,		tertiary	82
% of pop.	76.1		

Society

No. of households, m	57.2	Cost of living, Dec. 2018	
Av. no. per household	2.5	New York = 100	55
Marriages per 1,000 pop.	8.5	Cars per 1,000 pop.	307
Divorces per 1,000 pop.	4.7	Telephone lines per 100 pop.	22.2
Religion, % of pop.		Mobile telephone subscribers	
Christian	73.3	per 100 pop.	157.9
Non-religious	16.2	Internet access, %	76.0
Muslim	10.0	Broadband subs per 100 pop.	21.6
Jewish	0.2	Broadband speed, Mbps	11.6
Hindu	<0.1		
Other	<0.1		

SAUDI ARABIA

Area, sq km	2,206,714	Capital	Riyadh
Arable as % of total land	1.4	Currency	Riyal (SR)

People

Population, m	32.9	Life expectancy: men	74.3 yrs
Pop. per sq km	14.9	women	77.5 yrs
Total change in population		Adult literacy	94.4
2010–20, %	26.6	Fertility rate (per woman)	2.5
Pop. aged 0–19, %	30.7	Urban population, %	83.4
Pop. aged 65 and over, %	3.8		per 1,000 pop.
No. of men per 100 women	135.1	Crude birth rate	19.1
Human Development Index	85.3	Crude death rate	3.9

The economy

GDP	$687bn	GDP per head	$23,566
GDP	SR2,582bn	GDP per head in purchasing	
Av. ann. growth in real		power parity (USA=100)	89.4
GDP 2012–17	2.2%	Economic freedom index	60.7

Origins of GDP		Components of GDP	
	% of total		% of total
Agriculture	3	Private consumption	41
Industry, of which:	45	Public consumption	25
manufacturing	13	Investment	28
Services	52	Exports	35
		Imports	-29

Structure of employment

	% of total		% of labour force
Agriculture	4.9	Unemployed 2018	5.9
Industry	24.4	Av. ann. rate 2010–18	5.7
Services	70.7		

Energy

	m TOE		
Total output	741.7	Net energy imports as %	
Total consumption	273.2	of energy use	-192
Consumption per head			
kg oil equivalent	6,937		

Inflation and finance

Consumer price		% change 2017–18	
inflation 2018	2.5%	Narrow money (M1)	3.9
Av. ann. inflation 2013–18	1.4%	Broad money	2.8
Treasury bill rate, Feb. 2018	1.59%		

Exchange rates

	end 2018		December 2018
SR per $	3.75	Effective rates	2010 = 100
SR per SDR	5.22	– nominal	117.7
SR per €	4.31	– real	114.8

Trade

Principal exports		Principal imports	
	$bn fob		*$bn cif*
Crude oil	123.1	Machinery & transport equip.	53.3
Refined petroleum products	34.7	Foodstuffs	21.8
		Chemical & metal products	13.4
Total incl. others	**221.9**	Total incl. others	**135.3**

Main export destinations		Main origins of imports	
	% of total		*% of total*
Japan	12.2	China	15.4
China	11.7	United States	13.6
South Korea	9.0	United Arab Emirates	6.5
India	8.9	Germany	5.8

Balance of payments, reserves and aid, $bn

Visible exports fob	221.9	Change in reserves	-37.9
Visible imports fob	-123.4	Level of reserves	
Trade balance	98.5	end Dec.	509.4
Invisibles inflows	37.0	No. months of import cover	29.1
Invisibles outflows	-86.8	Official gold holdings, m oz	10.4
Net transfers	-38.3	Foreign debt	206.9
Current account balance	10.5	– as % of GDP	30.1
– as % of GDP	1.5	– as % of total exports	79.9
Capital balance	-48.7	Debt service ratio	7.3
Overall balance	-39.9		

Health and education

Health spending, % of GDP	5.7	Education spending, % of GDP	...
Doctors per 1,000 pop.	2.6	Enrolment, %: primary	116
Hospital beds per 1,000 pop.	2.7	secondary	...
At least basic drinking water,		tertiary	67
% of pop.	99.2		

Society

No. of households, m	5.9	Cost of living, Dec. 2018	
Av. no. per household	5.6	New York = 100	54
Marriages per 1,000 pop.	...	Cars per 1,000 pop.	136
Divorces per 1,000 pop.	...	Telephone lines per 100 pop.	11.0
Religion, % of pop.		Mobile telephone subscribers	
Muslim	93.0	per 100 pop.	122.1
Christian	4.4	Internet access, %	82.1
Hindu	1.1	Broadband subs per 100 pop.	7.6
Other	0.9	Broadband speed, Mbps	3.1
Non-religious	0.7		
Jewish	<0.1		

SINGAPORE

Area, sq km	718	Capital	Singapore
Arable as % of total land	0.9	Currency	Singapore dollar (S$)

People

Population, m	5.7	Life expectancy: men	82.2 yrs
Pop. per sq km	7,938.7	women	86.0 yrs
Total change in population		Adult literacy	97.0
2010–20, %	17.0	Fertility rate (per woman)	1.3
Pop. aged 0–19, %	19.9	Urban population, %	100.0
Pop. aged 65 and over, %	15.0		per 1,000 pop.
No. of men per 100 women	97.7	Crude birth rate	8.7
Human Development Index	93.2	Crude death rate	5.9

The economy

GDP	$324bn	GDP per head	$64,041
GDP	S$465bn	GDP per head in purchasing	
Av. ann. growth in real		power parity (USA=100)	160.3
GDP 2012–17	3.4%	Economic freedom index	89.4

Origins of GDP		**Components of GDP**	
	% of total		% of total
Agriculture	0	Private consumption	36
Industry, of which:	23	Public consumption	11
manufacturing	18	Investment	28
Services	77	Exports	173
		Imports	-149

Structure of employment

	% of total		% of labour force
Agriculture	0.5	Unemployed 2018	3.8
Industry	16.6	Av. ann. rate 2010–18	3.9
Services	82.9		

Energy

	m TOE		
Total output	1.3	Net energy imports as %	
Total consumption	88.6	of energy use	98
Consumption per head			
kg oil equivalent	5,122		

Inflation and finance

Consumer price			% change 2017–18
inflation 2018	0.4%	Narrow money (M1)	5.4
Av. ann. inflation 2013–18	0.2%	Broad money	3.9
Deposit rate, Dec. 2018	0.17%		

Exchange rates

	end 2018		December 2018
S$ per $	1.36	Effective rates	2010 = 100
S$ per SDR	1.90	– nominal	112.2
S$ per €	1.56	– real	107.3

Trade

Principal exports

	$bn fob
Machinery & transport equip.	182.8
Mineral fuels	65.3
Construction materials & metals	50.9
Chemicals & chemical products	50.3
Total incl.others	**373.1**

Principal imports

	$bn cif
Machinery & transport equip.	150.4
Mineral fuels	72.3
Chemicals & chemical products	27.8
Misc. manufactured articles	26.8
Total incl.others	**327.4**

Main export destinations

	% of total
China	14.4
Hong Kong	12.3
Malaysia	10.6
United States	6.5

Main origins of imports

	% of total
China	13.8
Malaysia	11.9
United States	10.6
Taiwan	8.3

Balance of payments, reserves and debt, $bn

Visible exports fob	399.9	Change in reserves	33.9
Visible imports fob	-308.8	Level of reserves	
Trade balance	91.1	end Dec.	285.0
Invisibles inflows	264.5	No. months of import cover	5.7
Invisibles outflows	-296.2	Official gold holdings, m oz	4.1
Net transfers	-5.5	Foreign debt	566.1
Current account balance	53.9	– as % of GDP	168.1
– as % of GDP	16.6	– as % of total exports	85.2
Capital balance	-26.6	Debt service ratio	8.9
Overall balance	27.4		

Health and education

Health spending, % of GDP	4.5	Education spending, % of GDP	...
Doctors per 1,000 pop.	2.3	Enrolment, %: primary	101
Hospital beds per 1,000 pop.	2.4	secondary	108
At least basic drinking water,		tertiary	84
% of pop.	99.5		

Society

No. of households, m	1.3	Cost of living, Dec. 2018	
Av. no. per household	4.4	New York = 100	107
Marriages per 1,000 pop.	7.1	Cars per 1,000 pop.	113
Divorces per 1,000 pop.	1.8	Telephone lines per 100 pop.	34.9
Religion, % of pop.		Mobile telephone subscribers	
Buddhist	33.9	per 100 pop.	146.8
Christian	18.2	Internet access, %	84.4
Non-religious	16.4	Broadband subs per 100 pop.	25.9
Muslim	14.3	Broadband speed, Mbps	55.1
Other	12.0		
Hindu	5.2		

SLOVAKIA

Area, sq km	49,035	Capital	Bratislava
Arable as % of total land	28.9	Currency	Euro (€)

People

Population, m	5.4	Life expectancy: men	74.3 yrs
Pop. per sq km	110.1	women	81.0 yrs
Total change in population		Adult literacy	...
2010–20, %	0.9	Fertility rate (per woman)	1.5
Pop. aged 0–19, %	20.4	Urban population, %	53.8
Pop. aged 65 and over, %	16.7		per 1,000 pop.
No. of men per 100 women	94.6	Crude birth rate	10.3
Human Development Index	85.5	Crude death rate	10.5

The economy

GDP	$96bn	GDP per head	$19,582
GDP	€85nb	GDP per head in purchasing	
Av. ann. growth in real		power parity (USA=100)	56.1
GDP 2012–17	3.0%	Economic freedom index	65.0

Origins of GDP

Components of GDP

	% of total		% of total
Agriculture	3	Private consumption	55
Industry, of which:	31	Public consumption	19
manufacturing	20	Investment	23
Services	66	Exports	97
		Imports	-94

Structure of employment

	% of total		% of labour force
Agriculture	2.7	Unemployed 2018	6.8
Industry	37.0	Av. ann. rate 2010–18	11.7
Services	60.3		

Energy

	m TOE		
Total output	6.5	Net energy imports as %	
Total consumption	17.9	of energy use	61
Consumption per head			
kg oil equivalent	3,004		

Inflation and finance

			% change 2017–18
Consumer price			
inflation 2018	2.5%	Narrow money (M1)	0.7
Av. ann. inflation 2013–18	0.6%	Broad money	4.2
Deposit rate, Dec. 2018	0.46%		

Exchange rates

	end 2018		December 2018
€ per $	0.87	Effective rates	2010 = 100
€ per SDR	1.21	– nominal	104.0
		– real	99.8

Trade

Principal exports

	$bn fob
Machinery & transport equip.	49.9
Chemicals & related products	3.7
Mineral fuels & lubricants	3.7
Food, drink & tobacco	2.8
Total incl. others	**84.4**

Principal imports

	$bn cif
Machinery & transport equip.	39.4
Chemicals & related products	7.3
Mineral fuels & lubricants	7.1
Food, drink & tobacco	4.4
Total incl. others	**81.1**

Main export destinations

	% of total
Germany	20.6
Czech Republic	11.6
Poland	7.8
France	6.3
EU28	85.7

Main origins of imports

	% of total
Germany	19.8
Czech Republic	16.6
Austria	10.5
Poland	6.7
EU28	79.8

Balance of payments, reserves and debt, $bn

Visible exports fob	80.7	Overall balance	0.5
Visible imports fob	-80.0	Change in reserves	0.7
Trade balance	0.8	Level of reserves	
Invisibles inflows	14.2	end Dec.	3.6
Invisibles outflows	-15.5	No. months of import cover	0.5
Net transfers	-1.4	Official gold holdings, m oz	1.0
Current account balance	-1.9	Aid given	0.1
– as % of GDP	-2.0	– as % of GNI	0.1
Capital balance	4.0		

Health and education

Health spending, % of GDP	7.1	Education spending, % of GDP	4.7
Doctors per 1,000 pop.	3.5	Enrolment, %: primary	98
Hospital beds per 1,000 pop.	5.8	secondary	91
At least basic drinking water,		tertiary	48
% of pop.	93.2		

Society

No. of households, m	1.8	Cost of living, Dec. 2018	
Av. no. per household	3.0	New York = 100	...
Marriages per 1,000 pop.	5.8	Cars per 1,000 pop.	377
Divorces per 1,000 pop.	1.9	Telephone lines per 100 pop.	13.9
Religion, % of pop.		Mobile telephone subscribers	
Christian	85.3	per 100 pop.	130.7
Non-religious	14.3	Internet access, %	81.6
Muslim	0.2	Broadband subs per 100 pop.	25.8
Other	0.1	Broadband speed, Mbps	18.9
Hindu	<0.1		
Jewish	<0.1		

SLOVENIA

Area, sq km	20,273	Capital	Ljubljana
Arable as % of total land	8.4	Currency	Euro (€)

People

Population, m	2.1	Life expectancy: men	79.5 yrs
Pop. per sq km	103.6	women	84.6 yrs
Total change in population		Adult literacy	99.7
2010–20, %	1.8	Fertility rate (per woman)	1.6
Pop. aged 0–19, %	19.7	Urban population, %	54.0
Pop. aged 65 and over, %	20.8		per 1,000 pop.
No. of men per 100 women	98.9	Crude birth rate	10.0
Human Development Index	89.6	Crude death rate	10.3

The economy

GDP	$49bn	GDP per head	$26,234
GDP	€43bn	GDP per head in purchasing	
Av. ann. growth in real		power parity (USA=100)	58.7
GDP 2012–17	2.4%	Economic freedom index	65.5

Origins of GDP

	% of total		% of total
		Components of GDP	
Agriculture	2	Private consumption	53
Industry, of which:	29	Public consumption	18
manufacturing	21	Investment	19
Services	69	Exports	82
		Imports	-73

Structure of employment

	% of total		% of labour force
Agriculture	5.5	Unemployed 2018	5.5
Industry	33.1	Av. ann. rate 2010–18	8.1
Services	61.4		

Energy

	m TOE		
Total output	3.6	Net energy imports as %	
Total consumption	7.1	of energy use	49
Consumption per head			
kg oil equivalent	3,175		

Inflation and finance

			% change 2017–18
Consumer price			
inflation 2018	1.7%	Narrow money (M1)	0.7
Av. ann. inflation 2013–18	0.6%	Broad money	4.2
Deposit rate, Dec. 2018	0.18%		

Exchange rates

	end 2018		December 2018
€ per $	0.87	Effective rates	2010 = 100
€ per SDR	1.21	– nominal	...
		– real	...

Trade

Principal exports		Principal imports	
	$bn fob		*$bn cif*
Machinery & transport equip.	15.6	Machinery & transport equip.	13.1
Manufactures	11.7	Manufactures	10.3
Chemicals	5.7	Chemicals	4.9
Miscellaneous manufactures	5.4	Mineral fuels & lubricants	3.1
Total incl. others	**38.4**	Total incl. others	**36.0**

Main export destinations		Main origins of imports	
	% of total		*% of total*
Germany	18.9	Germany	16.5
Italy	10.7	Italy	13.6
Austria	7.4	Austria	9.3
Croatia	7.1	Turkey	5.8
EU28	75.7	EU28	69.4

Balance of payments, reserves and debt, $bn

Visible exports fob	32.2	Overall balance	0.1
Visible imports fob	-30.4	Change in reserves	0.1
Trade balance	1.8	Level of reserves	
Invisibles inflows	10.1	end Dec.	0.9
Invisibles outflows	-8.1	No. months of import cover	0.3
Net transfers	-0.3	Official gold holdings, m oz	0.1
Current account balance	3.5	Aid given	0.1
– as % of GDP	7.1	– as % of GNI	0.2
Capital balance	-2.2		

Health and education

Health spending, % of GDP	8.5	Education spending, % of GDP	4.9
Doctors per 1,000 pop.	2.8	Enrolment, %: primary	99
Hospital beds per 1,000 pop.	4.6	secondary	115
At least basic drinking water,		tertiary	78
% of pop.	92.4		

Society

No. of households, m	0.9	Cost of living, Dec. 2018	
Av. no. per household	2.3	New York = 100	...
Marriages per 1,000 pop.	3.1	Cars per 1,000 pop.	518
Divorces per 1,000 pop.	1.2	Telephone lines per 100 pop.	34.5
Religion, % of pop.		Mobile telephone subscribers	
Christian	78.4	per 100 pop.	117.5
Non-religious	18.0	Internet access, %	78.9
Muslim	3.6	Broadband subs per 100 pop.	28.9
Hindu	<0.1	Broadband speed, Mbps	18.4
Jewish	<0.1		
Other	<0.1		

SOUTH AFRICA

Area, sq km	1,215,037	Capital	Pretoria
Arable as % of total land	9.9	Currency	Rand (R)

People

Population, m	56.7	Life expectancy: men	61.5 yrs
Pop. per sq km	46.7	women	68.3 yrs
Total change in population		Adult literacy	94.4
2010–20, %	13.8	Fertility rate (per woman)	2.4
Pop. aged 0–19, %	37.2	Urban population, %	65.3
Pop. aged 65 and over, %	5.7		per 1,000 pop.
No. of men per 100 women	96.2	Crude birth rate	20.5
Human Development Index	69.9	Crude death rate	9.4

The economy

GDP	$349bn	GDP per head	$6,377
GDP	R4,654bn	GDP per head in purchasing	
Av. ann. growth in real		power parity (USA=100)	21.8
GDP 2012–17	1.5%	Economic freedom index	58.3

Origins of GDP

Components of GDP

	% of total		% of total
Agriculture	2	Private consumption	59
Industry, of which:	26	Public consumption	21
manufacturing	12	Investment	19
Services	72	Exports	30
		Imports	-28

Structure of employment

	% of total		% of labour force
Agriculture	5.2	Unemployed 2018	27.0
Industry	23.2	Av. ann. rate 2010–18	25.5
Services	71.6		

Energy

	m TOE		
Total output	157.8	Net energy imports as %	
Total consumption	153.2	of energy use	-14
Consumption per head			
kg oil equivalent	2,696		

Inflation and finance

			% change 2017–18
Consumer price			
inflation 2018	4.6%	Narrow money (M1)	4.6
Av. ann. inflation 2013–18	5.4%	Broad money	5.6
Central bank policy rate, Dec. 2018	6.75%		

Exchange rates

	end 2018		December 2018
R per $	14.39	Effective rates	2010 = 100
R per SDR	20.02	– nominal	62.1
R per €	16.54	– real	78.5

Trade

Principal exports		**Principal imports**	
	$bn fob		*$bn cif*
Mineral products	22.3	Machinery & equipment	19.5
Precious metals	14.8	Mineral products	12.6
Iron & steel products	10.6	Chemicals	9.1
Vehicles, aircraft & vessels	10.6	Vehicles, aircraft & vessels	8.3
Total incl. others	**89.0**	Total incl. others	**83.2**

Main export destinations		**Main origins of imports**	
	% of total		*% of total*
China	9.6	China	19.4
Germany	7.5	Germany	12.3
United States	7.1	United States	7.0
India	4.7	India	5.0

Balance of payments, reserves and debt, $bn

Visible exports fob	87.6	Change in reserves	3.5
Visible imports fob	-82.8	Level of reserves	
Trade balance	4.9	end Dec.	50.7
Invisibles inflows	21.9	No. months of import cover	5.3
Invisibles outflows	-32.8	Official gold holdings, m oz	4.0
Net transfers	-2.9	Foreign debt	176.3
Current account balance	-8.9	– as % of GDP	50.4
– as % of GDP	-2.6	– as % of total exports	147.7
Capital balance	10.1	Debt service ratio	11.2
Overall balance	1.9		

Health and education

Health spending, % of GDP	8.1	Education spending, % of GDP	6.2
Doctors per 1,000 pop.	0.8	Enrolment, %: primary	102
Hospital beds per 1,000 pop.	...	secondary	100
At least basic drinking water,		tertiary	21
% of pop.	98.3		

Society

No. of households, m	16.9	Cost of living, Dec. 2018	
Av. no. per household	3.4	New York = 100	50
Marriages per 1,000 pop.	...	Cars per 1,000 pop.	114
Divorces per 1,000 pop.	...	Telephone lines per 100 pop.	8.5
Religion, % of pop.		Mobile telephone subscribers	
Christian	81.2	per 100 pop.	156.0
Non-religious	14.9	Internet access, %	56.2
Muslim	1.7	Broadband subs per 100 pop.	2.0
Hindu	1.1	Broadband speed, Mbps	4.4
Other	0.9		
Jewish	0.1		

SOUTH KOREA

Area, sq km	100,266	Capital	Seoul
Arable as % of total land	15.4	Currency	Won (W)

People

Population, m	51.0	Life expectancy: men	80.4 yrs
Pop. per sq km	508.6	women	86.2 yrs
Total change in population		Adult literacy	...
2010–20, %	3.9	Fertility rate (per woman)	1.3
Pop. aged 0–19, %	18.1	Urban population, %	81.6
Pop. aged 65 and over, %	15.7		per 1,000 pop.
No. of men per 100 women	100.0	Crude birth rate	8.9
Human Development Index	90.3	Crude death rate	6.8

The economy

GDP	$1,531bn	GDP per head	$31,346
GDP	W1,730trn	GDP per head in purchasing	
Av. ann. growth in real		power parity (USA=100)	66.0
GDP 2012–17	3.0%	Economic freedom index	72.3

Origins of GDP		Components of GDP	
	% of total		% of total
Agriculture	2	Private consumption	48
Industry, of which:	36	Public consumption	15
manufacturing	28	Investment	31
Services	62	Exports	43
		Imports	-38

Structure of employment

	% of total		% of labour force
Agriculture	4.9	Unemployed 2016	3.7
Industry	24.9	Av. ann. rate 2006–16	3.4
Services	70.2		

Energy

	m TOE		
Total output	42.2	Net energy imports as %	
Total consumption	287.5	of energy use	81
Consumption per head			
kg oil equivalent	5,413		

Inflation and finance

Consumer price			% change 2017–18
inflation 2018	1.5%	Narrow money (M1)	10.5
Av. ann. inflation 2013–18	1.8%	Broad money	6.7
Central bank policy rate, Dec. 2018	1.75%		

Exchange rates

	end 2018		December 2018
W per $	1,115.70	Effective rates	2010 = 100
W per SDR	1,551.71	– nominal	...
W per €	1,282.41	– real	...

Trade

Principal exports		Principal imports	
	$bn fob		*$bn cif*
Machinery & transport equip.	338.5	Machinery & transport equip.	162.7
Manufactured goods	71.7	Mineral fuels & lubricants	110.0
Chemicals & related products	70.5	Chemicals & related products	48.8
Mineral fuels & lubricants	36.4	Manufactured goods	48.4
Total incl. others	**572.9**	Total incl. others	**478.4**

Main export destinations		Main origins of imports	
	% of total		*% of total*
China	25.1	China	20.5
United States	12.2	Japan	11.5
Vietnam	8.2	United States	10.5
Hong Kong	6.9	Germany	4.2

Balance of payments, reserves and debt, $bn

Visible exports fob	580.3	Change in reserves	18.6
Visible imports fob	-466.7	Level of reserves	
Trade balance	113.6	end Dec.	388.8
Invisibles inflows	119.2	No. months of import cover	7.6
Invisibles outflows	-150.6	Official gold holdings, m oz	3.4
Net transfers	-7.0	Foreign debt	384.6
Current account balance	75.2	– as % of GDP	25.1
– as % of GDP	4.9	– as % of total exports	55.8
Capital balance	-80.1	Debt service ratio	5.3
Overall balance	4.5		

Health and education

Health spending, % of GDP	7.3	Education spending, % of GDP	5.2
Doctors per 1,000 pop.	2.3	Enrolment, %: primary	97
Hospital beds per 1,000 pop.	11.5	secondary	100
At least basic drinking water,		tertiary	94
% of pop.	99.6		

Society

No. of households, m	20.5	Cost of living, Dec. 2018	
Av. no. per household	2.5	New York = 100	100
Marriages per 1,000 pop.	5.1	Cars per 1,000 pop.	326
Divorces per 1,000 pop.	2.1	Telephone lines per 100 pop.	52.7
Religion, % of pop.		Mobile telephone subscribers	
Non-religious	46.4	per 100 pop.	124.9
Christian	29.4	Internet access, %	95.1
Buddhist	22.9	Broadband subs per 100 pop.	41.6
Other	1.0	Broadband speed, Mbps	22.9
Muslim	0.2		
Jewish	<0.1		

SPAIN

Area, sq km	505,992	Capital	Madrid
Arable as % of total land	25.1	Currency	Euro (€)

People

Population, m	46.4	Life expectancy: men	81.3 yrs
Pop. per sq km	91.7	women	86.7 yrs
Total change in population		Adult literacy	98.3
2010–20, %	-0.7	Fertility rate (per woman)	1.4
Pop. aged 0–19, %	19.2	Urban population, %	79.8
Pop. aged 65 and over, %	20.4		per 1,000 pop.
No. of men per 100 women	96.4	Crude birth rate	8.5
Human Development Index	89.1	Crude death rate	9.6

The economy

GDP	$1,314bn	GDP per head	$30,697
GDP	€1,166bn	GDP per head in purchasing	
Av. ann. growth in real		power parity (USA=100)	64.1
GDP 2012–17	1.9%	Economic freedom index	65.7

Origins of GDP		**Components of GDP**	
	% of total		% of total
Agriculture	3	Private consumption	58
Industry, of which:	22	Public consumption	18
manufacturing	13	Investment	21
Services	75	Exports	34
		Imports	-31

Structure of employment

	% of total		% of labour force
Agriculture	4.3	Unemployed 2018	15.5
Industry	19.9	Av. ann. rate 2010–18	21.2
Services	75.8		

Energy

	m TOE		
Total output	40.7	Net energy imports as %	
Total consumption	114.7	of energy use	71
Consumption per head			
kg oil equivalent	2,571		

Inflation and finance

			% change 2017–18
Consumer price			
inflation 2018	1.7%	Narrow money (M1)	0.7
Av. ann. inflation 2013–18	0.6%	Broad money	4.2
Treasury bill rate, Dec. 2018	-0.32%		

Exchange rates

	end 2018		December 2018
€ per $	0.87	Effective rates	2010 = 100
€ per SDR	1.21	– nominal	104.5
		– real	96.8

Trade

Principal exports		Principal imports	
	$bn fob		*$bn cif*
Machinery & transport equip.	106.1	Machinery & transport equip.	113.7
Food, drink & tobacco	47.8	Mineral fuels & lubricants	49.7
Chemicals & related products	42.2	Chemicals & related products	46.0
Mineral fuels & lubricants	22.5	Food, drink & tobacco	35.1
Total incl. others	**311.7**	Total incl. others	**341.6**

Main export destinations		Main origins of imports	
	% of total		*% of total*
France	15.5	Germany	14.6
Germany	11.5	France	12.3
Italy	8.0	China	7.1
Portugal	7.3	Italy	7.0
EU28	66.3	EU28	59.7

Balance of payments, reserves and aid, $bn

Visible exports fob	313.5	Overall balance	4.1
Visible imports fob	-338.3	Change in reserves	6.3
Trade balance	-24.7	Level of reserves	
Invisibles inflows	200.9	end Dec.	69.4
Invisibles outflows	-138.9	No. months of import cover	1.7
Net transfers	-12.2	Official gold holdings, m oz	9.1
Current account balance	25.0	Aid given	2.6
– as % of GDP	1.9	– as % of GNI	0.2
Capital balance	-18.6		

Health and education

Health spending, % of GDP	9.0	Education spending, % of GDP	4.3
Doctors per 1,000 pop.	3.9	Enrolment, %: primary	104
Hospital beds per 1,000 pop.	3.0	secondary	128
At least basic drinking water,		tertiary	91
% of pop.	95.1		

Society

No. of households, m	18.5	Cost of living, Dec. 2018	
Av. no. per household	2.5	New York = 100	80
Marriages per 1,000 pop.	3.7	Cars per 1,000 pop.	483
Divorces per 1,000 pop.	2.1	Telephone lines per 100 pop.	42.5
Religion, % of pop.		Mobile telephone subscribers	
Christian	78.6	per 100 pop.	113.3
Non-religious	19.0	Internet access, %	84.6
Muslim	2.1	Broadband subs per 100 pop.	31.6
Jewish	0.1	Broadband speed, Mbps	19.6
Other	0.1		
Hindu	<0.1		

SWEDEN

Area, sq km	450,295	Capital	Stockholm
Arable as % of total land	6.4	Currency	Swedish krona (Skr)

People

Population, m	9.9	Life expectancy: men	82.0 yrs
Pop. per sq km	22.0	women	85.0 yrs
Total change in population		Adult literacy	...
2010–20, %	7.8	Fertility rate (per woman)	1.9
Pop. aged 0–19, %	23.1	Urban population, %	86.9
Pop. aged 65 and over, %	20.3		per 1,000 pop.
No. of men per 100 women	100.5	Crude birth rate	12.3
Human Development Index	93.3	Crude death rate	9.0

The economy

GDP	$536bn	GDP per head	$53,873
GDP	Skr4,579bn	GDP per head in purchasing	
Av. ann. growth in real		power parity (USA=100)	84.6
GDP 2012–17	2.8%	Economic freedom index	75.2

Origins of GDP		Components of GDP	
	% of total		% of total
Agriculture	1	Private consumption	45
Industry, of which:	22	Public consumption	26
manufacturing	14	Investment	26
Services	77	Exports	45
		Imports	-42

Structure of employment

	% of total		% of labour force
Agriculture	1.8	Unemployed 2018	6.4
Industry	18.0	Av. ann. rate 2010–18	7.6
Services	80.2		

Energy

	m TOE		
Total output	36.6	Net energy imports as %	
Total consumption	54.7	of energy use	25
Consumption per head			
kg oil equivalent	5,103		

Inflation and finance

Consumer price		% change 2017–18	
inflation 2018	2.0%	Narrow money (M1)	7.6
Av. ann. inflation 2013–18	1.2%	Broad money	6.9
Central bank policy rate, Jun. 2018	-0.50%		

Exchange rates

	end 2018		December 2018
Skr per $	8.96	Effective rates	2010 = 100
Skr per SDR	12.46	– nominal	95.7
Skr per €	10.30	– real	89.0

Trade

Principal exports

	$bn fob
Machinery & transport equip.	60.8
Chemicals & related products	18.7
Mineral fuels & lubricants	10.6
Raw materials	10.3
Total incl. others	**152.9**

Principal imports

	$bn cif
Machinery & transport equip.	59.6
Chemicals & related products	16.8
Food, drink & tobacco	16.1
Mineral fuels & lubricants	15.5
Total incl. others	**154.2**

Main export destinations

	% of total
Germany	11.0
Norway	10.2
Finland	6.9
United States	6.9
EU28	59.2

Main origins of imports

	% of total
Germany	18.7
Netherlands	8.8
Norway	7.6
Denmark	7.2
EU28	71.0

Balance of payments, reserves and aid, $bn

Visible exports fob	165.2	Overall balance	0.1
Visible imports fob	-154.4	Change in reserves	2.8
Trade balance	10.8	Level of reserves	
Invisibles inflows	122.8	end Dec.	62.2
Invisibles outflows	-110.3	No. months of import cover	2.8
Net transfers	-8.3	Official gold holdings, m oz	4.0
Current account balance	15.0	Aid given	5.6
– as % of GDP	2.8	– as % of GNI	1.0
Capital balance	-20.8		

Health and education

Health spending, % of GDP	10.9	Education spending, % of GDP	7.6
Doctors per 1,000 pop.	4.2	Enrolment, %: primary	125
Hospital beds per 1,000 pop.	2.6	secondary	145
At least basic drinking water,		tertiary	64
% of pop.	100		

Society

No. of households, m	4.6	Cost of living, Dec. 2018	
Av. no. per household	2.2	New York = 100	73
Marriages per 1,000 pop.	5.2	Cars per 1,000 pop.	476
Divorces per 1,000 pop.	2.4	Telephone lines per 100 pop.	26.5
Religion, % of pop.		Mobile telephone subscribers	
Christian	67.2	per 100 pop.	126.3
Non-religious	27.0	Internet access, %	96.4
Muslim	4.6	Broadband subs per 100 pop.	39.0
Other	0.8	Broadband speed, Mbps	40.2
Hindu	0.2		
Jewish	0.1		

SWITZERLAND

| Area, sq km | 41,285 | Capital | Berne |
| Arable as % of total land | 10.1 | Currency | Swiss franc (SFr) |

People

Population, m	8.5	Life expectancy: men	82.5 yrs
Pop. per sq km	205.9	women	86.1 yrs
Total change in population		Adult literacy	...
2010–20, %	10.7	Fertility rate (per woman)	1.6
Pop. aged 0–19, %	19.9	Urban population, %	73.7
Pop. aged 65 and over, %	19.1		per 1,000 pop.
No. of men per 100 women	98.4	Crude birth rate	10.4
Human Development Index	94.4	Crude death rate	8.2

The economy

GDP	$679bn	GDP per head	$82,950
GDP	SFr669bn	GDP per head in purchasing	
Av. ann. growth in real		power parity (USA=100)	103.3
GDP 2012–17	1.6%	Economic freedom index	81.9

Origins of GDP

	% of total
Agriculture	1
Industry, of which:	25
manufacturing	18
Services	74

Components of GDP

	% of total
Private consumption	54
Public consumption	12
Investment	24
Exports	65
Imports	-54

Structure of employment

	% of total		% of labour force
Agriculture	3.1	Unemployed 2018	4.9
Industry	20.3	Av. ann. rate 2010–18	4.7
Services	76.6		

Energy

	m TOE		
Total output	14.3	Net energy imports as %	
Total consumption	29.9	of energy use	50
Consumption per head			
kg oil equivalent	2,960		

Inflation and finance

			% change 2017–18
Consumer price			
inflation 2018	0.9%	Narrow money (M1)	5.5
Av. ann. inflation 2013–18	0.0%	Broad money	3.5
Central bank policy rate, Dec. 2018	-0.25%		

Exchange rates

	end 2018		December 2018
SFr per $	0.98	Effective rates	2010 = 100
SFr per SDR	1.37	– nominal	122.4
SFr per €	1.13	– real	104.5

Trade

Principal exports

	$bn fob
Chemicals	100.1
Precision instruments, watches & jewellery	47.5
Machinery, equipment & electronics	32.5
Metals & metal manufactures	13.9
Total incl. others	**224.1**

Principal imports

	$bn cif
Chemicals	47.5
Machinery, equipment & electronics	31.0
Precision instruments, watches & jewellery	23.4
Motor vehicles	19.3
Total incl. others	**188.8**

Main export destinations

	% of total
Germany	20.3
United States	16.4
China	10.9
India	8.9
EU28	45.3

Main origins of imports

	% of total
Germany	29.2
United States	11.1
Italy	10.7
United Kingdom	10.3
EU28	59.7

Balance of payments, reserves and aid, $bn

Visible exports fob	315.8	Overall balance	61.7
Visible imports fob	-265.9	Change in reserves	131.9
Trade balance	49.9	Level of reserves	
Invisibles inflows	278.1	end Dec.	810.8
Invisibles outflows	-269.2	No. months of import cover	18.2
Net transfers	-13.5	Official gold holdings, m oz	33.4
Current account balance	45.4	Aid given	3.1
– as % of GDP	6.7	– as % of GNI	0.5
Capital balance	22.9		

Health and education

Health spending, % of GDP	12.2	Education spending, % of GDP	5.1
Doctors per 1,000 pop.	4.2	Enrolment, %: primary	104
Hospital beds per 1,000 pop.	4.7	secondary	102
At least basic drinking water, % of pop.	100	tertiary	58

Society

No. of households, m	3.7	Cost of living, Dec. 2018	
Av. no. per household	2.3	New York = 100	101
Marriages per 1,000 pop.	4.8	Cars per 1,000 pop.	536
Divorces per 1,000 pop.	...	Telephone lines per 100 pop.	43.1
Religion, % of pop.		Mobile telephone subscribers	
Christian	81.3	per 100 pop.	130.8
Non-religious	11.9	Internet access, %	93.7
Muslim	5.5	Broadband subs per 100 pop.	46.1
Other	0.6	Broadband speed, Mbps	22.9
Hindu	0.4		
Jewish	0.3		

TAIWAN

Area, sq km	36,179	Capital	Taipei
Arable as % of total land	...	Currency	Taiwan dollar (T$)

People

Population, m	23.6	Life expectancy: men	78.6 yrs
Pop. per sq km	652.3	women	83.7 yrs
Total change in population		Adult literacy	...
2010–20, %	3.1	Fertility rate (per woman)	1.2
Pop. aged 0–19, %	18.2	Urban population, %	77.3
Pop. aged 65 and over, %	15.6		per 1,000 pop.
No. of men per 100 women	99.0	Crude birth rate	9.0
Human Development Index	...	Crude death rate	8.0

The economy

GDP	$575bn	GDP per head	$24,971
GDP	T$17,501bn	GDP per head in purchasing	
Av. ann. growth in real		power parity (USA=100)	84.7
GDP 2012–17	2.3%	Economic freedom index	77.3

Origins of GDP

	% of total
Agriculture	2
Industry, of which:	35
manufacturing	31
Services	63

Components of GDP

	% of total
Private consumption	52
Public consumption	14
Investment	20
Exports	63
Imports	-51

Structure of employment

	% of total		% of labour force
Agriculture	...	Unemployed 2018	3.9
Industry	...	Av. ann. rate 2010–18	4.3
Services	...		
Energy			

Energy

	m TOE		
Total output	10.8	Net energy imports as %	
Total consumption	120.2	of energy use	...
Consumption per head			
kg oil equivalent	...		

Inflation and finance

			% change 2017–18
Consumer price			
inflation 2018	1.5%	Narrow money (M1)	5.8
Av. ann. inflation 2013–18	0.9%	Broad money	2.7
Deposit rate, Dec. 2018	...		

Exchange rates

	end 2018		December 2018
T$ per $	30.73	Effective rates	2010 = 100
T$ per SDR	42.74	– nominal	...
T$ per €	35.32	– real	...

Trade

Principal exports

	$bn fob
Machinery & electrical equip.	177.9
Basic metals & articles	29.0
Plastic & rubber articles	23.0
Chemicals	19.4
Total incl. others	**291.5**

Principal imports

	$bn cif
Machinery & electrical equip.	101.9
Minerals	44.1
Chemicals & related products	27.9
Basic metals & articles	20.5
Total incl. others	**258.5**

Main export destinations

	% of total
China	30.5
Hong Kong	14.1
United States	12.7
Japan	7.1

Main origins of imports

	% of total
China	19.4
Japan	16.2
United States	11.7
South Korea	6.5

Balance of payments, reserves and debt, $bn

Visible exports fob	349.8	Change in reserves	19.3
Visible imports fob	-269.0	Level of reserves	
Trade balance	80.9	end Dec.	469.1
Invisibles inflows	79.4	No. months of import cover	16.4
Invisibles outflows	-73.3	Official gold holdings, m oz	13.6
Net transfers	-4.1	Foreign debt	181.9
Current account balance	82.9	– as % of GDP	31.6
– as % of GDP	14.4	– as % of total exports	42.3
Capital balance	-65.9	Debt service ratio	2.6
Overall balance	12.5		

Health and education

Health spending, % of GDP	...	Education spending, % of GDP	...
Doctors per 1,000 pop.	...	Enrolment, %: primary	...
Hospital beds per 1,000 pop.	...	secondary	...
At least basic drinking water,		tertiary	...
% of pop.	...		

Society

No. of households, m	8.6	Cost of living, Dec. 2018	
Av. no. per household	2.7	New York = 100	73
Marriages per 1,000 pop.	...	Cars per 1,000 pop.	279
Divorces per 1,000 pop.	...	Telephone lines per 100 pop.	57.4
Religion, % of pop.		Mobile telephone subscribers	
Other	60.5	per 100 pop.	121.8
Buddhist	21.3	Internet access, %	...
Non-religious	12.7	Broadband subs per 100 pop.	24.2
Christian	5.5	Broadband speed, Mbps	34.4
Hindu	<0.1		
Jewish	<0.1		

THAILAND

Area, sq km	513,120	Capital	Bangkok
Arable as % of total land	30.8	Currency	Baht (Bt)

People

Population, m	69.0	Life expectancy: men	73.0 yrs
Pop. per sq km	134.5	women	80.2 yrs
Total change in population		Adult literacy	92.9
2010–20, %	3.3	Fertility rate (per woman)	1.5
Pop. aged 0–19, %	22.7	Urban population, %	48.4
Pop. aged 65 and over, %	12.9		per 1,000 pop.
No. of men per 100 women	94.8	Crude birth rate	10.0
Human Development Index	75.5	Crude death rate	8.8

The economy

GDP	$455bn	GDP per head	$7,187
GDP	Bt15,452bn	GDP per head in purchasing	
Av. ann. growth in real		power parity (USA=100)	31.1
GDP 2012–17	2.8%	Economic freedom index	68.3

Origins of GDP

	% of total
Agriculture	9
Industry, of which:	35
manufacturing	27
Services	56

Components of GDP

	% of total
Private consumption	49
Public consumption	16
Investment	23
Exports	68
Imports	-55

Structure of employment

	% of total		% of labour force
Agriculture	30.7	Unemployed 2018	0.7
Industry	23.5	Av. ann. rate 2010–18	0.6
Services	45.8		

Energy

	m TOE		
Total output	70.4	Net energy imports as %	
Total consumption	136.7	of energy use	42
Consumption per head			
kg oil equivalent	1,970		

Inflation and finance

		% change 2017–18	
Consumer price			
inflation 2018	1.1%	Narrow money (M1)	3.1
Av. ann. inflation 2013–18	0.6%	Broad money	4.7
Central bank policy rate, Dec. 2018	1.75%		

Exchange rates

	end 2018		December 2018
			2010 = 100
Bt per $	32.45	Effective rates	
Bt per SDR	45.13	– nominal	...
Bt per €	37.30	– real	...

Trade

Principal exports		Principal imports	
	$bn fob		*$bn cif*
Machinery, equip. & supplies	105.3	Machinery, equip. & supplies	82.3
Food	29.5	Manufactured goods	39.3
Manufactured goods	29.0	Fuel & lubricants	30.4
Chemicals	22.1	Chemicals	24.3
Total incl. others	**235.3**	Total incl. others	**223.8**

Main export destinations		Main origins of imports	
	% of total		*% of total*
China	12.5	China	20.0
United States	11.3	Japan	14.5
Japan	9.4	United States	6.7
Hong Kong	5.2	Malaysia	5.2

Balance of payments, reserves and debt, $bn

Visible exports fob	235.3	Change in reserves	30.7
Visible imports fob	-201.1	Level of reserves	
Trade balance	34.2	end Dec.	202.5
Invisibles inflows	84.1	No. months of import cover	8.8
Invisibles outflows	-75.6	Official gold holdings, m oz	5.0
Net transfers	7.5	Foreign debt	129.8
Current account balance	50.2	– as % of GDP	28.5
– as % of GDP	11.0	– as % of total exports	39.8
Capital balance	-12.4	Debt service ratio	4.6
Overall balance	26.0		

Health and education

Health spending, % of GDP	3.7	Education spending, % of GDP	...
Doctors per 1,000 pop.	0.5	Enrolment, %: primary	100
Hospital beds per 1,000 pop.	2.1	secondary	117
At least basic drinking water,		tertiary	49
% of pop.	99.6		

Society

No. of households, m	23.8	Cost of living, Dec. 2018	
Av. no. per household	2.9	New York = 100	78
Marriages per 1,000 pop.	...	Cars per 1,000 pop.	119
Divorces per 1,000 pop.	...	Telephone lines per 100 pop.	5.0
Religion, % of pop.		Mobile telephone subscribers	
Buddhist	93.2	per 100 pop.	176.0
Muslim	5.5	Internet access, %	52.9
Christian	0.9	Broadband subs per 100 pop.	11.9
Non-religious	0.3	Broadband speed, Mbps	16.9
Hindu	0.1		
Jewish	<0.1		

TURKEY

Area, sq km	783,562	Capital	Ankara
Arable as % of total land	26.7	Currency	Turkish Lira (YTL)

People

Population, m	80.7	Life expectancy: men	74.2 yrs
Pop. per sq km	103.0	women	80.4 yrs
Total change in population		Adult literacy	95.6
2010–20, %	15.9	Fertility rate (per woman)	2.0
Pop. aged 0–19, %	31.9	Urban population, %	74.1
Pop. aged 65 and over, %	8.8		*per 1,000 pop.*
No. of men per 100 women	97.3	Crude birth rate	15.8
Human Development Index	79.1	Crude death rate	6.0

The economy

GDP	$852bn	GDP per head	$9,346
GDP	YTL3,107bn	GDP per head in purchasing	
Av. ann. growth in real		power parity (USA=100)	44.7
GDP 2012–17	6.1%	Economic freedom index	64.6

Origins of GDP

	% of total
Agriculture	6
Industry, of which:	29
manufacturing	18
Services	65

Components of GDP

	% of total
Private consumption	59
Public consumption	15
Investment	31
Exports	25
Imports	-29

Structure of employment

	% of total		*% of labour force*
Agriculture	19.2	Unemployed 2018	10.9
Industry	26.3	Av. ann. rate 2010–18	9.9
Services	54.5		

Energy

	m TOE		
Total output	40.3	Net energy imports as %	
Total consumption	150.5	of energy use	75
Consumption per head			
kg oil equivalent	1,657		

Inflation and finance

			% change 2017–18
Consumer price			
inflation 2018	16.3%	Narrow money (M1)	7.3
Av. ann. inflation 2013–18	10.3%	Broad money	18.5
Central bank policy rate, Dec. 2018	22.50%		

Exchange rates

	end 2018		*December 2018*
YTL per $	5.27	Effective rates	*2010 = 100*
YTL per SDR	7.32	– nominal	...
YTL per €	6.06	– real	...

Trade

Principal exports		Principal imports	
	$bn fob		*$bn cif*
Transport equipment	28.9	Fuels	37.2
Agricultural products	26.5	Chemicals	33.1
Textiles & clothing	16.4	Transport equipment	20.9
Iron & steel	15.6	Mechanical equipment	20.4
Total incl. others	**157.0**	Total incl. others	**233.8**

Main export destinations		Main origins of imports	
	% of total		*% of total*
Germany	9.6	China	10.0
United Kingdom	6.1	Germany	9.1
Iraq	5.8	Russia	8.3
Italy	5.4	United States	5.1
EU28	47.1	EU28	36.4

Balance of payments, reserves and debt, $bn

Visible exports fob	166.2	Change in reserves	1.6
Visible imports fob	-225.1	Level of reserves	
Trade balance	-59.0	end Dec.	107.6
Invisibles inflows	49.0	No. months of import cover	4.9
Invisibles outflows	-40.1	Official gold holdings, m oz	18.2
Net transfers	2.7	Foreign debt	454.7
Current account balance	-47.3	– as % of GDP	53.6
– as % of GDP	-5.6	– as % of total exports	210.4
Capital balance	38.5	Debt service ratio	40.0
Overall balance	-8.2		

Health and education

Health spending, % of GDP	4.3	Education spending, % of GDP	4.3
Doctors per 1,000 pop.	1.7	Enrolment, %: primary	101
Hospital beds per 1,000 pop.	2.7	secondary	103
At least basic drinking water,		tertiary	104
% of pop.	96.2		

Society

No. of households, m	23.1	Cost of living, Dec. 2018	
Av. no. per household	3.5	New York = 100	46
Marriages per 1,000 pop.	7.4	Cars per 1,000 pop.	133
Divorces per 1,000 pop.	1.6	Telephone lines per 100 pop.	14.0
Religion, % of pop.		Mobile telephone subscribers	
Muslim	98.0	per 100 pop.	96.4
Non-religious	1.2	Internet access, %	64.7
Christian	0.4	Broadband subs per 100 pop.	14.8
Other	0.3	Broadband speed, Mbps	4.0
Hindu	<0.1		
Jewish	<0.1		

UKRAINE

Area, sq km	603,500	Capital	Kiev
Arable as % of total land	56.1	Currency	Hryvnia (UAH)

People

Population, m	44.2	Life expectancy: men	68.0 yrs
Pop. per sq km	73.2	women	77.8 yrs
Total change in population		Adult literacy	...
2010–20, %	-4.8	Fertility rate (per woman)	1.6
Pop. aged 0–19, %	20.6	Urban population, %	69.2
Pop. aged 65 and over, %	17.3		per 1,000 pop.
No. of men per 100 women	86.0	Crude birth rate	10.5
Human Development Index	75.1	Crude death rate	14.9

The economy

GDP	$112bn	GDP per head	$2,963
GDP	UAH2,983bn	GDP per head in purchasing	
Av. ann. growth in real		power parity (USA=100)	14.8
GDP 2012–17	-2.4%	Economic freedom index	52.3

Origins of GDP		Components of GDP	
	% of total		% of total
Agriculture	10	Private consumption	67
Industry, of which:	24	Public consumption	20
manufacturing	12	Investment	21
Services	66	Exports	48
		Imports	-56

Structure of employment

	% of total		% of labour force
Agriculture	15.3	Unemployed 2018	9.4
Industry	24.3	Av. ann. rate 2010–18	8.6
Services	60.4		

Energy

	m TOE		
Total output	63.9	Net energy imports as %	
Total consumption	98.1	of energy use	27
Consumption per head			
kg oil equivalent	2,334		

Inflation and finance

Consumer price			% change 2017–18
inflation 2018	10.9%	Narrow money (M1)	9.2
Av. ann. inflation 2013–18	19.2%	Broad money	5.7
Deposit rate, Dec. 2018	14.16%		

Exchange rates

	end 2018		December 2018
UAH per $	28.02	Effective rates	2010 = 100
UAH per SDR	38.97	– nominal	43.1
UAH per €	32.21	– real	83.7

Trade

Principal exports		Principal imports	
	$bn fob		*$bn cif*
Food & beverages	17.8	Machinery & equipment	14.1
Non-precious metals	10.1	Fuels	12.5
Machinery & equipment	4.9	Chemicals	6.5
Fuels	3.9	Food & beverages	4.3
Total incl. others	**43.3**	Total incl. others	**49.5**

Main export destinations		Main origins of imports	
	% of total		*% of total*
Russia	9.0	Russia	14.6
Poland	6.3	China	11.2
Turkey	5.8	Germany	10.9
Italy	5.4	Belarus	6.4
EU28	40.7	EU28	42.2

Balance of payments, reserves and debt, $bn

Visible exports fob	39.7	Change in reserves	3.3
Visible imports fob	-49.4	Level of reserves	
Trade balance	-9.7	end Dec.	18.8
Invisibles inflows	23.5	No. months of import cover	3.3
Invisibles outflows	-19.9	Official gold holdings, m oz	0.8
Net transfers	3.6	Foreign debt	113.3
Current account balance	-2.4	– as % of GDP	101.0
– as % of GDP	-2.2	– as % of total exports	150.4
Capital balance	4.5	Debt service ratio	19.3
Overall balance	2.6		

Health and education

Health spending, % of GDP	6.7	Education spending, % of GDP	5.0
Doctors per 1,000 pop.	3.0	Enrolment, %: primary	...
Hospital beds per 1,000 pop.	8.8	secondary	...
At least basic drinking water,		tertiary	...
% of pop.	99.7		

Society

No. of households, m	16.7	Cost of living, Dec. 2018	
Av. no. per household	2.6	New York = 100	52
Marriages per 1,000 pop.	5.4	Cars per 1,000 pop.	167
Divorces per 1,000 pop.	3.1	Telephone lines per 100 pop.	17.2
Religion, % of pop.		Mobile telephone subscribers	
Christian	83.8	per 100 pop.	133.5
Non-religious	14.7	Internet access, %	57.1
Muslim	1.2	Broadband subs per 100 pop.	12.6
Jewish	0.1	Broadband speed, Mbps	8.2
Other	0.1		
Hindu	<0.1		

UNITED ARAB EMIRATES

Area, sq km	83,600	Capital	Abu Dhabi
Arable as % of total land	0.6	Currency	Dirham (AED)

People

Population, m	9.4	Life expectancy: men	77.6 yrs
Pop. per sq km	112.4	women	79.8 yrs
Total change in population		Adult literacy	93.0
2010–20, %	18.7	Fertility rate (per woman)	1.7
Pop. aged 0–19, %	17.8	Urban population, %	86.0
Pop. aged 65 and over, %	1.4		per 1,000 pop.
No. of men per 100 women	249.8	Crude birth rate	9.2
Human Development Index	86.3	Crude death rate	2.0

The economy

GDP	$383bn	GDP per head	$40,711
GDP	AED1,405bn	GDP per head in purchasing	
Av. ann. growth in real		power parity (USA=100)	110.8
GDP 2012–17	3.6%	Economic freedom index	77.6

Origins of GDP

Components of GDP

	% of total		% of total
Agriculture	1	Private consumption	35
Industry, of which:	44	Public consumption	12
manufacturing	9	Investment	25
Services	55	Exports	100
		Imports	-72

Structure of employment

	% of total		% of labour force
Agriculture	3.7	Unemployed 2018	2.6
Industry	23.4	Av. ann. rate 2010–18	2.3
Services	72.9		

Energy

	m TOE		
Total output	251.6	Net energy imports as %	
Total consumption	118.8	of energy use	-184
Consumption per head			
kg oil equivalent	7,769		

Inflation and finance

			% change 2017–18
Consumer price			
inflation 2018	3.1%	Narrow money (M1)	0.6
Av. ann. inflation 2013–18	2.6%	Broad money	2.5
Deposit rate, Dec. 2018	...		

Exchange rates

	end 2018		December 2018
AED per $	3.67	Effective rates	2010 = 100
AED per SDR	5.11	– nominal	141.0
AED per €	4.22	– real	...

Trade

Principal exports		Principal imports	
	$bn fob		*$bn cif*
Re-exports	148.8	Machinery & electrical equip.	77.3
Crude oil	31.3	Precious stones & metals	54.7
Gas	19.3	Vehicles & other transport	
		equipment	31.3
		Base metals & related products	15.0
Total incl. others	**313.5**	Total incl. others	**273.7**

Main export destinations		Main origins of imports	
	% of total		*% of total*
India	11.0	China	18.7
Japan	9.8	United States	9.0
China	5.8	India	7.9
Oman	5.2	Japan	5.4

Balance of payments, reserves and debt, $bn

Visible exports fob	313.5	Change in reserves	10.0
Visible imports fob	-246.3	Level of reserves	
Trade balance	67.2	end Dec.	95.4
Invisibles inflows	91.9	No. months of import cover	3.4
Invisibles outflows	-90.4	Official gold holdings, m oz	0.2
Net transfers	-41.2	Foreign debt	237.6
Current account balance	27.5	– as % of GDP	62.1
– as % of GDP	7.2	– as % of total exports	59.4
Capital balance	17.0	Debt service ratio	4.9
Overall balance	44.0		

Health and education

Health spending, % of GDP	3.5	Education spending, % of GDP	...
Doctors per 1,000 pop.	1.6	Enrolment, %: primary	111
Hospital beds per 1,000 pop.	1.2	secondary	96
At least basic drinking water,		tertiary	...
% of pop.	94.5		

Society

No. of households, m	1.7	Cost of living, Dec. 2018	
Av. no. per household	5.5	New York = 100	76
Marriages per 1,000 pop.	...	Cars per 1,000 pop.	215
Divorces per 1,000 pop.	...	Telephone lines per 100 pop.	24.7
Religion, % of pop.		Mobile telephone subscribers	
Muslim	76.9	per 100 pop.	210.9
Christian	12.6	Internet access, %	94.8
Hindu	6.6	Broadband subs per 100 pop.	29.4
Other	2.8	Broadband speed, Mbps	4.2
Non-religious	1.1		
Jewish	<0.1		

UNITED KINGDOM

Area, sq km	242,495	Capital	London
Arable as % of total land	25.1	Currency	Pound (£)

People

Population, m	66.2	Life expectancy: men	81.0 yrs
Pop. per sq km	273.0	women	84.1 yrs
Total change in population		Adult literacy	...
2010–20, %	6.4	Fertility rate (per woman)	1.9
Pop. aged 0–19, %	23.3	Urban population, %	82.9
Pop. aged 65 and over, %	19.0		per 1,000 pop.
No. of men per 100 women	97.7	Crude birth rate	12.1
Human Development Index	92.2	Crude death rate	9.1

The economy

GDP	$2,638bn	GDP per head	$42,558
GDP	£2,050bn	GDP per head in purchasing	
Av. ann. growth in real		power parity (USA=100)	73.0
GDP 2012–17	2.2%	Economic freedom index	78.9

Origins of GDP		**Components of GDP**	
	% of total		% of total
Agriculture	1	Private consumption	66
Industry, of which:	18	Public consumption	18
manufacturing	9	Investment	17
Services	81	Exports	30
		Imports	-31

Structure of employment

	% of total		% of labour force
Agriculture	1.1	Unemployed 2018	4.0
Industry	18.1	Av. ann. rate 2010–18	6.2
Services	80.7		

Energy

	m TOE		
Total output	131.4	Net energy imports as %	
Total consumption	221.2	of energy use	35
Consumption per head			
kg oil equivalent	2,764		

Inflation and finance

			% change 2017–18
Consumer price			
inflation 2018	2.5%	Narrow money (M1)	-0.3
Av. ann. inflation 2013–18	1.5%	Broad money	2.2
Deposit rate, Dec. 2018			

Exchange rates

	end 2018		December 2018
£ per $	0.79	Effective rates	2010 = 100
£ per SDR	1.10	– nominal	96.1
£ per €	0.91	– real	97.1

Trade

Principal exports

	$bn fob
Machinery & transport equip.	169.9
Chemicals & related products	72.6
Food, drink & tobacco	35.9
Mineral fuels & lubricants	28.4
Total incl. others	**436.0**

Principal imports

	$bn cif
Machinery & transport equip.	235.9
Chemicals & related products	76.7
Mineral fuels & lubricants	58.6
Food, drink & tobacco	51.7
Total incl. others	**612.3**

Main export destinations

	% of total
United States	13.4
Germany	10.7
France	6.9
Netherlands	6.3
EU28	47.7

Main origins of imports

	% of total
Germany	14.4
China	9.9
United States	9.7
Netherlands	8.4
EU28	51.9

Balance of payments, reserves and aid, $bn

Visible exports fob	436.4	Overall balance	7.5
Visible imports fob	-613.0	Change in reserves	15.9
Trade balance	-176.5	Level of reserves	
Invisibles inflows	582.2	end Dec.	150.8
Invisibles outflows	-477.1	No. months of import cover	1.7
Net transfers	-27.0	Official gold holdings, m oz	10.0
Current account balance	-98.4	Aid given	18.1
– as % of GDP	-3.7	– as % of GNI	0.7
Capital balance	91.1		

Health and education

Health spending, % of GDP	9.8	Education spending, % of GDP	5.5
Doctors per 1,000 pop.	2.8	Enrolment, %: primary	101
Hospital beds per 1,000 pop.	2.8	secondary	152
At least basic drinking water,		tertiary	59
% of pop.	100		

Society

No. of households, m	28.8	Cost of living, Dec. 2018	
Av. no. per household	2.3	New York = 100	86
Marriages per 1,000 pop.	4.4	Cars per 1,000 pop.	510
Divorces per 1,000 pop.	1.8	Telephone lines per 100 pop.	50.1
Religion, % of pop.		Mobile telephone subscribers	
Christian	71.1	per 100 pop.	119.5
Non-religious	21.3	Internet access, %	94.6
Muslim	4.4	Broadband subs per 100 pop.	39.3
Other	1.4	Broadband speed, Mbps	16.5
Hindu	1.3		
Jewish	0.5		

UNITED STATES

Area, sq km	9,833,517	Capital	Washington DC
Arable as % of total land	17.5	Currency	US dollar ($)

People

Population, m	324.5	Life expectancy: men	78.2 yrs
Pop. per sq km	33.0	women	82.5 yrs
Total change in population		Adult literacy	...
2010–20, %	7.4	Fertility rate (per woman)	1.9
Pop. aged 0–19, %	25.0	Urban population, %	81.9
Pop. aged 65 and over, %	16.6		per 1,000 pop.
No. of men per 100 women	98.1	Crude birth rate	12.7
Human Development Index	92.4	Crude death rate	8.5

The economy

GDP	$19,485bn	GDP per head	$62,606
Av. ann. growth in real		GDP per head in purchasing	
GDP 2012–17	2.2%	power parity (USA=100)	100.0
		Economic freedom index	76.8

Origins of GDP		Components of GDP	
	% of total		% of total
Agriculture	1	Private consumption	68
Industry, of which:	19	Public consumption	14
manufacturing	12	Investment	21
Services	80	Exports	12
		Imports	-15

Structure of employment

	% of total		% of labour force
Agriculture	1.4	Unemployed 2018	3.9
Industry	19.4	Av. ann. rate 2010–18	6.5
Services	79.1		

Energy

	m TOE		
Total output	2,125.0	Net energy imports as %	
Total consumption	2,500.8	of energy use	7
Consumption per head			
kg oil equivalent	6,804		

Inflation and finance

Consumer price			% change 2017–18
inflation 2018	2.4%	Narrow money (M1)	-10.75
Av. ann. inflation 2013–18	1.5%	Broad money	4.1
Treasury bill rate, Dec. 2018	2.40%		

Exchange rates

	end 2018		December 2018
$ per SDR	1.39	Effective rates	2010 = 100
$ per €	1.15	– nominal	122.1
		– real	116.9

Trade

Principal exports		Principal imports	
	$bn fob		*$bn fob*
Capital goods, excl. vehicles	533.3	Capital goods, excl. vehicles	548.7
Industrial supplies	464.7	Consumer goods, excl. vehicles	516.9
Consumer goods, excl. vehicles	197.7	Industrial supplies	507.3
Vehicles & products	157.6	Vehicles & products	359.0
Total incl. others	**1,546.3**	Total incl. others	**2,342.0**

Main export destinations		Main origins of imports	
	% of total		*% of total*
Canada	18.2	China	21.6
Mexico	15.7	Mexico	13.4
China	8.4	Canada	12.8
Japan	4.4	Japan	5.8
EU28	18.4	EU28	18.6

Balance of payments, reserves and aid, $bn

Visible exports fob	1,553.4	Overall balance	-1.7
Visible imports fob	-2,360.9	Change in reserves	43.9
Trade balance	-807.5	Level of reserves	
Invisibles inflows	1,725.8	end Dec.	449.8
Invisibles outflows	-1,248.9	No. months of import cover	1.5
Net transfers	-118.6	Official gold holdings, m oz	261.5
Current account balance	-449.1	Aid given	34.7
– as % of GDP	-2.3	– as % of GNI	0.2
Capital balance	354.9		

Health and education

Health spending, % of GDP	17.1	Education spending, % of GDP	5.0
Doctors per 1,000 pop.	2.6	Enrolment, %: primary	101
Hospital beds per 1,000 pop.	2.9	secondary	99
At least basic drinking water,		tertiary	89
% of pop.	97.6		

Society

No. of households, m	126.2	Cost of living, Dec. 2018	
Av. no. per household	2.6	New York = 100	100
Marriages per 1,000 pop.	6.9	Cars per 1,000 pop.	380
Divorces per 1,000 pop.	2.5	Telephone lines per 100 pop.	37.0
Religion, % of pop.		Mobile telephone subscribers	
Christian	78.3	per 100 pop.	120.7
Non-religious	16.4	Internet access, %	75.2
Other	2.0	Broadband subs per 100 pop.	33.9
Jewish	1.8	Broadband speed, Mbps	20.0
Muslim	0.9		
Hindu	0.6		

VENEZUELA

Area, sq km	912,050	Capital	Caracas
Arable as % of total land	2.9	Currency	Bolivar (Bs)

People

Population, m	32.0	Life expectancy: men	71.8 yrs
Pop. per sq km	35.1	women	79.8 yrs
Total change in population		Adult literacy	97.1
2010–20, %	14.3	Fertility rate (per woman)	2.3
Pop. aged 0–19, %	35.3	Urban population, %	88.2
Pop. aged 65 and over, %	7.2		per 1,000 pop.
No. of men per 100 women	98.7	Crude birth rate	18.6
Human Development Index	76.1	Crude death rate	6.0

The economy

GDP	$144bn	GDP per head	$3,374
GDP	...	GDP per head in purchasing	
Av. ann. growth in real		power parity (USA=100)	19.5
GDP 2012–17	-8.1%	Economic freedom index	25.9

Origins of GDP[a]

	% of total
Agriculture	5
Industry, of which:	37
manufacturing	17
Services	58

Components of GDP[a]

	% of total
Private consumption	75
Public consumption	15
Investment	25
Exports	17
Imports	-34

Structure of employment

	% of total		% of labour force
Agriculture	7.2	Unemployed 2018	8.4
Industry	21.1	Av. ann. rate 2010–18	7.4
Services	71.7		

Energy

	m TOE		
Total output	174.4	Net energy imports as %	
Total consumption	69.4	of energy use	...
Consumption per head			
kg oil equivalent	...		

Inflation and finance

		% change 2017–18	
Consumer price			
inflation 2018	929,790%	Narrow money (M1)	...
Av. ann. inflation 2013–18	1,355%	Broad money	...
Deposit rate, Sep. 2018	14.88%		

Exchange rates

	end 2018		December 2018
Bs per $	95,760.00	Effective rates	2010 = 100
Bs per SDR	134,693.40	– nominal	...
Bs per €	110,068.97	– real	...

Trade

Principal exports[b]		Principal imports[b]	
	$bn fob		*$bn cif*
Oil	26.6	Manufactured goods	9.6
non-oil	0.9	Agricultural products	3.1
		Fuels & mining products	1.2
Total	**27.4**	Total incl. others	**14.1**

Main export destinations		Main origins of imports	
	% of total		*% of total*
United States	34.5	United States	30.6
India	17.0	China	17.5
China	15.9	Mexico	11.7
Netherlands Antilles	7.7	Brazil	4.6

Balance of payments[b], reserves[b] and debt, $bn

Visible exports fob	27.4	Change in reserves	-5.4
Visible imports fob	-16.3	Level of reserves	
Trade balance	11.1	end Dec.	10.1
Invisibles Inflows	1.9	No. months of import cover	3.7
Invisibles outflows	-17.0	Official gold holdings, m oz	6.0
Net transfers	0.2	Foreign debt	105.6
Current account balance	-3.9	– as % of GDP	33.0
– as % of GDP	-2.7	– as % of total exports	310.7
Capital balance	0.3	Debt service ratio	39.4
Overall balance	-6.3		

Health and education

Health spending, % of GDP	3.2	Education spending, % of GDP	...
Doctors per 1,000 pop.	...	Enrolment, %: primary	94
Hospital beds per 1,000 pop.	0.8	secondary	84
At least basic drinking water,		tertiary	...
% of pop.	93.1		

Society

No. of households, m	8.6	Cost of living, Dec. 2018	
Av. no. per household	3.7	New York = 100	15
Marriages per 1,000 pop.	2.5	Cars per 1,000 pop.	114
Divorces per 1,000 pop.	...	Telephone lines per 100 pop.	18.5
Religion, % of pop.		Mobile telephone subscribers	
Christian	89.3	per 100 pop.	78.5
Non-religious	10.0	Internet access, %	64.3
Muslim	0.3	Broadband subs per 100 pop.	8.2
Other	0.3	Broadband speed, Mbps	0.7
Hindu	<0.1		
Jewish	<0.1		

a 2014   b 2016

VIETNAM

Area, sq km	330,967	Capital	Hanoi
Arable as % of total land	21.0	Currency	Dong (D)

People

Population, m	95.5	Life expectancy: men	73.1 yrs
Pop. per sq km	288.5	women	81.9 yrs
Total change in population		Adult literacy	94.5
2010–20, %	11.2	Fertility rate (per woman)	2.0
Pop. aged 0–19, %	29.6	Urban population, %	34.5
Pop. aged 65 and over, %	8.1		per 1,000 pop.
No. of men per 100 women	98.0	Crude birth rate	16.2
Human Development Index	69.4	Crude death rate	6.0

The economy

GDP	$224bn	GDP per head	$2,551
GDP	D5,006trn	GDP per head in purchasing	
Av. ann. growth in real		power parity (USA=100)	12.0
GDP 2012–17	6.2%	Economic freedom index	55.3

Origins of GDP

Components of GDP

	% of total		% of total
Agriculture	15	Private consumption	68
Industry, of which:	33	Public consumption	7
manufacturing	15	Investment	27
Services	52	Exports	102
		Imports	-99

Structure of employment

	% of total		% of labour force
Agriculture	39.8	Unemployed 2018	1.9
Industry	25.8	Av. ann. rate 2010–18	1.5
Services	34.4		

Energy

	m TOE		
Total output	65.7	Net energy imports as %	
Total consumption	80.7	of energy use	...
Consumption per head			
kg oil equivalent	...		

Inflation and finance

			% change 2017–18
Consumer price			
inflation 2018	3.5%	Narrow money (M1)	6.9
Av. ann. inflation 2013–18	2.9%	Broad money	12.7
Deposit rate, Sep. 2018	4.65%		

Exchange rates

	end 2018		December 2018
D per $	22,825.00	Effective rates	2010 = 100
D per SDR	31,744.82	– nominal	...
D per €	26,235.63	– real	...

Trade

Principal exports

	$bn fob
Telephones & mobile phones	45.3
Textiles & garments	26.1
Computers & electronic products	26.0
Footwear	14.7
Total incl. others	**215.0**

Principal imports

	$bn cif
Electronics, computers & parts	37.8
Machinery & equipment	33.9
Telephones & mobile phones	16.4
Textiles	11.4
Total incl. others	**213.0**

Main export destinations

	% of total
United States	19.5
China	16.6
Japan	7.9
South Korea	6.9

Main origins of imports

	% of total
China	27.6
South Korea	22.1
Japan	8.0
Taiwan	6.5

Balance of payments, reserves and debt, $bn

Visible exports fob	214.1	Change in reserves	12.5
Visible imports fob	-202.6	Level of reserves	
Trade balance	11.5	end Dec.	49.1
Invisibles inflows	13.8	No. months of import cover	2.6
Invisibles outflows	-27.6	Official gold holdings, m oz	0.0
Net transfers	8.4	Foreign debt	104.1
Current account balance	6.1	– as % of GDP	47.2
– as % of GDP	2.7	– as % of total exports	43.1
Capital balance	20.2	Debt service ratio	5.6
Overall balance	12.5		

Health and education

Health spending, % of GDP	5.7	Education spending, % of GDP	...
Doctors per 1,000 pop.	0.8	Enrolment, %: primary	108
Hospital beds per 1,000 pop.	2.6	secondary	...
At least basic drinking water,		tertiary	28
% of pop.	97.6		

Society

No. of households, m	28.9	Cost of living, Dec. 2018	
Av. no. per household	3.3	New York = 100	71
Marriages per 1,000 pop.	...	Cars per 1,000 pop.	21
Divorces per 1,000 pop.	...	Telephone lines per 100 pop.	4.6
Religion, % of pop.		Mobile telephone subscribers	
Other	45.6	per 100 pop.	125.6
Non-religious	29.6	Internet access, %	49.6
Buddhist	16.4	Broadband subs per 100 pop.	11.8
Christian	8.2	Broadband speed, Mbps	5.5
Muslim	0.2		
Jewish	<0.1		

ZIMBABWE

Area, sq km	390,757	Capital	Harare
Arable as % of total land	10.6	Currency	Zimbabwe dollar (Z$)

People

Population, m	16.5	Life expectancy: men	60.9 yrs
Pop. per sq km	42.2	women	64.6 yrs
Total change in population		Adult literacy	88.7
2010–20, %	25.5	Fertility rate (per woman)	3.6
Pop. aged 0–19, %	50.8	Urban population, %	32.3
Pop. aged 65 and over, %	2.9		per 1,000 pop.
No. of men per 100 women	95.3	Crude birth rate	31.7
Human Development Index	53.5	Crude death rate	7.4

The economy

GDP	$22bn	GDP per head	$1,712
GDP	...	GDP per head in purchasing	
Av. ann. growth in real		power parity (USA=100)	4.5
GDP 2012–17	2.3%	Economic freedom index	40.4

Origins of GDP		Components of GDP	
	% of total		% of total
Agriculture	8	Private consumption	79
Industry, of which:	21	Public consumption	22
manufacturing	11	Investment	10
Services	71	Exports	20
		Imports	-30

Structure of employment

	% of total		% of labour force
Agriculture	67.2	Unemployed 2018	4.9
Industry	7.2	Av. ann. rate 2010–18	5.3
Services	25.6		

Energy

	m TOE		
Total output	2.4	Net energy imports as %	
Total consumption	4.0	of energy use	...
Consumption per head			
kg oil equivalent	...		

Inflation and finance

		% change 2017–18	
Consumer price			
inflation 2018	10.6%	Narrow money (M1)	22.1
Av. ann. inflation 2013–18	1.4%	Broad money	28.0
Deposit rate, Dec. 2018	2.61%		

Exchange rates

	end 2018		December 2018
Z$ per $	...	Effective rates	2010 = 100
Z$ per SDR	...	– nominal	...
Z$ per €	...	– real	...

Trade

Principal exports[a]		Principal imports[a]	
	$bn fob		$bn cif
Gold	0.9	Manufactured products	2.1
Tobacco	0.9	Fuels & mining products	1.2
Nickel ores & concentrates	0.3	Agricultural products	0.9
Ferro-alloys	0.1		
Total incl. others	**3.3**	Total	**4.2**

Main export destinations		Main origins of imports	
	% of total		% of total
South Africa	73.8	South Africa	50.1
Mozambique	12.4	Zambia	21.7
United Arab Emirates	7.6	United States	3.4
Zambia	2.0	China	3.3

Balance of payments, reserves and debt, $bn

Visible exports fob	4.3	Change in reserves	-0.1
Visible imports fob	-5.5	Level of reserves	
Trade balance	-1.2	end Dec.	0.3
Invisibles inflows	0.6	No. months of import cover	0.5
Invisibles outflows	-1.5	Official gold holdings, m oz	0.0
Net transfers	1.7	Foreign debt	9.3
Current account balance	-0.3	– as % of GDP	52.3
– as % of GDP	-1.4	– as % of total exports	149.4
Capital balance	0.1	Debt service ratio	11.9
Overall balance	-0.6		

Health and education

Health spending, % of GDP	9.4	Education spending, % of GDP	7.5
Doctors per 1,000 pop.	0.1	Enrolment, %: primary	...
Hospital beds per 1,000 pop.	1.7	secondary	...
At least basic drinking water,		tertiary	9
% of pop.	76.9		

Society

No. of households, m	3.1	Cost of living, Dec. 2018	
Av. no. per household	5.3	New York = 100	...
Marriages per 1,000 pop.	...	Cars per 1,000 pop.	51
Divorces per 1,000 pop.	...	Telephone lines per 100 pop.	1.6
Religion, % of pop.		Mobile telephone subscribers	
Christian	87.0	per 100 pop.	85.3
Non-religious	7.9	Internet access, %	27.1
Other	4.2	Broadband subs per 100 pop.	1.1
Muslim	0.9	Broadband speed, Mbps	2.5
Hindu	<0.1		
Jewish	<0.1		

a 2016

EURO AREA[a]

Area, sq km	2,578,704	Capital	–
Arable as % of total land	24.2	Currency	Euro (€)

People

Population, m	337.7	Life expectancy: men	80.5 yrs
Pop. per sq km	131.0	women	85.3 yrs
Total change in population		Adult literacy	98.9
2010–20, %	0.9	Fertility rate (per woman)	1.7
Pop. aged 0–19, %	19.9	Urban population, %	76.5
Pop. aged 65 and over, %	21.4		per 1,000 pop.
No. of men per 100 women	96.5	Crude birth rate	9.5
Human Development Index	90.3	Crude death rate	10.4

The economy

GDP	$12.7trn	GDP per head	$45,538
GDP	€11.6trn	GDP per head in purchasing	
Av. ann. growth in real		power parity (USA=100)	72.7
GDP 2012–17	1.5%	Economic freedom index	67.6

Origins of GDP		Components of GDP	
	% of total		% of total
Agriculture	2	Private consumption	54
Industry, of which:	25	Public consumption	20
manufacturing	17	Investment	21
Services	73	Exports	47
		Imports	-43

Structure of employment

	% of total		% of labour force
Agriculture	3.1	Unemployed 2018	8.2
Industry	23.3	Av. ann. rate 2010–18	10.3
Services	73.6		

Energy

	m TOE		
Total output	434.8	Net energy imports as %	
Total consumption	1,236.7	of energy use	60
Consumption per head			
kg oil equivalent	3,329		

Inflation and finance

Consumer price			% change 2017–18
inflation 2018	1.8%	Narrow money (M1)	0.7
Av. ann. inflation 2013–18	0.8%	Broad money	4.2
Deposit rate, Dec. 2018	-0.40%		

Exchange rates

	end 2018		December 2018
€ per $	0.78	Effective rates	2010 = 100
€ per SDR	1.21	– nominal	107.9
		– real	93.9

Trade[b]

Principal exports

	$bn fob
Machinery & transport equip.	896.8
Other manufactured goods	479.1
Chemicals & related products	376.0
Food, drink & tobacco	137.3
Mineral fuels & lubricants	112.2
Total incl. others	**2,122.8**

Principal imports

	$bn cif
Machinery & transport equip.	673.3
Other manufactured goods	539.0
Mineral fuels & lubricants	377.6
Chemicals & related products	221.8
Food, drink & tobacco	126.5
Total incl. others	**2,099.0**

Main export destinations

	% of total
United States	20.0
China	10.5
Switzerland	8.0
Turkey	4.5

Main origins of imports

	% of total
China	20.2
United States	13.8
Russia	7.8
Switzerland	6.0

Balance of payments, reserves and aid, $bn

Visible exports fob	2,543.0	Overall balance	16.9
Visible imports fob	-2,182.4	Change in reserves	59.0
Trade balance	360.6	Level of reserves	
Invisibles inflows	1,775.2	end Dec.	800.8
Invisibles outflows	-1,566.3	No. months of import cover	2.6
Net transfers	-154.3	Official gold holdings, m oz	346.7
Current account balance	415.3	Aid given	56.5
– as % of GDP	3.3	– as % of GNI	0.5
Capital balance	-434.9		

Health and education

Health spending, % of GDP	10.1	Education spending, % of GDP	5.3
Doctors per 1,000 pop.	3.9	Enrolment, %: primary	103
Hospital beds per 1,000 pop.	6.2	secondary	111
At least basic drinking water,		tertiary	72
% of pop.	99.9		

Society

No. of households, m, m	149.3	Telephone lines per 100 pop.	37.2
Av. no. per household	2.3	Mobile telephone subscribers	
Marriages per 1,000 pop.	4.1	per 100 pop.	129.3
Divorces per 1,000 pop.	1.9	Internet access, %	79.4
Cost of living, Dec. 2018		Broadband subs per 100 pop.	34.5
New York = 100	...	Broadband speed, Mbps	...
Cars per 1,000 pop.	524		

a Data generally refer to the 19 EU members that had adopted the euro as at December 31 2017: Austria, Belgium, Cyprus, Estonia, Finland, France, Germany, Greece, Ireland, Italy, Latvia, Lithuania, Luxembourg, Malta, Netherlands, Portugal, Slovakia, Slovenia and Spain.

b EU28, excluding intra-trade.

WORLD

Area, sq km	148,698,382	Capital	...
Arable as % of total land	10.8	Currency	...

People

Population, m	7,550.3	Life expectancy: men	70.7 yrs
Pop. per sq km	50.8	women	75.3 yrs
Total change in population		Adult literacy	86.2
2010–20, %	12.0	Fertility rate (per woman)	2.5
Pop. aged 0–19, %	33.3	Urban population, %	54.4
Pop. aged 65 and over, %	9.4		per 1,000 pop.
No. of men per 100 women	101.8	Crude birth rate	18.6
Human Development Index	72.8	Crude death rate	7.8

The economy

GDP	$80.1trn	GDP per head	$17,100
Av. ann. growth in real		GDP per head in purchasing	
GDP 2012–17	3.5%	power parity (USA=100)	27.3
		Economic freedom index	59.4

Origins of GDP		**Components of GDP**	
	% of total		% of total
Agriculture	4	Private consumption	58
Industry, of which:	27	Public consumption	17
manufacturing	17	Investment	24
Services	69	Exports	29
		Imports	-28

Structure of employment

	% of total		% of labour force
Agriculture	28.3	Unemployed 2018	5.0
Industry	22.9	Av. ann. rate 2010–18	5.2
Services	48.8		

Energy

	m TOE		
Total output	14,235.7	Net energy imports as %	
Total consumption	14,615.7	of energy use	...
Consumption per head			
kg oil equivalent	1,936		

Inflation and finance

		% change 2017–18	
Consumer price			
inflation 2018	3.6%	Narrow money (M1)	6.0
Av. ann. inflation 2013–18	3.1%	Broad money	5.0
LIBOR $ rate, 3-month, Dec. 2018	2.81%		

Trade

World exports

	$bn fob		$bn fob
Manufactures	12,670	Ores & minerals	714
Food	1,981	Agricultural raw materials	268
Fuels	1,660		
		Total incl. others	**17,846**

Main export destinations

	% of total
United States	13.2
China	9.7
Germany	6.7
United Kingdom	3.8
France	3.7

Main origins of imports

	% of total
China	13.9
United States	8.6
Germany	8.0
Japan	4.2
South Korea	3.5

Balance of payments, reserves and aid, $bn

Visible exports fob	17,396.6	Capital balance	-216.1
Visible imports fob	-17,015.6	Overall balance	-0.2
Trade balance	381.0	Change in reserves	908.8
Invisibles inflows	9,391.5	Level of reserves	
Invisibles outflows	-9,190.0	end Dec.	13,186.5
Net transfers	-137.6	No. months of import cover	6.0
Current account balance	444.9	Official gold holdings, m oz	1,081.9
– as % of GDP	0.5		

Health and education

Health spending, % of GDP	9.9	Education spending, % of GDP	4.7
Doctors per 1,000 pop.	1.5	Enrolment, %: primary	104
Hospital beds per 1,000 pop.	...	secondary	76
At least basic drinking water,		tertiary	37
% of pop.	91.0		

Society

No. of households, m, m	2,012.2	Cost of living, Dec. 2018	
Av. no. per household	3.8	New York = 100	...
Marriages per 1,000 pop.	...	Cars per 1,000 pop.	129
Divorces per 1,000 pop.	...	Telephone lines per 100 pop.	18.1
Religion, % of pop.		Mobile telephone subscribers	
Christian	31.5	per 100 pop.	109.1
Muslim	23.2	Internet access, %	48.6
Non-religious	16.3	Broadband subs per 100 pop.	15.1
Hindu	15.0	Broadband speed, Mbps	...
Other	13.8		
Jewish	0.2		

WORLD RANKINGS QUIZ

Test your knowledge with our world rankings quiz. Answers can be found on the pages indicated.

Geography and demographics

1   Which country has the largest marine area relative to its land area?
    a France **b** Australia **c** Portugal **d** Denmark   *page 12*

2   Which is the largest desert?
    a Arabian **b** Sahara **c** Gobi **d** Syrian   *page 13*

3   Which river is longest?
    a Yangtze **b** Amazon **c** Nile   *page 13*

4   Which is the largest of the Great Lakes?
    a Superior **b** Michigan **c** Erie   *page 13*

5   Ethiopia has a larger population than Germany.
    a True **b** False   *page 14*

6   In 2040, which of these countries is expected to have the most people?
    a Brazil **b** Mexico **c** Russia **d** Nigeria   *page 14*

7   Which country has the fastest-growing population?
    a Iraq **b** Kuwait **c** Lebanon **d** Oman   *page 15*

8   Which country recorded the highest number of total births?
    a Brazil **b** Egypt **c** Pakistan **d** United States   *page 16*

9   Which country has the highest median age?
    a Germany **b** Greece **c** Italy **d** Netherlands   *page 18*

10 The world's most populated city is in China.
    a True **b** False   *page 19*

11 Which of these cities has the slowest population-growth rate?
    a Athens **b** Bucharest **c** Detroit **d** Naples   *page 19*

12 More than half of Israel's population lives in Tel Aviv.
    a True **b** False   *page 21*

13 Which country has the biggest rural population?
    a Bangladesh **b** Nigeria **c** United States **d** Vietnam *page 21*

Business and economics

1 Which country scores lowest in the world on the UN Human Development Index?
   a South Sudan **b** Syria **c** Niger **d** Yemen   *page 28*

2 Which is not in the top three countries/areas with the most millionaires?
   a China **b** Euro area **c** Japan **d** United States   *page 29*

3 Which country's economy shrank the most over the past decade?
   a Greece **b** Libya **c** Venezuela **d** Yemen   *page 30*

4 Which country receives the highest level of remittances from workers in foreign countries?
   a Mexico **b** India **c** France **d** Bangladesh   *page 36*

5 Brazil has the world's highest foreign debt.
   a True **b** False   *page 40*

6 Which country receives the most aid?
   a Afghanistan **b** Iraq **c** Syria **d** Yemen   *page 42*

7 Between 2007 and 2017 which country had the highest average annual growth in industrial output?
   a Ethiopia **b** Liberia **c** Congo-Kinshasa **d** China   *page 44*

8 Italy has a larger manufacturing output than France.
   a True **b** False   *page 45*

9 Which of these countries has the highest dependence on agriculture?
   a Nigeria **b** Madagascar **c** North Korea **d** Haiti   *page 46*

10 Argentina produces more cereal than Canada.
   a True **b** False   *page 47*

11 Which of these countries is the biggest producer of cereals?
   a Turkey **b** Australia **c** Canada **d** Pakistan   *page 48*

12 Which country/area is the biggest consumer of sugar?
   a China **b** EU28 **c** India **d** United States   *page 48*

13 China consumes almost twice as much tea as India.
   a True **b** False   *page 49*

14 Which of these countries is the biggest consumer of cocoa?
a Ghana **b** Indonesia **c** Netherlands **d** Germany *page 49*

15 Which country is the world's biggest producer of copper?
a United States **b** China **c** Chile **d** Peru *page 50*

16 Which of these countries is the biggest consumer of lead?
a South Korea **b** Germany **c** India **d** Russia *page 50*

17 Germany consumes over a third of the tin in the EU28.
a True **b** False *page 50*

18 Which country is the world's biggest producer of nickel?
a Indonesia **b** China **c** Philippines **d** New Caledonia *page 51*

19 Which country is the world's biggest producer of rubber?
a Brazil **b** Thailand **c** China **d** United States *page 52*

20 Which country produces the most oil?
a Saudi Arabia **b** United States **c** Russia **d** Iran *page 53*

21 Which country uses the most energy?
a Mexico **b** Iran **c** Japan **d** India *page 54*

22 South Sudan is the most energy efficient country.
a True **b** False *page 54*

23 Modern slavery is most prevalent in which of these countries?
a Brunei **b** Rwanda **c** Iran **d** Burundi *page 57*

24 Which country has the most unpaid work on average?
a Portugal **b** France **c** Slovenia **d** United States *page 58*

25 The gender pay gap is biggest in which country?
a Estonia **b** South Korea **c** Israel **d** United Kingdom *page 58*

26 Which country has highest foreign direct investment inflows?
a China **b** Switzerland **c** India **d** United States *page 59*

27 Which country has the lowest brain-drain score?
a Switzerland **b** United States **c** Japan **d** Egypt *page 60*

28 Which stockmarket has the most listed companies?
a BSE India **b** Japan Exchange Group **c** Nasdaq-US *page 65*

Politics and society

1 Which country has the highest tertiary enrolment?
   a Turkey **b** United States **c** Greece **d** Norway page 68

2 Education spending is lower in Monaco than South Sudan.
   a True **b** False page 69

3 Which of these countries has the lower marriage rate?
   a Argentina **b** France **c** Japan **d** United Kingdom page 70

4 What is the mean age at which women in India first marry?
   a 18.1 **b** 19.5 **c** 20.7 **d** 21.1 page 71

5 Which country has the lowest number of households?
   a North Korea **b** Kenya **c** Ethiopia **d** Uganda page 72

6 Which country gives most generously?
   a China **b** United States **c** Indonesia **d** Sri Lanka page 73

7 Which country has the longest roads relative to its land area?
   a Malawi **b** Venezuela **c** Togo **d** Somalia page 74

8 Which country suffers the highest rate of road deaths?
   a London **b** Moscow **c** Paris **d** Mexico page 75

9 Which country had the biggest increase in car registrations in 2016–17?
   a Chile **b** Romania **c** Ecuador **d** Ukraine page 77

10 Which airport is the busiest?
   a Beijing **b** Amsterdam **c** Atlanta **d** JFK, New York page 78

11 In which country do people travel most by rail?
   a Japan **b** Switzerland **c** Austria **d** Germany page 79

12 Germany has a bigger merchant fleet than the United States.
   a True **b** False page 80

13 Which country spends most on defence as % of GDP?
   a Saudi Arabia **b** Afghanistan **c** Oman **d** Germany page 82

14 Which country had the highest number of terrorist incidents in 2017?
   a India **b** Afghanistan **c** Pakistan **d** Iraq page 83

Health and welfare

1 Life expectancy in Greece is higher than that in Denmark.
   a True **b** False   *page 90*

2 In Japan, women live how many years longer on average
   than men?
   a 3.4 **b** 4.6 **c** 5.2 **d** 6.5   *page 90*

3 Which country has the lowest life expectancy?
   a Central African Republic **b** Chad **c** Lesotho
   d Sierra Leone   *page 91*

4 Which of these countries has the highest death rate?
   a China **b** Germany **c** Nigeria **d** South Africa   *page 92*

5 Which country has the highest rate of infant mortality?
   a Central African Republic **b** Chad **c** Lesotho
   d Sierra Leone   *page 93*

6 Diabetes in adults is highest in which country?
   a Guam **b** Egypt **c** New Caledonia **d** Mexico   *page 94*

7 Which country has the highest rate of death by
   cardiovascular disease?
   a Belarus **b** Georgia **c** Russia **d** Ukraine   *page 94*

8 Cancer is most prevalent in which country?
   a Croatia **b** Hungary **c** Japan **d** Greece   *page 94*

9 The United States has a higher suicide rate than Sweden.
   a True **b** False   *page 94*

10 Afghanistan immunises more infants against measles than
   South Africa does.
   a True **b** False   *page 95*

11 Which of these countries has the highest rate of deaths
   from AIDS?
   a Lesotho **b** Mozambique **c** South Africa **d** Swaziland
                                                             page 95

12 Health spending is lower in South Sudan than in Sierra Leone.
   a True **b** False   *page 96*

13 Obesity is highest in which country?
   a Kuwait **b** Qatar **c** Fiji **d** United States   *page 97*

Culture and entertainment

1 In a ranking of the top 50, most countries have more than one mobile phone per person.
   a True **b** False *page 98*

2 Which country has the most landline telephones per person?
   a Germany **b** United Kingdom **c** United States **d** Taiwan *page 98*

3 Which country has the fastest broadband?
   a United States **b** France **c** Taiwan **d** Singapore *page 99*

4 Which country has the highest % of music income from performance rights?
   a Japan **b** United Kingdom **c** Brazil **d** Germany *page 100*

5 Which country recorded the most visits to the cinema?
   a China **b** India **c** Mexico **d** United States *page 101*

6 Which country produces the most feature films?
   a Japan **b** China **c** India **d** United Kingdom *page 101*

7 Which country's press is the most free?
   a Finland **b** Jamaica **c** New Zealand **d** Norway *page 102*

8 Which country has produced the most Nobel prize winners in literature?
   a Canada **b** Russia **c** France **d** United States *page 103*

9 Australia's women's cricket team is more successful than the men's.
   a True **b** False *page 104*

10 Which country has won most gold medals at summer Olympics?
   a France **b** Germany **c** Canada **d** United Kingdom *page 105*

11 In which of these countries is the most beer consumed per person?
   a Ireland **b** Poland **c** Romania **d** Spain *page 106*

12 Portugal consumes more wine per person than France.
   a True **b** False *page 106*

Glossary

Balance of payments The record of a country's transactions with the rest of the world. The **current account** of the balance of payments consists of: visible trade (goods); "invisible" trade (services and income); private transfer payments (eg, remittances from those working abroad); official transfers (eg, payments to international organisations, famine relief). Visible imports and exports are normally compiled on rather different definitions to those used in the trade statistics (shown in principal imports and exports) and therefore the statistics do not match. The **capital account** consists of long- and short-term transactions relating to a country's assets and liabilities (eg, loans and borrowings). The **current and capital accounts**, plus an errors and omissions item, make up the **overall balance**. **Changes in reserves** include gold at market prices and are shown without the practice often followed in balance of payments presentations of reversing the sign.

Big Mac index A light-hearted way of looking at exchange rates. If the dollar price of a burger at McDonald's in any country is higher than the price in the United States, converting at market exchange rates, then that country's currency could be thought to be over-valued against the dollar and vice versa.

Body-mass index A measure for assessing obesity – weight in kilograms divided by height in metres squared. An index of 30 or more is regarded as an indicator of obesity; 25 to 29.9 as over-weight. Guidelines vary for men and for women and may be adjusted for age.

CFA Communauté Financière Africaine. Its members, most of the francophone African nations, share a common currency, the CFA franc, pegged to the euro.

Cif/fob Measures of the value of merchandise trade. Imports include the cost of "carriage, insurance and freight" (cif) from the exporting country to the importing. The value of exports does not include these elements and is recorded "free on board" (fob). Balance of payments statistics are generally adjusted so that both exports and imports are shown fob; the cif elements are included in invisibles.

CIS is the Commonwealth of Independent States, including Georgia, Turkmenistan and Ukraine.

Crude birth rate The number of live births in a year per 1,000 population. The crude rate will automatically be relatively high if a large proportion of the population is of childbearing age.

Crude death rate The number of deaths in a year per 1,000 population. Also affected by the population's age structure.

Debt, foreign Financial obligations owed by a country to the rest of the world and repayable in foreign currency. The **debt service ratio** is debt service (principal repayments plus interest payments) expressed as a percentage of the country's earnings from exports of goods and services.

Debt, household All liabilities that require payment of interest or principal in the future.

Economic Freedom Index The ranking includes data on labour and business freedom as well as trade policy, taxation, monetary policy, the banking system, foreign-investment rules, property rights, government spending, regulation policy, the level of corruption and the extent of wage and price controls.

Effective exchange rate The nominal index measures a currency's depreciation (figures below 100) or appreciation (figures over 100) from a base date against a trade-weighted basket of the currencies of the country's main trading partners. The real effective exchange rate reflects adjustments for relative movements in prices or costs.

EU European Union. Members as at mid 2019 are: Austria, Belgium, Bulgaria, Croatia, Cyprus, Czech Republic, Denmark, Estonia, Finland, France, Germany, Greece, Hungary, Ireland, Italy, Latvia, Lithuania, Luxembourg, Malta,

Netherlands, Poland, Portugal, Romania, Slovakia, Slovenia, Spain, Sweden and the United Kingdom.

Euro area The 19 euro area members of the EU are Austria, Belgium, Cyprus, Estonia, Finland, France, Germany, Greece, Ireland, Italy, Latvia, Lithuania, Luxembourg, Malta, Netherlands, Portugal, Slovakia, Slovenia and Spain. Their common currency is the euro.

Fertility rate The average number of children born to a woman who completes her childbearing years.

G7 Group of seven countries: United States, Japan, Germany, United Kingdom, France, Italy and Canada.

GDP Gross domestic product. The sum of all output produced by economic activity within a country. GNP (gross national product) and GNI (gross national income) include net income from abroad, eg, rent, profits.

Import cover The number of months of imports covered by reserves, ie, reserves ÷ ¹⁄₁₂ annual imports (visibles and invisibles).

Inflation The annual rate at which prices are increasing. The most common measure and the one shown here is the increase in the consumer price index.

Life expectancy The average length of time a baby born today can expect to live.

Literacy is defined by UNESCO as the ability to read and write a simple sentence, but definitions can vary from country to country.

Median age Divides the age distribution into two halves. Half of the population is above and half below the median age.

Money supply A measure of the "money" available to buy goods and services. Various definitions exist. The measures shown here are based on definitions used by the IMF and may differ from measures used nationally. Narrow money (M1) consists of cash in circulation and demand deposits (bank deposits that can be withdrawn on demand). "Quasi-money"

(time, savings and foreign currency deposits) is added to this to create broad money.

OECD Organisation for Economic Co-operation and Development. The "rich countries" club was established in 1961 to promote economic growth and the expansion of world trade. It is based in Paris and now has 36 members from May 2018, when Lithuania joined.

Official reserves The stock of gold and foreign currency held by a country to finance any calls that may be made for the settlement of foreign debt.

Opec Set up in 1960 and based in Vienna, Opec is mainly concerned with oil pricing and production issues. The current members (2017) are: Algeria, Angola, Congo-Brazzaville, Ecuador, Equatorial Guinea, Gabon, Iran, Iraq, Kuwait, Libya, Nigeria, Qatar (until January 1st 2019), Saudi Arabia, United Arab Emirates and Venezuela.

PPP Purchasing power parity. PPP statistics adjust for cost of living differences by replacing normal exchange rates with rates designed to equalise the prices of a standard "basket" of goods and services. These are used to obtain PPP estimates of GDP per head. PPP estimates are shown on an index, taking the United States as 100.

Real terms Figures adjusted to exclude the effect of inflation.

SDR Special drawing right. The reserve currency, introduced by the IMF in 1970, was intended to replace gold and national currencies in settling international transactions. The IMF uses SDRs for book-keeping purposes and issues them to member countries. Their value is based on a basket of the US dollar (with a weight of 41.73%), the euro (30.93%), the Chinese renminbi (10.92%), the Japanese yen (8.33%), and the pound sterling (8.09%).

List of countries

	Population	GDP	GDP per head	Area	Median age
	m, 2017	$bn, 2017	$PPP, 2017	'000 sq km	yrs, 2017
Afghanistan	35.5	20	1,955	653	17.8
Albania	2.9	13	12,521	29	36.9
Algeria	41.3	168	15,100	2,382	28.1
Andorra	0.08	3	49,900	0	43.0
Angola	29.8	122	6,988	1,247	16.6
Argentina	44.3	637	20,830	2,780	31.2
Armenia	2.9	12	9,476	30	34.6
Australia	24.5	1,323	50,609	7,741	37.6
Austria	8.7	417	50,035	84	43.7
Azerbaijan	9.8	41	17,651	87	31.1
Bahamas	0.4	12	32,377	14	33.2
Bahrain	1.5	35	49,035	1	31.7
Bangladesh	164.7	250	4,237	148	26.4
Barbados	0.3	5	18,263	0	39.0
Belarus	9.5	54	18,892	208	39.9
Belgium	11.4	495	46,755	31	41.5
Benin	11.2	9	2,287	115	18.4
Bermuda	0.06	6	52,547	0	42.0
Bolivia	11.1	38	7,123	1,099	24.6
Bosnia & Herz.	3.5	18	12,784	51	41.6
Botswana	2.3	17	17,110	582	25.0
Brazil	209.3	2,054	15,739	8,516	32.2
Brunei	0.4	12	78,971	6	31.0
Bulgaria	7.1	58	21,818	111	44.0
Burkina Faso	19.2	12	1,867	274	17.2
Burundi	10.9	3	737	28	17.6
Cambodia	16.0	22	4,012	181	24.6
Cameroon	24.1	35	3,688	475	18.5
Canada	36.6	1,647	48,342	9,985	40.9
Central African Rep.	4.7	2	680	623	18.0
Chad	14.9	10	2,349	1,284	16.3
Channel Islands	0.2	9	...	0	43.2
Chile	18.1	277	24,676	756	34.4
China	1,409.5	12,238	16,682	9,563	37.7
Colombia	49.1	314	14,392	1,142	30.9
Congo-Brazzaville	5.3	9	6,761	342	18.9
Congo-Kinshasa	81.3	38	744	2,345	16.9
Costa Rica	4.9	57	16,920	51	32.3
Croatia	4.2	55	24,792	57	43.2
Cuba	11.5	97	12,300	110	41.9
Cyprus	1.2	22	38,048	9	35.9
Czech Republic	10.6	216	35,560	79	42.2
Denmark	5.7	330	50,643	43	41.9
Dominican Rep.	10.8	76	17,008	49	26.7
Ecuador	16.6	104	11,507	256	27.2
Egypt	97.6	235	12,698	1,001	24.9
El Salvador	6.4	25	7,738	21	26.5

	Population	GDP	GDP per head	Area '000 sq	Median age
	m, 2017	$bn, 2017	$PPP, 2017	km	yrs, 2017
Equatorial Guinea	1.3	12	24,417	28	22.3
Eritrea	5.1	6	1,585	118	19.1
Estonia	1.3	27	32,130	45	42.0
Ethiopia	105.0	81	2,151	1,104	19.1
Fiji	0.9	5	9,751	18	28.0
Finland	5.5	252	44,492	338	42.6
France	65.0	2,583	44,168	549	41.5
French Guiana	0.3	...	...	84	24.8
French Polynesia	0.3	3	...	4	31.6
Gabon	2.0	15	18,116	268	22.8
Gambia, The	2.1	1	2,642	11	17.2
Georgia	3.9	15	10,679	70	38.3
Germany	82.1	3,693	50,804	357	46.2
Ghana	28.8	59	6,099	239	20.7
Greece	11.2	203	27,812	132	44.1
Guadeloupe	0.4	...	...	2	42.3
Guam	0.2	6	35,600	1	30.6
Guatemala	16.9	76	8,165	109	21.9
Guinea	12.7	10	2,189	246	18.6
Guinea-Bissau	1.9	1	1,865	36	19.1
Guyana	0.8	4	8,101	215	25.3
Haiti	11.0	8	1,819	28	23.5
Honduras	9.3	23	5,000	112	23.5
Hong Kong	7.4	341	61,529	1	43.8
Hungary	9.7	140	29,670	93	42.4
Iceland	0.3	24	53,834	103	36.5
India	1,339.2	2,651	7,287	3,287	27.3
Indonesia	264.0	1,015	12,434	1,911	28.5
Iran	81.2	454	20,136	1,745	30.7
Iraq	38.3	192	17,625	435	19.6
Ireland	4.8	331	73,215	70	37.6
Israel	8.3	353	36,662	22	30.4
Italy	59.4	1,944	38,358	301	46.7
Ivory Coast	24.3	37	3,902	322	18.5
Jamaica	2.9	15	9,161	11	30.2
Japan	127.5	4,872	42,819	378	47.1
Jordan	9.7	40	9,232	89	22.5
Kazakhstan	18.2	163	26,265	2,725	29.8
Kenya	49.7	79	3,502	580	19.4
Kosovo	1.9	7	10,949	11	28.0
Kuwait	4.1	120	66,197	18	33.5
Kyrgyzstan	6.0	8	3,706	200	25.7
Laos	6.9	17	7,382	237	23.4
Latvia	1.9	30	27,685	64	43.1
Lebanon	6.1	54	14,351	10	29.5
Lesotho	2.2	3	3,294	30	21.7
Liberia	4.7	3	1,405	111	18.8

	Population	GDP	GDP per head	Area '000 sq	Median age
	m, 2017	$bn, 2017	$PPP, 2017	km	yrs, 2017
Libya	6.4	38	9,610	1,760	27.9
Liechtenstein	0.04	6	139,100	0	42.0
Lithuania	2.9	48	32,463	65	43.0
Luxembourg	0.6	62	103,298	3	39.5
Macau	0.6	50	110,592	0	38.2
Macedonia	2.1	11	14,976	26	38.1
Madagascar	25.6	11	1,558	587	19.1
Malawi	18.6	6	1,170	118	17.7
Malaysia	31.6	315	29,144	331	28.6
Maldives	0.4	5	20,223	0	29.0
Mali	18.5	15	2,290	1,240	16.2
Malta	0.4	13	42,532	0	41.5
Martinique	0.4	...	...	1	44.5
Mauritania	4.4	5	3,896	1,031	19.9
Mauritius	1.3	13	22,354	2	36.3
Mexico	129.2	1,151	19,949	1,964	28.2
Moldova	4.1	8	6,864	34	36.4
Monaco	0.04	6	115,900	0	52.0
Mongolia	3.1	11	12,529	1,564	27.7
Montenegro	0.6	5	17,833	14	38.3
Morocco	35.7	110	8,566	447	28.6
Mozambique	29.7	13	1,256	799	17.4
Myanmar	53.4	67	6,259	677	28.3
Namibia	2.5	13	11,200	824	21.4
Nepal	29.3	25	2,702	147	23.9
Netherlands	17.0	831	53,933	42	42.5
New Caledonia	0.3	3	31,100	19	33.0
New Zealand	4.7	204	38,776	268	37.5
Nicaragua	6.2	14	5,855	130	26.0
Niger	21.5	8	1,166	1,267	15.0
Nigeria	190.9	376	5,941	924	18.0
North Korea	25.5	32	1,700	121	34.5
Norway	5.3	399	72,170	385	39.4
Oman	4.6	71	46,011	310	29.7
Pakistan	197.0	305	5,378	796	22.9
Panama	4.1	62	24,524	75	28.9
Papua New Guinea	8.3	21	3,656	463	22.1
Paraguay	6.8	40	12,810	407	25.5
Peru	32.2	211	13,518	1,285	28.1
Philippines	104.9	314	8,360	300	24.5
Poland	38.2	526	29,722	313	40.5
Portugal	10.3	219	30,622	92	44.8
Puerto Rico	3.7	104	39,389	9	37.1
Qatar	2.6	167	127,785	12	31.5
Réunion	0.9	...	...	3	35.1
Romania	19.7	212	24,686	238	42.0
Russia	144.0	1,578	27,964	17,098	39.1

	Population	GDP	GDP per head	Area '000 sq	Median age
	m, 2017	$bn, 2017	$PPP, 2017	km	yrs, 2017
Rwanda	12.2	9	2,090	26	19.8
Saudi Arabia	32.9	687	54,595	2,150	30.6
Senegal	15.9	21	3,459	197	18.5
Serbia	8.8	41	16,386	88	40.5
Sierra Leone	7.6	4	1,561	72	18.6
Singapore	5.7	324	95,508	1	41.0
Slovakia	5.4	96	33,042	49	40.0
Slovenia	2.1	49	34,420	20	43.6
Somalia	14.7	7	0	638	16.6
South Africa	56.7	349	13,552	1,219	26.6
South Korea	51.0	1,531	39,548	100	41.8
South Sudan	12.6	3	1,533	644	18.8
Spain	46.4	1,314	38,320	506	44.1
Sri Lanka	20.9	87	12,863	66	33.0
Sudan	40.5	117	4,353	1,879	19.2
Suriname	0.6	3	14,671	164	28.9
Swaziland	1.4	4	10,830	17	20.8
Sweden	9.9	536	51,180	447	40.9
Switzerland	8.5	679	62,131	41	42.6
Syria	18.3	17	2,900	185	20.8
Taiwan	23.6	575	50,593	36	40.6
Tajikistan	8.9	7	3,187	141	22.8
Tanzania	57.3	53	3,223	947	17.5
Thailand	69.0	455	18,330	513	38.7
Timor-Leste	1.3	3	5,700	15	17.6
Togo	7.8	5	1,671	57	19.1
Trinidad & Tobago	1.4	22	31,585	5	34.8
Tunisia	11.5	40	11,936	164	31.7
Turkey	80.7	852	27,049	785	30.6
Turkmenistan	5.8	38	18,164	488	26.1
Uganda	42.9	26	2,370	242	16.0
Ukraine	44.2	112	8,754	604	40.7
United Arab Emirates	9.4	383	68,639	84	33.6
United Kingdom	66.2	2,638	44,365	244	40.4
United States	324.5	19,485	59,895	9,832	37.9
Uruguay	3.5	56	22,374	176	35.2
Uzbekistan	31.9	50	7,259	447	27.1
Venezuela	32.0	144	12,185	912	28.0
Vietnam	95.5	224	6,928	331	31.3
Virgin Islands (US)	0.1	4	...	0	41.6
West Bank & Gaza	4.9	14	4,300	6	19.7
Yemen	28.3	31	2,456	528	19.6
Zambia	17.1	26	3,999	753	17.3
Zimbabwe	16.5	22	2,704	391	19.2
Euro area (19)	337.7	12,652	45,076	2,759	44.2
World	7,550.3	80,144	17,100	134,325	30.1

Sources

AFM Research
Airports Council International, *Worldwide Airport Traffic Report*

Bank of East Asia
Bloomberg
BP, *Statistical Review of World Energy*

Cable
CAF, *The World Giving Index*
CBRE, *Global Prime Office Occupancy Costs*
Central banks
Central Intelligence Agency, *The World Factbook*
Company reports
Cornell University
Council of Tall Buildings and Urban Habitat
Credit Suisse

The Economist, www.economist.com
Economist Intelligence Unit, *Cost of Living Survey; Country Forecasts; Country Reports; Liveability Index*
Encyclopaedia Britannica
Eurostat, *Statistics in Focus*

FIFA
Finance ministries
Food and Agriculture Organisation

Global Democracy Ranking
Global Entrepreneurship Monitor
Global Internal Displacement Database
Global Terrorism Database, University of Maryland
Government statistics

H2 Gambling Capital
The Heritage Foundation, *Index of Economic Freedom*

Holman Fenwick Willan

IFPI
IMD, *World Competitiveness Yearbook*
IMF, *International Financial Statistics; World Economic Outlook*
INSEAD
Institute for Criminal Policy Research
International Civil Aviation Organisation
International Cocoa Organisation, *Quarterly Bulletin of Cocoa Statistics*
International Coffee Organisation
International Cotton Advisory Committee, *March Bulletin*
International Cricket Council
International Diabetes Federation, *Diabetes Atlas*
International Grains Council
International Institute for Strategic Studies, *Military Balance*
International Labour Organisation
International Olympic Committee
International Organisation of Motor Vehicle Manufacturers
International Publishers Association
International Rubber Study Group, *Rubber Statistical Bulletin*
International Sugar Organisation, *Statistical Bulletin*
International Telecommunication Union, *ITU Indicators*
International Union of Railways
Inter-Parliamentary Union

Johnson Matthey

McDonald's

National Institute of Statistics and Economic Studies

National statistics offices
Nobel Foundation

OECD, *Development Assistance Committee Report; Economic Outlook; Government at a Glance; OECD.Stat; Revenue Statistics*

Pew Research Centre, *The Global Religious Landscape*
Progressive Media

Reporters Without Borders, *Press Freedom Index*

Sovereign Wealth Fund Institute
Space Launch Report
Stockholm International Peace Research Institute
Swiss Re

Taiwan Statistical Data Book
The Times, *Atlas of the World*
Thomson Reuters
Trade Data & Analysis

Union of Concerned Scientists
UN, *Demographic Yearbook; National Accounts; State of World Population Report; World Fertility Report*
UNAIDS
UNCTAD, *Review of Maritime Transport; World Investment Report*
UNCTAD/WTO International Trade Centre
UN Development Programme, *Human Development Report*

UNESCO Institute for Statistics
UN High Commissioner for Refugees
UN Office on Drugs and Crime
UN, Population Division
US Department of Agriculture
US Energy Information Administration
US Federal Aviation Administration
US Geological Survey

Visionofhumanity.org

Walk Free Foundation
WHO, *Global Health Observatory; Global Immunisation Data; World Health Statistics*
World Bank, *Doing Business; Global Development Finance; Migration and Remittances Data; World Development Indicators; World Development Report*
World Bureau of Metal Statistics, *World Metal Statistics*
World Economic Forum, *Global Competitiveness Report*
World Federation of Exchanges
World Health Organisation
World Intellectual Property Organization
World Tourism Organisation, *Yearbook of Tourism Statistics*
World Trade Organisation, *Annual Report*

Yale University